Empireland

Empireland

How Imperialism Has Shaped Modern Britain

SATHNAM SANGHERA

VIKING
an imprint of
PENGUIN BOOKS

VIKING

UK | USA | Canada | Ireland | Australia
India | New Zealand | South Africa

Viking is part of the Penguin Random House group of companies
whose addresses can be found at global.penguinrandomhouse.com.

First published 2021

008

The Satanic Verses by Salman Rushdie published by Viking. Copyright © Salman Rushdie, 1988.
Reprinted by permission of Penguin Books Limited.
Used by permission of The Wylie Agency (UK) Limited

Copyright © Sathnam Sanghera, 2021

The moral right of the author has been asserted

Set in 12/14.75 pt Bembo Book MT Std
Typeset by Jouve (UK), Milton Keynes
Printed and bound in Great Britain by Clays Ltd, Elcograf S.p.A.

The authorized representative in the EEA is Penguin Random House Ireland,
Morrison Chambers, 32 Nassau Street, Dublin D02 YH68

A CIP catalogue record for this book is available from the British Library

ISBN: 978–0–241–44529–7

www.greenpenguin.co.uk

Penguin Random House is committed to a
sustainable future for our business, our readers
and our planet. This book is made from Forest
Stewardship Council® certified paper.

In memory of Robin Roberts
1953–2019

The trouble with the Engenglish is that their hiss hiss history happened overseas, so they dodo don't know what it means.

Whisky Sisodia, in Salman Rushdie, *The Satanic Verses*

Contents

Acknowledgements

This is a book about how modern Britain has been shaped by its past, and it would have been impossible to write without the enormous number of history books and articles I consulted during my research. I hope readers will consult the plethora of sources cited and I also hope that, in efforts to synthesize, I have not slipped at any stage into plagiarism. A small amount of material may have originally appeared in different form under my byline in *The Times*.

I will refer to the violent events of 1857, when Indian soldiers rebelled against their colonizers, as the Indian Uprising, though they also go by other names, such as the Indian Mutiny, the Indian Rebellion, the Sepoy Mutiny, the Sepoy Revolt and the First War of Independence, depending on your perspective. The changing nature of Ireland's relationship to Britain is just as contentious, and for reasons that will become evident I will be talking about nineteenth-century Ireland as if it were an imperial colony, though it officially became part of the United Kingdom as a result of the Act of Union, passed in 1801.

I take the view that slavery was an aspect of the British empire: this nation wasn't the first into the slave trade, and the slaves weren't taken from a part of the world that was part of British empire at the time, but they were transported to British colonies where they helped sustain vital imperial trade. Britain participated to such a degree that, according to the *Financial Times*, slave-related businesses in the eighteenth century accounted for about the same proportion of GDP as the professional and support services sector does today. As Linda Colley puts it in *Captives: Britain, Empire and the World, 1600– 1850*: 'Africans transported as slaves across the Atlantic experienced an atrocity that was not peculiar to the British empire, but was certainly fostered by it.'

Where useful, I will translate historical amounts of money into modern equivalents on the detailed advice of an economic historian:

xii   *Acknowledgements*

comparisons are difficult when it comes to long-run inflation calculations.[1] And I'm going to spend as little time as possible fretting about definitions: almost every term used in discussion of empire, from 'colony' to 'commonwealth' to 'colonialism', to say nothing of 'race' and 'racism', can be contested, their meanings changing over time. Even 'the British empire' itself has changed in definition, with Nicholas Canny explaining in an essay in *The Oxford History of the British Empire* that 'the adjective "British" meant little to most inhabitants of Britain and Ireland' during the sixteenth and seventeenth centuries, and when England was described as an 'empire' then it was 'with a view to emphasizing the long tradition of independence from foreign potentates, including the Pope, enjoyed by its monarchs through the centuries'.

If we immerse ourselves in definitions, however, we will end up with yet another forbiddingly long academic book on empire, when my ambition is to create something resembling the opposite. Any errors are, of course, entirely my own, but I am grateful for the many people who have helped me navigate the almost infinite amount of material on the subject. Particular thanks to Emanuel Besorai, Helen Carr, Sarah Chalfant, Leigh Gardner, Peter James, Simran Kular, Amandeep Madra, Peter Mitchell, Lottie Moggach, Ferdinand Mount, Mary Mount, Rebecca Rideal, Angela Saini, Assallah Tahir, Ella Taylor, Kim Wagner, Colin Yeo, Alba Ziegler-Bailey.

1. Empire Day 2.0

My inbox at work is a nightmare. It currently holds 87,875 unread emails, a reflection not of my popularity (a colleague has more than 200,000), but of the fact that public relations professionals vastly out-number journalists, and sending anyone they know news of the latest printer/teabag they're promoting seems to be part of their job. Inten-sifying the tedium is that around a third of these messages begin with the greeting: 'I hope your [sic] well'. To which I am always tempted to reply 'My well what? Never runs dry?' or with a precise descrip-tion of the well my family actually owns on a farm in India. But most enervating of all is the fact that another third of the messages are marketing some kind of awareness event.

It seems that when you can't think of any other way of generating attention for your cause, establishing an 'awareness day' is always an option. There are thousands of them, from National French Bread Day to National Skipping Day, Nude Gardening Day and National Corndog Day. Pointless? Not entirely: I've just been inspired by this research to look up corndogs and am now not only aware of corndogs but desire a corndog for my tea. Inane? More often than not. Which makes it even more surprising that nearly two years after I started looking into how imperialism has shaped modern Britain, I find myself wishing a new one into existence: Empire Awareness Day.

Despite a recent surge of interest in British colonial history, with statues being torn down (or defended), concert halls and schools being renamed (or councils refusing to submit to demands) and com-panies apologizing for past deeds (or trying to ignore it all), the effect of British empire upon this country is poorly understood. Many of us have learned more about British imperialism in a few months of statuecide than we did during our entire schooling, but there seems to be a view that if you pull down enough statues/change enough names or fight to keep enough statues up/refuse to change names, you can delete or defend British imperialism. But British empire defines us more deeply than these controversies suggest and an Empire Day could help explain how.

Such a thing actually existed for decades in the twentieth century. This half-day school holiday was established by the Earl of Meath, to celebrate the splendour of the empire on 24 May each year, the late Queen Victoria's birthday, with the aim of creating a bond between imperial subjects and counteracting what Meath felt was lamentable ignorance about its achievements. The story goes that he once asked a bunch of teenagers whether they had heard of the Indian Uprising, a key event in empire history, and, to his dismay, received just one positive response. For a man who, at Eton, was told that brushing snow off his knees was spineless and unimperial, the implications were unconscionable. Convinced that such ignorance was widespread and undermining faith in civilization's greatest achievement, worried that the British empire might die like most other empires, he started campaigning for the establishment of an annual Empire Day, which had originally been pioneered in Canada in the 1890s.

By 1916, in the middle of the war, when patriotic feeling was at its height, Meath got his way: the British government inaugurated an official Empire Day. He would later claim that his movement had inspired the 'rush to the colours' to fight in the First World War, which seems grandiose, but it certainly did become an institution.[1] The BBC promoted it in their programmes, notably an Empire Day special in 1929 presented by Sir Henry Newbolt. An Empire Day thanksgiving service at Wembley Stadium attracted around 90,000 people. Most British towns marked the occasion, with marches, music, bonfires and fireworks, and celebrations were reported as far away as Australia. And while Empire Day formally died in 1958 when Prime Minister Harold Macmillan announced in Parliament it would be renamed British Commonwealth Day, Empire Day continued to be marked in Protestant schools in Northern Ireland into the 1960s.

I'm not saying it should return in its old form, with children reading about the downfall of previous empires at school in order to learn about 'the dangers of subordinating', receiving a free mug with the news that empire was glorious, saluting the flag, turning up to celebrations in blackface and carrying colonial goods such as tea or sugar. Nor do I envisage Empire Awareness Day having the same aims as Empire Day: the latter focused on sustaining enthusiasm for colonialism, whereas I would want Empire Day 2.0 to explain how the experience of having colonized shapes Britain now. What might it actually involve? Well, as Empire Day is primarily remembered as an annual half-day holiday for most children in most schools, with Meath claiming that the festival was being observed throughout empire in some 55,000 schools by 1909, there would need to be a focus on education. And the simplest thing would be to persuade schools to allocate chunks of the timetable to the cause, with the most obvious candidate being foreign-language lessons.

For one day a year, instead of being taught French or Spanish, the children of Britain could instead be instructed on how the English language itself exists as a living monument to Britain's deep and complex relationship with the world through empire. More specifically, they could consult the glorious *Hobson-Jobson Dictionary*, a remarkable 1,000-page 'glossary of colloquial Anglo-Indian words and phrases, and of kindred terms etymological, historical, geographical and discursive' compiled by Colonel Henry Yule and A. C. Burnell in 1886, which provides testament to the enormous number of Indian words that have entered English. Many of the citations function as time capsules into the British Raj. 'Dam' originally referred to a copper coin, for example, 'the fortieth part of a rupee' and so low in value that it led to Britons in India employing the phrase 'I won't give a dumri,' which in turn led to the popular expression 'I don't give a dam[n].' And 'Juggernaut' is a corruption of the Sanskrit 'Jagannatha', 'Lord of the Universe, a name of Krishna worshipped as Vishnu at the famous shrine of Puri in Orissa', the idol of which 'was, and is, annually dragged forth in procession on a monstrous car, and ... occasionally persons, sometimes sufferers of painful disease, cast themselves before the advancing wheels'.*

* In *Pax Britannica*, Jan Morris produces an unlikely passage that makes use of two dozen examples of English words of Indian origin: 'Returning to the *bungalow* through the *jungle*, she threw her *calico* bonnet on to the *teak* table, put on her *gingham* apron and slipped into a pair of *sandals*. There was the *tea caddy* to fill, the

If there is time, or, perhaps, if there is a spare period of English going, it could be dedicated to tracing how the definitions of hundreds of other words in the *Oxford English Dictionary* illustrate the linguistic influence of empire beyond India. Students could learn, for instance, how 'toboggan' was originally a native American word ('A light sledge which curves upwards and backwards at the front, and has either a flat bottom or runners'). And how 'Zombie' is of West African origin ('In the West Indies and southern states of America, a soulless corpse said to have been revived by witchcraft; formerly, the name of a snake-deity in voodoo cults of or deriving from West Africa and Haiti').

Another school lesson that could be usefully hijacked in the name of empire awareness: economics. Many famous enterprises still trading today have their roots in imperial trade, not least Liberty of London, founded by Arthur Lasenby Liberty, the son of a Chesham lace manufacturer who began by selling silks and cashmere shawls from the East when South Asian textiles became popular in the Victorian age. The popularity of South Asian textiles was boosted by the British royal family, with Queen Victoria accepting a shawl from the Maharajah of Kashmir each year, and Kashmiri shawl fabric becoming so important that when the Kashmir Valley was officially annexed to the empire in 1846, the treaty stated that the local maharajah was to pay a yearly tribute of 'one horse, twelve shawl goats . . . and three pairs of Kashmir shawls'.[2] In the entry for 'shawl' in her 2013 edition of *Hobson-Jobson*, Kate Teltscher explains that the expense of the genuine article led to the creation of a domestic shawl industry in Norwich and Paisley that 'copied Indian designs at a fraction of the price'. Liberty soon moved on to sell oriental goods of all kinds, with records showing that the shop buildings, which were named East India House, were constructed out of more than 24,000 cubic feet of

---

chutney to prepare for the *curry, pepper* and *cheroots* to order from the *bazaar* – she would give the boy a *chit*. The children were out in the *dinghy*, and their *khaki dungarees* were sure to be wet. She needed a *shampoo*, she still had to mend Tom's *pyjamas*, and she never had finished those *chintz* hangings for the *veranda*. Ah well! she didn't really give a *dam*, and putting a *shawl* around her shoulders, she poured herself a *punch*.'

ships' timbers – one of the boats, which measured the length and height of the Liberty building, being HMS *Hindustan*.[3]

Then there is Shell, established in the nineteenth century by one Marcus Samuel, who started off selling antiques and importing oriental seashells from the Far East, which were at the time fashionable in interior design, establishing the process for a successful import–export business which eventually morphed into one of the world's best-known energy companies (after it had merged with Royal Dutch Petroleum, which came out of the Dutch empire in the East Indies). We also have the Bass Brewery founded in 1777 by William Bass in Burton-upon-Trent, Staffordshire, England – whose distinctive red triangle became the UK's first registered trademark, and which had become the largest brewery in the world by 1877, with an annual output of 1 million barrels, in part because of the 'pale ale' it exported throughout the British empire. India pale ale had originally been developed elsewhere, when the long sea voyage to India was found to greatly improve the taste of 'stock' beer – four to five months of being gently rocked by the ship and the gradual introduction of heat as the ship neared India resulting in great depth of flavour – but Bass marketed it brilliantly to the shopkeeper-and-clerk class, and in the process helped to transform the brewing industry and put Burton at its centre.[4]

Admittedly, students who had already had foreign languages, English and economics lessons might have had enough of British empire by this point of the day, but I'm afraid PE or Games would offer no respite if I had anything to do with it. Playing football? The perfect opportunity to tell students that 'kop', the colloquial name for rising single-tier terraces at football grounds, originally comes from 'Spion Kop', a hill where, according to the historian Robert Tombs, 'British soldiers were picked off by a concealed enemy with Mauser rifles and smokeless ammunition.' Playing cricket? From the nineteenth century, the game became innate to empire, the Imperial Cricket Conference's efforts to standardize the rules of the game helping to bring the many disparate parts of empire together, while the values of fair play, courage and resilience nurtured on the games fields of public schools were seen as key to developing the imperial ruling race. As the historian John MacKenzie has put it: 'Games became . . . an analogue of war which, with cadet corps and rifle clubs, could prepare the nation's officer class not just for imperial campaigns, but for a global defence against any European rival.'

Though as Empire Day was not exclusively for children, with adults observing it in all sorts of ways, from conducting ceremonies at the London memorial to Lord Meath at Lancaster Gate (which still stands) to singing the National Anthem on the roofs of company headquarters, it would make sense for certain Empire Day 2.0 activities to cater for grown-ups too. And my next suggestion – a day trip around imperial London – would work for all ages. Recent protests have alerted us to how the dark history of colonialism is evident in London through many of its memorials, and of the hundreds of city statues surveyed by one A. Byron in a 1981 book, around 8 per cent have direct links to empire. They include tributes to Major-General Charles Napier, General Gordon and Robert Clive, the pioneer of a territorial empire in India, who didn't let his loathing of India and Indians hold him back from generating huge wealth from the place.

In the centre of town, we also have the Foreign and Commonwealth Office, opened in 1866 as the home for the India Office and Colonial Office, and existing as an expression of Britain's late nineteenth-century ideas about itself in a riot of colonially inflected neo-classical excess.[5] Large statues of East India Company and India Office administrators and military generals stand about dressed in togas and Roman breastplates; a Grand Durbar Court, made for the reception of Indian dignitaries, features allegorical statues in a style that is supposed to be half classical and half Indian; elsewhere, Spiridione Roma's painting *The East Offering its Riches to Britannia* stands proud, originally commissioned by the East India Company for the Revenue Committee room in East India House and depicting a dark-skinned character representing India willingly offering a pale Britannia all her jewellery and treasures, turning violent looting into an act of peaceful benevolence.

But our capital's former role as the metropole of the British empire is evident in numerous other ways, not least its famous museums (the British Museum not only housing a load of imperial loot but being founded on the original collection of Sir Hans Sloane, whose fortune came from marrying the widow of a plantation owner) and the very existence of Wembley Stadium. The stadium has recently been entirely rebuilt, but the former twin towers were an art-deco approximation of Mughal architecture from the colonized subcontinent, and it was originally known as the Empire Stadium, having been established for the 1924 Empire Exhibition, itself described as 'a stock-taking of the whole resources of empire' and attended by some 17 million visitors in 1924 and some 10 million in 1925.[6] As part of the enterprise, 15 miles of walkways and surrounding streets were named by Rudyard Kipling – they included Dominion Way, Union Approach, Atlantic Slope, Craftsman's Way, and a few of these, like Empire Way and Engineers Way, still exist. Across the river, in Wandsworth, a residential area between Battersea Park Road and Falcon Road known as 'Little India' has road names such as Afghan, Cabul, Candahar and Khyber, commemorating the Second Afghan War of 1878–80, complete with the nineteenth-century British spellings of the places they commemorate.

It would, of course, be a public relations catastrophe for any awareness campaign in the twenty-first century to be London-centric, so there would have to be a parallel programme of Empire Day 2.0 tours across the country, a task that would, as it happens, be no harder than planning the London itinerary, so many of our cities having been shaped by empire. The tearing down in Bristol of the statue of Edward Colston, some of whose wealth came directly from the slave trade, which he personally oversaw as Deputy Governor of the Royal African Company, and the (disputed) claim that Liverpool's Penny Lane commemorates the slave trader James Penny, have made the influence of empire on provincial life the stuff of general knowledge. But, as with London, the imperial heritage goes much deeper. Bristol is also the city from which the pioneer John Cabot set sail in 1497 in one of the voyages that arguably laid the foundations for the British empire. Liverpool, a city which Karl Marx famously claimed 'waxed fat on the slave trade', has its imperial legacy reflected not just in its size, growing as it did from a handful of streets in 1207 to a vigorous eighteenth-century city, but also in a frieze around the handsome

Town Hall illustrating trading routes and featuring lions, crocodiles, elephants and African faces. Meanwhile, in Belfast, Empire Awareness Day participants could be encouraged to visit Bombay Street, Kashmir Street, Cawnpore Street, Lucknow Street and Benares Street, all named in celebration of famous campaigns of the British empire, with nests of similar imperial street names existing across Britain, wherever terraced housing was being built at the height of imperialism in the late nineteenth and early twentieth centuries.

Meanwhile, in Glasgow, the so-called second city of the empire, which from the mid-eighteenth century became a major port for rum, sugar and tobacco grown by slaves, participants in Empire Day 2.0 could be directed to the street names such as Jamaica Street, Tobago Street and Antigua Street, commemorating historic associations with sugar plantations and the so-called Tobacco Lords, who grew rich as exports from British colonial settlements rose from around 30 million pounds of the American plant in 1700 to about 76 million pounds in 1800.[7] And as for my home region, the Black Country, the complicated legacy of empire is reflected in the inclusion of a chain in the official flag – featured because Wolverhampton was once a leading producer of iron goods such as manacles, chains, fetters and locks (but also a reminder that the region supplied shackles to pin down slaves), in the statue of Prince Albert in the middle of the city (which stands as an inadvertent reminder of the fact that the Consort became a staunch supporter of abolition, and was President of the African Civilization Society for the Extinction of the Slave Trade) and in the name of the famous local football ground for the mighty Wolverhampton Wanderers, Molineux (the Molineux family in Wolverhampton had some involvement in the Jamaican rum industry, and a sea captain gave them as a present a Sierra Leonean child slave whom they named George John Scipio Africanus and proceeded to educate).

Eating is, of course, a necessary part of both the school day and sightseeing, and lunchtime would, you've guessed it, be an opportunity to continue the spirit of the enterprise. Any school lunch provides the perfect occasion to teach people that free school meals are arguably a legacy of empire – some historians maintaining that many of the social reforms that led to the modern-day welfare state came about because politicians worried that the poor health of the newly urbanized working classes was endangering Britain's ability to maintain an empire and hold its own against growing competition from Germany, America and Japan. These concerns peaked around the time of the Boer Wars, when a national scandal erupted over the poor physical and educational quality of the recruits, more than a third of whom had been dismissed as unfit. This converged with the growing acceptance of eugenics – the idea that the success of the nation depended on breeding and maintaining a healthy Anglo-Saxon 'stock'. Horrified by the idea that poor housing, adulterated food, malnutrition, lack of healthcare and deficits in both literacy and moral and religious education might be causing the British race to degenerate until it resembled the races it was born to rule over, politicians introduced a raft of measures from the state pension to compulsory school medical services, unemployment and sickness insurance, maternity benefits paid direct to nursing mothers rather than through their husbands, and the new Mental Health Act of 1913 which allowed for the involuntary segregation of 'mental defectives' in institutions.[8]

Empire Day 2.0 menus could teach a great deal too, and they wouldn't necessarily have to focus on obviously colonial dishes like Mulligatawny soup (still available in the Heinz tinned range, but consumed by no one I know, and originating, according to *Hobson-Jobson*, from the Tamil *milagu-tannir*, meaning 'pepper-water'). Many of our more mainstream dishes are also of imperial origin. The popularity of curry, arguably our national dish now, is of course a testament to how empire changed our tastes. The great Sunday roast first became possible on a mass scale after the development of refrigeration and imports of meat could be brought in from the colonies (and elsewhere): by the late nineteenth century, Britain absorbed 60 per cent of all meat traded globally, the imports from places like Australia and New Zealand permitting the working classes their weekly roast.

The great British institution of the Christmas pudding is undeniably English in origin, but it nevertheless became a symbol of unity within empire when, in the 1920s, a quango called the Empire Marketing

Board used it to create the notion of the 'Empire Pudding'. In a promotional exercise worthy of the organizers of the International Day of the Nacho, they came up with the idea of creating a Christmas pudding for the royal family, where 'each ingredient had been sourced from one of the British colonies'. Such a focus on imperial foodstuffs and raw materials was a common visual aid at the time for schools teaching of imperialism, so-called object lessons, featuring boxes full of everything from raw cotton to loaf sugar, saffron, rice and camphor.* Then there is sugar, the addiction to which propelled the endless need for labourers on plantations, which in turn drove the slave trade, for a long time a key element of British empire.

Moreover, many aspects of the *way* we get our food originate from the age of empire. Food miles? Colonial imports of perishable food and drink were transported over huge distances to become everyday staples for the general population. Processed food? The British pioneered the technology, thanks to centuries of experience in transporting foods to feed their colonists at every corner of the globe, with the first food-canning factory opened in Bermondsey in 1813. One of the major companies, Crosse & Blackwell, still operates, although its imperial slogan, 'The name that is known to the ends of the earth', has been consigned to history.

Meanwhile, there is no shortage of drinks with imperial origins:

---

* In 1911 Rudyard Kipling supplied a poem, entitled 'Big Steamers', for a textbook which conveyed how much Britain relied on empire. It opens:

> 'OH, where are you going to, all you Big Steamers,
> With England's own coal, up and down the salt seas?'
> 'We are going to fetch you your bread and your butter,
> Your beef, pork, and mutton, eggs, apples, and cheese.'
> 'And where will you fetch it from, all you Big Steamers,
> And where shall I write you when you are away?'
> 'We fetch it from Melbourne, Quebec, and Vancouver.
> Address us at Hobart, Hong-kong, and Bombay.'
> 'But if anything happened to all you Big Steamers,
> And suppose you were wrecked up and down the salt sea?'
> 'Why, you'd have no coffee or bacon for breakfast,
> And you'd have no muffins or toast for your tea.'

Rose's Lime Juice Cordial was, for instance, devised in the 1860s by Lauchlan Rose as a method of preserving juice without alcohol, the world's first concentrated fruit drink making use of imported lime juice from the West Indies; it was discovered that, as with pale ale, the flavour of madeira wine was improved by being shipped around the globe; spotting the potential of rum, British merchants turned it from a niche Caribbean drink into a global phenomenon; and the great British gin and tonic originally became popular among the British abroad when they learned that the quinine in tonic had anti-malarial properties. This led to an upper-class character in the woeful 1976 British comedy *Spanish Fly* observing that 'gin and tonic was the cornerstone of the British empire'. Played by Terry-Thomas, the character continued: 'The empire was built on gin and tonic. Gin to fight the boredom of exile and quinine to fight malaria. How else do you think we could have carried the cross of responsibility for the life of millions without the friendly fortitude of gin and tonic?'[9] But there is, of course, nothing more imperial than the most British drink of all: a cup of sweetened tea. After all, tea was originally a Chinese plant traded for opium grown in Bengal (and the subcontinent later grew tea itself); the sugar to sweeten it was originally cultivated by African slaves on West Indian plantations (and later by Indian indentured labourers). Nonetheless, the drink became central to our national identity, while sugar also transformed our cuisine, increasing the consumption of vegetables and fruit by making them more palatable in tarts, preserves and pies.

Which brings us to the fact that a whole host of great British institutions actually came about or flourished because of empire. The Scouts? Conceived and founded by Sir Robert Baden-Powell to turn a new generation of boys 'into good citizens or useful colonists', he wanted to call them the Imperial Scouts, but was talked out of it by his publisher. Baden-Powell also founded the Girl Guides Association in 1909, setting its principles with his sister Agnes in its first handbook, entitled *How Girls Can Help to Build up the Empire*. Panto? Well, *Aladdin* is the most famous, and it features Widow Twankey, of course, as Aladdin's mother, with Twankay or 'twankey' being a substandard Chinese green tea. Our famous security services which inspire blockbusters like

James Bond? It has been pointed out that this country has a history of first developing and perfecting its policing methods in the colonies before bringing them to Britain. For instance, our very first official police system was tried out in Ireland before being initiated in Britain in 1829; fingerprinting was developed in India as a tool to control the population, before being brought to Britain to be used in the detection of crimes;* then, in 1883, the Special Branch of the London Metropolitan Police was established in order to deal with Irish troublemakers, and was led by those with experience in Ireland and India.[10]

And then we have the royal family. As British as you get, right? Well, leaving aside the family's foreign roots, reflected in the fact that Queen Victoria was known to speak to Prince Albert in German, many academics maintain that our reverence for the royals was closely bound up with empire, and vice versa, such patriotic feeling reaching its peak during a period which saw Queen Victoria being dubbed 'Empress of India' (in 1876) and which witnessed extravagant Diamond Jubilee celebrations (in 1897). Victoria famously enjoyed signing herself 'V.R. & I.' – Victoria Regina et Imperatrix – and entertaining imperial visitors at her palaces; the future George V went on tours of empire (with his brother Albert Victor, then heir to the throne, in 1879–82 and for almost eight months in 1901) and, when he took the throne, his first two Christmas broadcasts are thought to have been written by the arch-imperialist Rudyard Kipling; his first Christmas message was preceded by an hour-long programme about the empire, and the first speech of his that was ever broadcast was his opening address at the Empire Exhibition of 1924.[11] In her Christmas messages Queen Elizabeth II was referring to empire until the 1960s, while 'the confetti of empire' was, according to Britain's envoy to India, still noticeable at her coronation in 1953.[12]

---

* When achieving one of the earliest prosecutions using fingerprint evidence in Britain, Richard Muir, the prosecutor at the Old Bailey, emphasized the imperial connection. The technique, he declared in 1902, was 'of the greatest importance in the administration of the criminal law, and was now being introduced into this country on a very large scale for the purpose of identifying habitual criminals, as well as being applied to the detection of individual crimes. The system had had an extensive trial in our dependency in India.'

Lord Meath was enthusiastic about using the monarchy and empire to promote one another, and when the Empire Marketing Board came up with the notion of the 'Empire pudding' for the royal family, he got involved in the project. He arranged for the dessert to be made at Vernon House, the headquarters of the Royal Over-Seas League in London, an occasion which was filmed for a newsreel called *Think and Eat Imperially*,[13] and watching it on YouTube more than ninety years later is a mildly unsettling experience. It depicts Lord Meath, labelled as 'Empire Movement Veteran', awkwardly encouraging a series of representatives from the Dominions to take turns to throw relevant ingredients into the mix of the King's empire Christmas pudding. So we see Zanzibar cloves being presented by black men in fez hats, South African raisins being presented by white women in uniforms, English beer being presented by a sturdy man with a moustache and a barrel on his shoulder, and the overall vibe is a cross between that of a stilted Indian wedding, a Jamie Oliver cookery demonstration and, with Lord Meath sporting a top hat, all-black clothes and a heavy chain, a rap video. There is mercifully no blackface but, frankly, it's a struggle to imagine how it was considered entertainment then, or why it was deemed worthy of release.

The only explanation I can conceive is that perhaps, in the 1920s, simply seeing people from around the world interacting with the British was intrinsically fascinating. Such cosmopolitanism is a humdrum feature of London life now, of course, our multiculturalism largely being a consequence of our once having colonized a quarter of the world. The reason I am sitting here, as a person of colour in Britain, talking about this country as my home, is because several hundred years ago some Britons decided to take control of parts of the Asian subcontinent. In turn, this serves to highlight the fact that the things we have touched upon so far as legacies of empire are actually small fry. It's all very well highlighting empire awareness by talking about how our honours list still hands out Orders of the British Empire, how many of our common garden plants were originally imported into Britain by imperialists, or how Worcestershire sauce might originally have been an Indian recipe, reportedly brought back to Britain by an ex-governor of Bengal. But our imperial past has had a much more profound effect on modern Britain.

Empire explains why we have a diaspora of millions of Britons spread around the world. Empire explains the global pretensions of our Foreign and Defence secretaries. Empire explains the feeling that we are exceptional and can go it alone when it comes to everything from Brexit to dealing with global pandemics. Empire helped to establish the position of the City of London as one of the world's major financial centres, and also ensures that the interests of finance trump the interests of so many other groups in the twenty-first century. Empire explains how some of our richest families and institutions and cities became wealthy. Empire explains our particular brand of racism, it explains our distrust of cleverness, our propensity for jingoism. Let's face it, imperialism is not something that can be erased with a few statues being torn down or a few institutions facing up to their dark pasts; it exists as a legacy in my very being and, more widely, explains nothing less than who we are as a nation.

2. Imperialism and Me

The Punjab has always interested me, but I never saw it as fun. When I visited with my mother – twice, as a child and as a young man – it was where I was dragged around countless temples and relatives' houses in enervating heat, where strangers mocked my Indian-language skills, calling people from other parts of the village to listen to me struggling to articulate the most basic sentiments in a Black Country accent, and where I was encouraged to play with farm animals when all I actually wanted was access to a Nintendo. At home in Wolverhampton, where I grew up feeling as English as I did Asian, it was a part of the world where National Front yobs wanted to boot me back to, and the place where a substantial portion of my extended family seemed to succumb to substance abuse (a startling number of my fifty-four first cousins dying as a result of alcohol and drug addictions in the Punjab), to religious fanaticism (one got involved with the Sikh separatist movement and was killed) and to other violence (one of my uncles murdered another).

It turns out, however, that visiting the Punjab as an adult in the twenty-first century is a wholly different experience. My Punjabi is ropier than ever – when I try to buy a 'lathi' (stick), one shopkeeper seems to think I'm asking for a 'lassi' (the drink) – but it's the first time I feel at home in India. What was regarded as the 'third world' in the 1980s and 1990s is now a key state in an emerging superpower, and while Mumbai and Delhi are increasingly indistinguishable from most global cities, Amritsar has so much colour and character it feels like walking around inside a feature in *National Geographic*. Sikhs are a minority in both Britain and India and it feels extraordinary to be somewhere where, for once, my people are everywhere. I encounter Sikh policemen, Sikh pilots, Sikh doctors, even Sikh vagrants – my astonishment at the sight of the latter an inversion of the surprise my immigrant parents felt on arriving in Britain and discovering that even white people could be poor. In the middle of the city stands the Golden Temple, home to hundreds of volunteers feeding tens of thousands of people each day in the name of humanity and epitomizing the best of Sikhism. And then, the cuisine! The late Anthony Bourdain once said that the Punjab was the only place where vegetarian food didn't feel like a chore – which feels like an understatement. As a result, this visit to the Punjab, where I have come to make a documentary, feels more like a holiday than work and the luxury of the experience is accentuated by the fact that I am being guided around Amritsar by some leading historians, who know this amazing city better than anyone.

Chief among them is Kim Wagner, who, as we walk off our jet lag, highlights objects and places of interest, including a memorial built in the middle of Amritsar to honour the Sikhs – namely the twenty-one soldiers of the 36th Sikh Regiment who fought to the last man at the Battle of Saragarhi, on 12 September 1897, during one of the British campaigns on the North-West Frontier. Standing in front of it, Kim tells me that the battle occurred at a time when the situation in Afghanistan was as flammable as it is now, and when ongoing tensions between the British empire and Russia over various territories were referred to as 'the Great Game'. The twenty-one Sikh soldiers stood their ground against an onslaught of 10,000 enemy tribesmen – the Sikhs making a valiant and suicidal last stand, forcing the enemy to pay a high price for their victory, with around 180 dead. To commemorate their bravery, this Sikh temple, or *gurdwara*, was unveiled by the British in 1904. And as Kim continues regaling me with the details, that when news of the battle reached London both Houses of Parliament gave a rare standing ovation in honour of the Sikhs who had died holding the post, and that the events prompted Viscount Slim to remark that 'You are never disappointed when you are with Sikhs,' I feel pride.

I should confess that at this point of my journey into the story of British empire my history is poor. I have a GCSE in history under my belt, but it left me with little more than superficial knowledge of the world wars, the Tudors and Tollund Man. Meanwhile, my education in British empire was almost non-existent. In fact, looking back, it's almost as if teachers went out of their way to avoid telling us about it: we explored both world wars at length, for example, but I don't recall it once being mentioned that tens of thousands of brown people from across empire were fighting for Britain and that empire made great financial contributions too; and while we studied the Irish Potato Famine, no one cared to illustrate the tragedy by comparison to famines in India. At this stage I am aware, however, that we Sikhs did better than other colonized people out of empire.

I know that, although we were finally defeated by the British during the Anglo-Sikh Wars of 1845–6 and 1848–9,* Sikhs were generally respected by the British, largely taking the side of the colonizers during the Uprising of 1857, fighting in large numbers for Britain in both world wars – according to the WWI Sikh Memorial Fund, around 130,000 Sikhs took part, making up 20 per cent of the British Indian Army (despite making up less than 1 per cent of the population) – and being posted to Singapore and Hong Kong. I recall my grandfather comparing British empire favourably to the 1980s government of Indira Gandhi and telling me how the British had transformed the once forsaken Punjab by tapping the waters of its five rivers to make it one of the most productive and prosperous provinces in India. And Sikhs have traditionally been keen to make the most of opportunities for relocation within empire, whether it was travelling en masse to build a railway in East Africa, or in smaller numbers to work as pedlars in Britain in the early twentieth century, or in larger numbers again to staff British factories in the 1960s and 1970s.

---

* Before this, Maharajah Ranjit Singh enjoyed cordial relations with the British, who signed the Sutlej Treaty with the Sikh empire in April 1809. In *Empire of the Sikhs*, Patwant Singh writes: 'According to its provisions the Lahore Durbar would not relinquish its sovereignty over the territories acquired by it south of the Sutlej prior to 1806. The "perpetual friendship", according to the treaty, would rest on these four main clauses: that the British would leave control of the territories north of the Sutlej to the Sikh state; Ranjit Singh would not maintain "more troops than are necessary for the internal duties" of his territories south of the Sutlej; he would "not commit or suffer any encroachments on the possessions or rights of the chiefs in its vicinity"; in the event of a violation of these articles, or a "departure from the rules of friendship", the treaty would be considered terminated.'

Indeed, as the relevant Wikipedia entry states: 'British Sikhs are considered one of the best examples of cultural integration in the United Kingdom.' The 'Indian' food in British curry houses is no such thing, rather a merging of dishes from different regions tweaked for a conservative British palate by mostly Bangladeshi chefs, but many of the staples of what is now our national cuisine – the pakoras, the samosas, the saag – are recognizably Punjabi. Perhaps because the army set a precedent by allowing Sikh soldiers to keep their turbans, Sikhs in Britain have had the kind of success fighting for specific entitlements, such as the right to be exempted from laws requiring motorcyclists to wear helmets, and the right to carry the ceremonial kirpan (dagger), that many other minority groups have not enjoyed. There are now Sikhs in the Commons and the Lords, and a diamond that once belonged to a Sikh maharajah is among the Crown Jewels and likely to be worn by Camilla and Kate in their role as consorts to the King.

In short, it seems the Sikhs did relatively well out of empire and, frankly, it feels good to be admiring this impressive monument in our most sacred city to the historically fruitful relations between the two aspects of my dual identity. But the positivity doesn't last, because our next stop in Amritsar is a park down the road: Jallianwala Bagh. This pleasant open space, about the size of Trafalgar Square, is where, almost exactly a century before my visit, at 5.15pm on a Sunday, General Reginald Dyer stormed in with what he called his 'special party' of fifty armed infantry. Having recently arrived in the city to quash a supposed uprising against the British, and having hours earlier issued what he claimed were clear warnings against public gatherings, he concluded that the people assembled there – between 15,000 and 20,000 men, women and children – were intentionally resisting Raj rule. With no further warning, he ordered his troops to fire. As one, the huge crowd 'seemed to sink to the ground' according to witness Sergeant W. J. Anderson, 'a whole flutter of white garments'. There were few opportunities to escape: those climbing walls were targeted and shot, as was anyone seen running to the exit. At one point, according to a British eyewitness, Dyer asked one of his officers, 'Do you think they've had enough?', before adding, 'No, we'll give them four rounds more.' And at the end of ten minutes of carnage, 1,650 shots had been fired, an average of thirty-three bullets per soldier. The official number of deaths was eventually set at 379, with around three times as many wounded, but Kim puts the number of deaths at between 600 and 1,000, and other estimates put both tallies in their thousands.[1]

The Jallianwala Bagh Massacre is one of the key events of the twentieth century, arguably marking the moment the Raj lost its grip on the largest empire in human history, and after which the momentum for Indian independence became unstoppable. The Nobel laureate Rabindranath Tagore described it as 'without parallel in the history of civilised governments' and returned his knighthood in protest. The independence activist Motilal Nehru, father of the first Prime Minister of India, symbolically burned his European furniture and clothes. Gandhi declared that he had lost his trust in British justice, saying that he had 'underrated the forces of evil' in the empire. And in Britain, even the imperialist Winston Churchill famously described the incident as 'monstrous', while the Labour politician J. C. Wedgwood declared it had 'destroyed our reputation throughout the world . . . and damns us for all time'. With the centenary of the atrocity just months away in 2019, it is also the reason I'm in Amritsar with a TV documentary crew. But, to my shame, I know barely anything about it before coming here, what little knowledge I have deriving from the pivotal scene in Richard Attenborough's *Gandhi*, which I once watched when getting progressively tipsy on a long flight.

Just when I think I've learned the worst about the massacre, Kim proffers more devastating detail. The crowd at Jallianwala Bagh on 13 April 1919 had gathered in peace. Some were there to listen to a political speech, but the majority were ordinary students, watchmakers, barbers, hawkers, pedlars and pilgrims visiting the Golden Temple to mark the festival of Vaisakhi,* just as I have

---

* The Sikh equivalent of Easter, Vaisakhi commemorates Guru Gobind Singh's creation of the fellowship of the Khalsa, and is considered so auspicious that Maharajah Ranjit Singh chose the day of the festival in April 1801 to proclaim himself the ruler of the Sikh empire.

done on earlier trips with my mum, and as my own extended family in nearby villages still do. The victims, most of whom were entirely unaware of the warnings Dyer had erratically issued across the city, included women and more than forty children, some as young as one. Dyer remarked afterwards that he would have used the machine guns on his armoured cars if he could have physically got them into the Bagh, but the rifles used by troops were deadly enough. A single bullet from a .303 Lee Enfield rifle of the type used in the massacre could rip through several bodies – stray shots killed at least one woman outside the Bagh – and the weapons could fire tens of rounds a minute. A military curfew meant that the injured were not tended to, and many of them subsequently died.

Accounts show that doctors who later treated victims were harassed by the authorities for the details of their patients, because anyone who had been at Jallianwala Bagh was labelled a potential enemy of the state. Groups of men who were, with no evidence whatsoever, deemed to have been involved in 'riots' or disturbances before the massacre were arrested, ordered to stand in the brutal heat for hours, flogged until they passed out, dragged by the beard, kicked up and down streets and subjected to the sexual violence that was routine in colonial India. Although eventually forced to resign by the Army Council, Dyer was subsequently effectively exonerated by the House of Lords, and the *Morning Post*, which was eventually absorbed into the *Daily Telegraph*, started a public fund to support him. Contributors to the fund, who included Rudyard Kipling and 'one who remembers 1857', raised £26,000 (the equivalent today of £4.4 million). In contrast, the relatives of those killed received on average just 8,700 rupees each (modern equivalent, £141,537).

Later that afternoon, I go to a different part of the city, to look at the spot on a street where a British missionary, Marcia Sherwood, had been attacked in the riots that preceded the massacre, which led Dyer to pronounce that the area should be turned into a 'sacred space'. He had already subjected Amritsar to collective punishment for what he considered an uprising: both the water and electricity supplies to the city had been cut off and all Indians were subject to flogging if they did not salute/salaam to every Englishman they encountered.

But now Dyer decided that no Indians were allowed to set foot on this 'sacred' street, and ordered each end to be barricaded. If a local really had to go down it, they had to do so on all fours. The British soldiers who enforced the order at the end of bayonets, occasionally pissing into the well at the end of the street as they did so, made no exceptions, even forcing a blind elderly beggar named Kahan Chand to crawl when he unwittingly stumbled on to the scene.

Walking down this 'crawling lane' a hundred years later, I wouldn't have wanted to get down on my hands and knees even with modern sewage systems, but this is what members of my family could have been forced to do had they been in Amritsar then, purely because of the colour of their skin. As Kim points out in his book, this method of punishment is reminiscent of the British response to the Siege of Cawnpore in 1857, when General Neill forced Indian prisoners to lick up the blood in the house where British women and children had been killed, essentially an exercise in ritualized racial humiliation. But then it is apparent that everything about the way empire operated during this period of history was racialized. Speaking decades after the event, a British soldier from 1919 is recorded describing the Amritsar protestors as 'striking niggers'. One of Dyer's colleagues, Brigadier-General Drake-Brockman, who led British troops during uprisings in Delhi a few weeks before Jallianwala Bagh, openly called the rioting crowd 'scum'. He went on: 'I am of firm opinion that if they had got a bit more firing given them it would have done them a world of good and their attitude would be much more amenable and respectful, as force is the only thing that an Asiatic has any respect for.'

Jallianwala Bagh was not a uniquely Sikh tragedy by any means: there were more Hindu and Muslim deaths in the initial British report, and indeed some of Dyer's lethal riflemen were Sikhs. More than anything else, it was a formative national event for the whole of India. But it was nonetheless a defining event for the Sikh community and my investigation into it leaves me as depressed about British–Sikh relations as the Saragarhi memorial had made me feel uplifted about them. The massacre and its aftermath illustrate that, as well as being indulged, the Sikhs were seen by some imperial Brits as racially inferior and dispensable. What I learn leaves me bitter that my education didn't instil this crucial knowledge into me, ashamed I didn't find out about it myself, and the TV broadcast of my documentary reveals that I'm not alone in my ignorance. By far the most common response from viewers is 'I had no idea' and 'I was taught nothing about empire at school,' and among those who had heard of the Amritsar Massacre, details were sketchy: some fellow British Sikhs even confessed that they had confused the events of 1919 with the Indian government's actions against Sikhs during Operation Blue Star in 1984. Above all, I feel embarrassed that I have written two books about the British Sikh experience without really understanding the crucial position of Sikhs during empire.

There turn out to be many more demonstrations of anti-Sikh racism beyond what happened at Jallianwala Bagh. Here, during the Battle of Gujarat (1849), an encounter during the Second Anglo-Sikh War, we see Britons dehumanizing Sikhs, losing just 96 men in the course of slaughtering some 3,000 Sikhs, an officer of the 9th Lancers remarking in the process that enemies running for their lives were 'of course shot', with Sikhs hiding in trees providing 'great sport for our men, who were firing up at them as at so many rooks . . . down they would come like a bird, head downward, and bleeding most profusely'.[2] Here, in the Indian Pavilion of the 1851 Crystal Palace exhibition, we have Sikhs being described as lacking 'a ray of intelligence'. Here, in 1872, we have Deputy Commissioner J. L. Cowan summarily executing sixty-eight Namdhari Sikh prisoners in a form of collective punishment following an attack on the small Muslim principality of Malerkotla in the Punjab: the method he chose was to fire the victims from cannons, meaning that their body parts were so scattered they could not be retrieved for funeral rites.

And as for the famous Koh-i-Noor diamond: far from being a celebratory reflection of great British–Sikh relations, the brutal truth is that it ended up in the Crown Jewels only after it had been seized from Maharajah Ranjit Singh's family by the East India Company: the campaign to have it returned is very much alive. It's true, Sikhs volunteered in massive numbers for the First World War, to fight for a nation that had annexed their empire, but they were not rewarded for their loyal service: one of the many things that had been fuelling discontent among the protestors who had been rioting in the days leading up to the Jallianwala Bagh Massacre – alongside economic distress, rising food prices and the sudden arrest of two local nationalist leaders – was the fact that Sikhs and other Punjabis were faced with repressive legislation at the hands of the British. Furthermore, after the massacre, Dyer had sought and achieved an 'honour' in the Golden Temple thanks to priests allied to the British government: this caused so much outrage in the Sikh community that it contributed to the creation of a new political movement, the Shiromani Akali Dal, which remains a force in India to this day.

The most shocking revelation for me, however, is that the Sikh reputation for being a warrior race, which you probably wouldn't pick up on if you glanced at my physique, but which is nevertheless more central to our self-identity than beards, turbans and private numberplates on BMWs, was popularized by the British in their efforts to divide and rule imperial India after the Uprising of 1857. When the British first started recruiting soldiers they didn't take a man's ethnic group and social caste into account, but the 1857 Uprising, when thousands of Indian solders rose up against them, led to a change in thinking. The new notion had it that certain 'martial races', not coincidentally the ones that proved loyal to Britain during the Uprising, made particularly good soldiers, and so should be sought out. Recruiting officers could even consult handbooks that listed in exhaustive detail the physical characteristics of each of the desired martial races, such as smartness, soldierly bearing, the length of their limbs, broad jaws, clear eyes and 'alert expressions'. 'Today many of the ethnic groups that compose the martial races still believe that they are part of a martial race and that they always have been,' concludes Pradeep Barua in 'Inventing Race: The British and India's Martial Races'. 'More than a century after the Sepoy Revolt and almost a half century following independence, a significant proportion of the army of the Republic of India is still recruited along ethnic lines based on the Victorian theories of the martial races of India.' Tayyab Mahmud adds in 'Colonialism and Modern Constructions of Race: A Preliminary Inquiry': 'Sikh as a martial race was not discovered; it was created.'

I don't buy this claim entirely: Sikhs had some role in creating the image of themselves as fighters. The conception of Sikhs as spiritual warriors had originally been established by the sixth of the ten gurus who established the faith, Guru Hargobind, tradition having it that, on his coronation, he declared that he would wear a sword on each hip, and the tenth guru, Guru Gobind Singh, channelled this martial outlook when he fortified the city of Anandpur Sahib and established the Sikh warrior community called Khalsa in 1699.[3] This was a necessary move given that Sikhism was a minority faith in India when it emerged around 500 years ago in what was then the Mughal empire, challenged many ideas prevalent at the time and found itself threatened as a result. In *Empire of the Sikhs*, Patwant Singh estimates that the first seventy years of the eighteenth century saw around 200,000 Sikhs killed. But I accept it was British colonialists who did most to entrench and propagate this view of Sikhs in the world, and who, in their obsession with classification, accentuated the boundaries between Sikhs and other religious groups in India.

In other words, the way the British *saw* Sikhs in relation to other groups changed after 1857 and their views were so influential that they partly explain the way we see ourselves in relation to others. There are arguably numerous contemporary manifestations of the divisions, Sikhs being accepted in modern Britain as 'good immigrants', winning legal privileges and even being the subject of a campaign to recreate a Sikh regiment in the British Army, while other minority ethnic immigrant communities are demonized. And the realization blows my mind. Empire explains more about British Sikhs than the simple fact that we are here. Moreover, as I continue to educate myself, I begin to appreciate that many of the experiences of Sikhs in post-war Britain, and more specifically in post-war Wolverhampton, were also essentially colonial.

I read of coarse racist generalizations that could have come from the mouth of General Dyer himself, including remarks from the likes of Canon Selwyn Gummer and future Conservative minister John Selwyn Gummer in a book about Punjabi emigration to Britain in 1966 that 'the Sikhs are strangers in a strange land and are intellectually and educationally ill-equipped to deal with the complexities of a modern civilization'. I learn of rows in Midlands factories about hygiene, which led to one factory building a special lavatory for its 'unsanitary' Sikh workers, only to find it to be much better looked after than those used by its white workforce,[4] and the fact that some South Asian women disembarking at London's airports in the 1970s were obliged to undergo 'virginity tests' because the immigration service had absorbed colonial notions of gender and sexuality and assumed 'genuine' brides would be virgins.[5] Then there are the experiences many Sikhs had in my own home town with racial violence.

Clearly, there has never been a Jallianwala Bagh-style massacre of Sikhs in Britain, but the tone of the violence used against Sikhs in imperial India and the dehumanizing way imperial Britons talked about all Indians in general at the time will feel all too familiar to any-one of colour who, like me, grew up under the shadow of 'Paki-bashing' skinhead gangs in the second half of the twentieth century. Hundreds weren't mowed down in parks, but our lives were circumscribed by racial violence of a colonial tenor, whether it was a white mob attack-ing a black household in Wolverhampton (1965), twelve discrete incidents in the city which included one where fourteen white men chanted 'Powell' at a black christening, inspired by Enoch Powell's Rivers of Blood speech (1968), a judge at Birmingham Crown Court complaining that 'roughing up of coloureds is almost a hobby in some parts of the Black Country' (1973), five assaults on Indians in one week in Wolverhampton pubs (1976) and civil disturbances in Wolverhamp-ton involving gratuitous police violence and football supporters sporting K K K-style hoods (1978). I'm a fair-weather Wolves supporter nowadays, but when I was a child my mother wouldn't allow us out of the house on match days, and one of my earliest childhood memories is hiding, with tens of other Sikh families, in the local temple, as far-right gangs terrorized Wolverhampton.[6]

Then there was the routine employment discrimination that all people of colour faced in Wolverhampton – a mirror of what hap-pened in imperial India. On the subcontinent institutionalized racial discrimination saw brown people being kept out of senior roles and Sikhs, despite occasional indulgence, being allowed to do only the most demeaning work on the railways,* while in Wolverhampton it saw transport workers banning overtime in protest at the recruitment of black labour (1955), a Sikh bus driver being sent home from Wolverhampton Transport Department when he turned up for work sporting a beard (1967), a newspaper revealing that there was not one single 'coloured worker' in the West Midlands police force or working as a clerk in a bank or among the 1,000 members of staff in the large department store Beatties (1968) and an Indian teacher being appointed to a post at a local comprehensive only to have the decision reversed by the School Management Committee (1978).

A third imperial parallel lies in the discrimination Sikhs faced, along with other people of colour, in housing. In Amritsar in 1919, the British lived away from the 'native city' behind the 'civil lines', while elsewhere in India Britons talked about Indians living in 'Black Town' or the 'native quarter', reflecting a widespread attitude across empire that the ruling race should not mix with 'darkies' − an attitude that immigrants of my parents' generation found themselves facing in Wolverhampton. It was manifested in residents of Wordsworth Avenue and Beverley Crescent in Lanesfield (a few hundred yards from where I spent my teenage years) forming a residents' association of seventy-eight people to exclude black syndicates from buying houses in their area (1958), a firm declaring it had banned coloured people from Lyndale Park estate 'to protect whites' (1965), a hundred council tenants holding an open-air meeting to protest at a decision to offer a

---

* In his book on the Indian railways, *Railways & the Raj*, Christian Wolmar explains that the British-owned railway companies' system of employment was grotesquely racist: there were wild wage disparities between white and Indian employees; the companies created a special class of mixed-raced Eurasian labourer, as they were deemed more reliable than 'natives'; and the colonialists simply didn't think Indians could be trusted to do important tasks. Local workers were banned from most managerial, technical and supervisory jobs and imperial Brits 'placed a series of overt and covert barriers in the way of Indians progressing up the career ladder'. At one point they were persuaded to give Sikhs the chance to break 'the separation of office tasks between Europeans and locals but concluded they were only suited to lesser tasks in each area of work . . . shunting locomotives around yards or driving goods trains on branch lines, rather than operating services that carried passengers'.

one-bedroom flat to an Indian (1965), Wolverhampton housing committee regulations forcing immigrants who wished to be eligible for a
council property to be registered on a separate, longer waiting list
(1968) and house purchases being so difficult that one Dayabhai Patel
remarked (in 1968) that 'the only property we can buy is a slum house.
Then the whites turn around and say we're creating slums.' This legacy is only being slowly dismantled in the twenty-first century: when
I grew up in Wolverhampton, there were distinct 'Asian', 'black' and
'white' areas.

Yet another imperial import was colour bars. In Amritsar, the social
separation of races was so routine that Indians were forced to buy plat-
form tickets at the railway station while Europeans could go on the
platforms freely, European clubs allowed no Indian members and
Indian servants lived entirely separately from their British masters.
These were attitudes that were imported into Wolverhampton to various degrees, with a local journalist admitting that a colour bar existed
in the town (in 1955), the Scala ballroom baldly stating that it operated
one (in 1958), Wolverhampton's West End Working Men's Club introducing a colour bar after two Indians had applied to join (in 1961), a
colour bar still operating in some working men's clubs, according to
local historians, as late as 1984, and separate 'black', 'Asian' and 'white'
pubs being a fact of my upbringing even later than this. We are, as a
nation, rather smug about not having had formal racial segregation
like the United States (in itself not much of a boast anyway), but you
could argue it has operated informally for decades.

Of course, when considering race in Wolverhampton, there is no
avoiding the former local MP Enoch Powell, who cast a huge shadow
not only over local Wolverhampton politics, but over national politics
too.[7] With the twenty-first-century triumph of Nigel Farage, who
routinely cites Powell as a hero and inspiration, you could even argue
that Powell has been one of the most influential political figures of the
modern age, helping to inspire Brexit. And a glance at his life story
reveals how Powell's life and politics were, in turn, heavily influenced
by empire. Powell was an ardent imperialist from childhood, believing empire to be running in the blood and fibre of every Englishman.
His youthful commitment to empire ran deep, carrying him to

Australia in his twenties and then to Egypt and India during the Second World War. By his own admission, he fell helplessly in love with India, his devotion to the imperial cause creating the desire to become Viceroy of India. His ambitions, however, coincided with mounting pressure on the government to grant independence to India. Powell lobbied desperately against the move, attempting to justify empire on economic grounds, claiming that only with its colonies could Britain hold its own against the heft of America and the USSR. When, in 1947, power was transferred to India, he was devastated, 'spending the whole of one night walking the streets of London trying to come to terms with it' – struggling to accept that 'one's whole world had been altered'. Nevertheless, when he stood as a Conservative MP in the general election of 1951, his election address featured the declaration that 'I BELIEVE IN THE BRITISH EMPIRE. Without the empire, Britain would be like a head without a body.'

Looking back, Powell's attitudes to race were sometimes complicated: he talked about falling in love with India and studied Urdu at the School of Oriental and African Studies, but writing to his parents about his first impressions of India he talked in deeply racist terms: 'I was glad to be through India, where I felt a certain oppressiveness in the atmosphere difficult to describe. The people have not the spontaneity which makes the populations further east attractive, but a kind of dumb, almost animal, servility which to me came as a painful affront; largely, but not entirely, I think this is a projection of a fundamentally insubordinate nature.' Regardless, his embrace of racist politics in the 1960s was clearly a consequence of his imperialism. After all, his stated 'three enduring principles of Englishness' – 'unity under the Crown in Parliament, its historical continuity, and its racial homogeneity' – echoed the racial structure of empire. One of the central images in his infamous Rivers of Blood speech of 1968 involved the racial norms of empire being inverted, when he cited the fear that 'in this country in fifteen or twenty years the black man will have the whip hand over the white man'. He also warned against the 'communalism' of the Sikh population, as he saw it in imperial India, meaning that despite historically being a minority group they had an overriding loyalty to their own kind that would prevent them from making rational decisions and accepting the decision of the majority.

Furthermore, many of his supporters responded to his speech referencing the empire, one correspondent remarking in a letter that 'our British working classes have been sacrificed on the altar of a dead colonialism'. As the academic Shirin Hirsch puts it, Powell's racial hierarchies were 'framed by a history of British colonialism', where white imperialists were seen to be guiding and protecting the dark 'natives'. Notions of racial equality subverted the whole system. Modern multiculturalism, in which, according to one dictionary definition, 'all the different cultural or racial groups in a society have equal rights and opportunities, and none is ignored or regarded as unimportant', was an impossibility for Powell, because it didn't fit in with his views of how race worked in empire, where whites ruled over browns. The idea of brown people having equality was, for him, as much of a calamity as his politics were for us.

We all know from endless books and TV programmes on the subject that British empire has shaped the world – how it is responsible for the international prevalence of everything from cricket to polo, football, racquet sports, snooker, English literature, the English language, the Englishman's style of dressing, driving on the right-hand side of the road, Parliamentary politics, judges wearing wigs in court, the Anglican Church and the structures of contemporary international finance. It is also well known how empire is responsible for many of our intractable international disputes and crises, with Kwasi Kwarteng describing in *Ghosts of Empire* six cases where its impact is still felt most acutely – Iraq, Nigeria, Sudan, Hong Kong, Kashmir and Burma – the Tory politician going as far as to argue that 'much of the instability in the world is a product of its legacy of individualism and haphazard policy-making'. But what about us? Having faced up to how British has shaped and defined my life in deep ways I had never realized, I can't help but wonder how imperialism may have shaped modern Britain itself.

3.   Difficult History

Before I start examining how Britain has been shaped by the experience of empire, I realize I need to plug the gaps in my historical
knowledge. And the reading that follows is intense. Part of the challenge is that empire went on for so long: for between four and five
centuries, according to some estimates. Part of it is that empire was so
large: according to a turn-of-the-century school gazette, it consisted
of 'one continent, a hundred peninsulas, five hundred promontories,
a thousand lakes, two thousand rivers, ten thousand islands'. And part
of it is that empire has inspired so many books (mention you're writing about empire and people will invariably recommend a couple
which they insist are essential and which you've not heard of), that
these books are so long (Jan Morris' *Pax Britannica* trilogy extends to
well over 1,500 pages, Lawrence James' *Rise and Fall of the British
Empire* comprises 736 pages of densely printed text, and so on) and
that the stories they tell are so violent (it's not conducive to sleep to go
to bed reading about how, in 1818, the British were responsible for the
deaths of 10,000 people in the course of battling the Kandyan kingdom of Ceylon, how the 1838 Myall Creek massacre saw up to fifty
Indigenous Australians, including women, children and the aged,
being brutally murdered by a group of colonist cattle ranchers, or
how the Hola Camp for Mau Mau rehabilitation in Kenya was so
brutal that eleven prisoners were beaten to death by guards under the
watch of a British prison official).[1]

Nevertheless, it is also relentlessly fascinating. Did you know that
when the British empire was at its territorial peak in the early 1920s,
it covered 13.71 million square miles, which represents 24 per cent of
the earth's land area or equivalent to 94 per cent of the moon's surface
area or almost exactly twice as large as the surface area of Pluto?[2] Did
you know that despite Canada's vast resources Britain actually considered handing it back to France during peace negotiations, in

exchange for the sugar island of Guadeloupe?[3] That Adolf Hitler was fascinated by Britain's global strength and once remarked that Germany should 'learn from the English, who, with 250,000 men in all, govern four hundred million Indians!' That in the early seventeenth century, a pageant was arranged on the Thames to mark the flourishing trade with the East India Company's new ports, which included several artificial floating islands featuring unusual spice trees and international fruit?[4] That Lord Curzon, Viceroy of India from 1899 to 1905, had such a passion for detail that he even ordered the removal of pigeon droppings from Calcutta's Public Library? That we inherited Bombay, as it was known then, as a dowry, when in the 1660s Charles II of England entered an arranged marriage with Catherine of Braganza, daughter of King John IV of Portugal? That, initially, as a result of a missing map, no one at court knew where 'Bumbye' was located, with the Lord High Chancellor wondering out loud whether it was 'somewhere near Brazil'.[5] And that Britain inherited the now mighty island of Manhattan from the Dutch as part of a 1667 settlement of a dispute about some obscure islands located to the east of what is nowadays known as Indonesia?

I find myself particularly taken by this last story, as it is told by John Keay in his 1991 book *The Honourable Company: A History of the English East India Company*. In his version he focuses on the smallest of these islands, Run – full name Pulo Run, and sometimes called Rhun – which is so tiny (2 miles long by half a mile wide) that it takes about an hour to walk around and has no source of fresh water. But what it does have are groves and groves of nutmeg trees. And the thing that made the Banda Islands interesting to Europeans was that they were for many centuries the world's only source of prized nutmeg and mace. Nutmegs flourished here like nowhere else in the world and they were cheap. On Run, ten pounds of the spice cost less than half a penny. In Europe the same amount could be sold for £1.60 – an appreciation of around 32,000 per cent. And when, in 1603, English employees of the East India Company first landed on tiny, remote Run the Dutch had been in the area for two years.

It turned out that while nearby Banda Islands such as Neira and Lonthor had agreed to some Dutch control, Run and the neighbouring island Ai preferred to deal with the English. When, in 1616, Run was pressured by the Dutch (pressure, invasion and occupation which would ultimately result in the death of most of the Bandanese population and which is considered genocide by some), the village headmen voted to formally pledge allegiance to the East India Company. The headmen did this by swearing an oath and presenting the East India Company representatives with a nutmeg seedling rooted in Run soil. This was a statement of trust: as they were fully aware of their monopoly of this precious nut, seedlings were closely guarded and destroyed rather than surrendered. But there was a problem with the deal – the East India Company did not actually have the power to hold overseas territories. Its Royal Charter laid out trading rights and maritime conduct only. So, in a highly significant move, Run's allegiance was accepted by the East India Company on behalf of the Crown and on that day in 1616 James I, whose official title for a period was 'King of England, Scotland, Ireland, France, Puloway and Puloroon', became sovereign of the island. The Dutch weren't happy, and blockaded the island for years. The siege wore down the enthusiasm of the East India Company and they lost interest in Run: in 1667, the same year that the company took over Bombay, Charles II relinquished his rights to the island of Run. Under the Treaty of Breda, the British Crown ceded to the Dutch all rights in the Bandas, receiving by way of compensation a place on the North American coast called New Amsterdam, which would become New York City.

John Keay claims that Run is as fundamental to the story of empire as Runnymede, forever associated with the sealing of Magna Carta, is to British constitutional history – not only because of all these events, but also because it was with Run in mind that Oliver Cromwell made a hugely consequential move and issued the East India Company with a new charter which included the authority to hold, fortify and settle overseas territories. The tiny island of Run, which you could actually run around in a matter of minutes, is not only how the British inherited an island which would become the centre of a world city (incredibly, in an echo of what happened with Canada, the British weren't thrilled about it, and they tried to pawn it off for rich sugar-producing territory in South America),[6] but it was how St Helena, Calcutta, Bengal and other large parts of the East would eventually also come under British rule. And given that you could make the case that this was where British empire began, I decide to visit. To start my story where it all started, to get as close as possible to the actual roots of British empire.

I assume from the fact that the Maluku Province Tourism Office casually conducts its business through WhatsApp rather than email, and consistently refers to me as 'Mrs Sathnam' throughout our correspondence, that it doesn't get many requests for visits from Britain. But they seem keen to help me 'meet with community leaders' and if it doesn't end up happening it's for a bunch of reasons beyond their control. First, it turns out that going to see a few nutmeg trees (are they still there even?) will probably involve a month of travel: nearly two days of air travel to get to a nearby international airport; twelve hours of travel by road and boat from the remote Indonesian province of Papua to the island of Run; a week-long trip to Australia, because if I don't go when I'm so close I never will; and then, of course, some time in New Zealand because if I don't go when I'm so close I never will. Second, it turns out the trip involves travel through Papua, which, on the day I'm about to book, is the scene of brutal violence with dozens of people killed, scores injured and hundreds more arrested.[7] Third, by the time I'm ready to book again, the coronavirus outbreak has made travelling even to Wolverhampton to see my mother illegal. And then, as I continue to fail to get to Run and continue to inform myself about British imperialism, the final nail in the coffin: there turns out to be no consensus on where or when British empire actually began.

I'd gathered from reading about Jallianwala Bagh, and from newspaper coverage over the decades, that the question of when empire ended was the subject of debate. Some posit it was the massacre in the Punjab in 1919 when the British lost the moral argument, some say it was the 1930s when Gandhi gained traction against the British, some argue it was 1947 when the British formally withdrew from India, some pinpoint it to the handover of Hong Kong to the Chinese in July 1997, some gesture towards the Suez crisis of 1956, some insist it continues to exist in the remaining British Overseas Territories we still possess, which in 2020 consisted of Anguilla, Bermuda, the British Antarctic Territory, the British Indian Ocean Territory, the British Virgin Islands, the Cayman Islands, the Falkland Islands, Gibraltar, Montserrat, the Pitcairn Islands, South Georgia & the South Sandwich Islands, the Sovereign Base Areas of Akrotiri and Dhekelia, St Helena, Ascension & Tristan da Cunha and the Turks and Caicos Islands.

That its inception may be just as intangible is a novel notion. In *The Hungry Empire*, Lizzie Collingham dismantles the idea that the foundation of empire lay in 'terms of sea exploration and desire for spices', arguing that it 'was cod fishermen from the West Country who were the first Englishmen to acquire knowledge of the Atlantic currents and winds . . . The British empire was born on Newfoundland's stony beaches.' The first volume of *The Oxford History of the British Empire*, entitled *The Origins of Empire*, mentions Run and the Banda Islands only in passing in an essay by P. J. Marshall. Instead, authors in the collection focus on various early colonial escapades in the Irish province of Ulster, Chesapeake, New England, the Caribbean, Western Africa, Newfoundland and India. Elsewhere other historians point variously to 1497, the year that John Cabot sailed from Bristol on the *Matthew* and 'discovered' the coast of North America under the commission of Henry VII of England, or to 1708, which saw the publication of John Oldmixon's *The British Empire in America* (a year after the Act of Union between England and Scotland officially made Britain a thing), or to 1757, when Indians lost the Battle of Plassey to the East India Company, or to 1858, when the Government of India Act resulted in the abolition of the East India Company and the supremacy of the British Crown. And this is far from the last elastic aspect of British empire. Perhaps the main lesson I imbibe from my reading is that there is very little about British empire that is certain or knowable, the books I consult teaching me, among other things, that:

Britain's relationship with its colonies varied across the globe and over time. Mention 'empire', and I'd hazard that most people's first thought is of British India at the end of the nineteenth century, when Queen Victoria was the 'Empress' of the subcontinent and it was overseen by a viceroy on behalf of Britain.[8] But other territories of empire saw quite different approaches to power, at different times. It's helpful here to remember that there were two distinct phases of empire. The first British empire, which ran from the seventeenth century to the 1780s, was founded on the development of sugar plantations in the West Indies and involved large numbers of settlers to the American colonies and the Caribbean. Essentially, it was shaped by the endeavours of a number of different companies and private individuals, with no single authority. This phase ended with the American War of Independence. The second British empire was a more concerted power grab of India and Africa, at first dominated by the East India Company, which had the authority to print its own cash, set its own taxes, embark on wars on its own, on behalf of the national interest. It was an unusual organization, to say the least, beginning as a conventional international trading corporation, dealing in silks and spices, and becoming an aggressive colonial power: in the space of a few decades it had with a private army twice the size of the British Army conquered the subcontinent, ruling it from anonymous buildings in London. The historian William Dalrymple has pointed out that while the East India Company was the prototype for many of today's joint-stock corporations, it has no contemporary equivalent: Walmart, one of the biggest companies in the world, does not own nuclear submarines; Facebook doesn't possess infantry. If you're struggling to get your head around what it did, don't worry: the Company was so complex that even those involved with it at the time did not necessarily understand it. Judging from his written correspondence, Mir Jafar, the military general who became the first dependent Nawab of Bengal of the British East India Company, imagined the Company to be an individual.* Meanwhile, in

---

* The East India Company was often referred to as 'John Company' in India. As *Hobson-Jobson* explains in its entry for the term: 'An old personification of the East India Company, by the natives often taken seriously, and so used, in former days . . . It has been suggested, but apparently without real reason, that the phrase is a corruption of Company Jahān, which has a fine sounding smack about it, recalling Shah Jehan and Jehāngir, and the golden age of the Moguls.'

London, the East India Company directors could be just as confused: when receiving news of the overthrow and murder of one Siraj ud-Daula, one anxious Company director asked another: 'was it true that the recently assassinated Sir Roger Daulat was a baronet?'

The British state took over from the East India Company in 1858, and India become empire's most considerable colony, but even then there was nothing particularly consistent about how the government ran its realms. The way power worked on the subcontinent was unique: even as Britain's grip tightened there, it loosened in the so-called white dominions like Canada, New Zealand, South Africa and Australia, where it has been argued that settler inhabitants had more freedom than Britons at home. While some 'dependencies' and 'protectorates' were under the direct control of Britain, others were more or less self-governing. Furthermore, academics have shown that empire meant different things to different people at certain points even within single states such as India,[9] while in Latin America and Egypt there was also what could be classed as an informal empire, where Britain wielded power through financial dominance. More generally, it is important to remember that parts of the empire were still expanding in the 1870s (the Scramble for Africa was just beginning) when in other areas it was very old (the Caribbean) or had already collapsed (the USA).

The tone and culture of empire varied wildly during its history. There was an extended period between 1660 and 1807 when Britain profiteered from the evils of the Atlantic slave trade, shipping around 3 million Africans to America, but then, after Parliament had outlawed slavery, it took a leading role in abolishing it. There was a long period when missionaries were discouraged, for fear that they might disrupt the imperialists' work, but then missionaries were encouraged, with empire beginning to see itself as a civilizing mission. There were periods when colonialism was seemingly popular among the British people, most notably during a phase of great territorial conquest in the late nineteenth and early twentieth centuries which historians often refer to as 'New Imperialism', and which Sir Henry Campbell-Bannerman, the Liberal Prime Minister of the United Kingdom from 1905 to 1908, called 'the vulgar and bastard

imperialism of irritation and provocation and aggression . . . of grab-
bing everything even if we have no use for it ourselves', but there
were also times when the public were oblivious to Britain's overseas
adventures.

Then there were the varying attitudes to cultural integration with
'natives'. As we've already heard, in the early twentieth century India
was divided along racial lines, with Europeans living, working and
socializing separately from the people they colonised. In *Amritsar
1919*, Kim Wagner relates an extraordinary story about an Indian servant who dared to touch a memsahib, to warn her that she was about
to step upon a krait – one of the most venomous snakes in India. 'He
put his hand on my shoulder and pulled me back,' she recalled. 'My
shoe came off and I stopped. Of course, if he hadn't done that I should
undoubtedly have been killed; but I didn't like it all the same, and got
rid of him soon after.' But Britons in India weren't always so stand-
offish. At one stage of its history, many employees of the East India
Company enthusiastically embraced their exotic new milieu, dining
on curry and arak, chewing betel and smoking hookahs, forsaking
beef, donning dhotis and growing moustaches. One officer in the
East India Company army, Charles Stuart, was nicknamed Hindoo
Stuart for his wholehearted adoption of Hindu culture, writing
books extolling its traditions and virtues. At times, the British Indian
Army paid respect to Indian gods and goddesses, and Brahmins were
revered. Indian mistresses and intermarriage were common, with the
directors of the East India Company even actively encouraging these
interracial relationships, financially contributing to weddings and
christenings, in the belief that the unions added strength to their rapidly expanding army. However, as time went on, relationships with
Indians changed. In 1786, Charles Cornwallis became Governor-
General of India* and enacted a series of reforms of the East India
Company, including disqualifying mixed-race Anglo-Indians from
holding civil or military office or serving in the army and preventing
the training of Indians at Government House. Then, in the wake of

---

* When control of India was transferred from the East India Company to the
British Crown, the Governor-General became known as the Viceroy.

the Uprising of 1857, and with the increasing ability of British women to travel to India, it became more and more frowned upon for officers to socialize with the 'natives' and to keep Indian women as mistresses, let alone marry them. By the 1860s, the use of the word 'nigger' to describe Indians became commonplace.

Empire was never unanimous. The imperial project had no shortage of establishment champions at its height, ranging from Lord Cromer to Lord Curzon, General Kitchener, Lord Milner, Rudyard Kipling, Joseph Chamberlain, Lord Rosebery, Cecil Rhodes, Empire Day's Lord Meath and the Conservative Prime Minister Benjamin Disraeli, who in 1877 had Queen Victoria proclaimed as Empress of India and ensured celebrations were held to mark the fact in Delhi, in what is known as the Delhi Durbar. But equally there was not a single phase of empire when the enterprise was not being criticized, with establishment voices of opposition including Robert Graves, H. G. Wells, E. M. Forster, George Orwell, H. H. Munro ('Saki') and the Liberal heavyweight William Gladstone. Gladstone, who served four terms as Prime Minister between 1868 and 1894, famously complained that in South Africa 10,000 Zulus had been slaughtered 'for no other offence than their attempt to defend against your artillery with their naked bodies, their hearths and homes, their wives and families', and campaigned for election to Parliament in late 1879 with a speech about the injustice of the ongoing Afghan campaign, in which the British invaded and occupied Afghanistan with punitive brutality in response to the massacre of their legation in Kabul during an uprising. Gladstone urged people to 'Remember the rights of the savage! Remember that the happiness of his humble home, remember that the sanctity of life in the hill villages of Afghanistan . . . is as inviolable in the eye of Almighty God as is your own!'[10]

Elsewhere, censure of empire came from many quarters: economists who believed it was financially unsound; humanitarians who viewed it as a sin; Marxists who saw it as a branch of capitalism. In 1838, concern about the mistreatment of indigenous peoples led Parliament to appoint 'Protectors of Aborigines' in Western Australia and New South Wales. In 1861, a House of Commons Select Committee recommended a complete withdrawal from West Africa.

When, in 1893, the socialist Annie Besant emigrated to India, she dedicated herself to urging Indians to shake off the colonists, and wore Hindu mourning robes in recognition of what the British had done to the country. Most significantly, there was the extraordinary backlash against the East India Company, when the press ran articles exposing the alleged crimes by the Company on the subcontinent, and the riches accumulated in India by the likes of Lord Clive and Warren Hastings led to Parliamentary inquiries and impeachment proceedings. The political theorist Edmund Burke led the attack on Hastings and in his opening speech labelled him variously 'a robber', 'a professor, a doctor upon the subject of crime', 'a rat', 'a weasel', 'a keeper of a pigsty, wallowing in corruption', and charged him 'with injustice and treachery against the faith of nations . . . With various instances of extortion and other deeds of maladministration . . . With impoverishing and depopulating the whole country . . . with a wanton, and unjust, and pernicious, exercise of his powers'.*

There are intense disagreements about what happened during empire and what it means. Frankly, it's difficult to find any aspect of empire that isn't subject to animated academic argument. Was 1783 the point when the first empire became the second empire, or was there an overlap? There are reams of articles and books taking opposite positions, and some arguing that there was such a thing as a third empire. When did empire reach its peak? Jan Morris says it was in 1933 when it became 'the greatest expanse of territory ever presided over by one ruler in the history of mankind', while the National Archives rather vaguely claim that 'the British empire reached its height in the 1920s and 1930s', and other experts give different dates.

---

* He also accused him of 'cruelties unheard of and devastations almost without name . . . Crimes which have their rise in the wicked dispositions of men – in avarice, rapacity, pride, cruelty, malignity, haughtiness, insolence, ferocity, treachery, cruelty, malignity of temper – in short, nothing that does not argue a total extinction of all moral principle, that does not manifest an inveterate blackness of heart, a heart blackened to the very blackest, a heart corrupted, gangrene to the core . . . We have brought before you the head, the Captain General of Iniquity . . . one in whom all the frauds, all the peculations, all the violence, all the tyranny in India are embodied.'

Then there is the biggest argument of all: was the British empire good or bad? This 'balance sheet' view of history, with 'colonial crimes' such as the use of poison gas and the deaths of millions in famines being weighed against the supposed elimination of 'native crimes' such as sati, foot-binding, infanticide, slavery and cannibalism, is futile and misleading. History and the people who made it were complicated. You can't apply modern ethics to the past. To read history as a series of events that instil pride and shame, or a balance of rights and wrongs, is as inane as listing the events in your own life as good and bad. But one of the most startling discoveries I made as a result of the broadcast of my documentary on Jallianwala Bagh is that this debate has a gravitational force of its own. It's impossible to discuss British empire in the twenty-first century, or even admit to ignorance or curiosity about it, without getting dragged into this binary consideration.

And Lord is it bitter. I've tackled some controversial subjects in my journalism career – racism, social mobility, schizophrenia, Islamic sex gangs, Conservative Party politics, pianos in train stations (which attracted a bizarre amount of correspondence when I said I disliked them), but none of them proved as problematic as tackling the subject of British empire on TV. At the time I couldn't explain the vehement reaction, but now I get it: empire is a veritable industrial oven of hot potatoes. As Ashley Jackson has put it, 'any study of imperialism embraces a range of controversial topics, including unequal power relations, nationalism, race, cultural confrontations, economics, warfare, and ideology.' Or to put it another way, empire is yet another of those topics, alongside trans rights, Brexit, the merits of Dyson vacuum cleaners over Henrys, that has become a locum of tension in the culture wars. You can't explore the issue casually, or express curiosity, or admit ignorance: you need to take sides. It extends even to party politics, with former Labour leader Jeremy Corbyn announcing in the run-up to a general election that under his party children would be taught about the 'historical injustice' and 'colonialism' as part of the national curriculum,[11] while Michael Gove announced early in his tenure as Secretary of State for Education that history lessons in schools needed to 'celebrate' the legacy of the British empire.

And the pressure continues as I tell people what I'm reading. I mention I'm consulting Jan Morris, Niall Ferguson or Jeremy Paxman and get told they're not to be trusted because they're imperialists or racists. I mention works by Pankaj Mishra or Shashi Tharoor and get told I can't trust them because they're Marxists. Both sides label the other as oversimplistic and posturing, whereas their own position is nuanced and thoughtful, and claim their opponents are guilty of being culture warriors, even as they engage in the culture wars themselves. At the same time, despite inciting such powerful emotions, empire, bewilderingly, remains untaught in most schools: its absence in my education, it transpires, is typical.

There was no clear motivation for the establishment and development of empire. One of the few things historians actually agree upon is that empire was both unplanned and a nebulous construct. Unlike history's other famous empires – Rome's being the most obvious example – it was never a legal entity, and had no constitution or emperor issuing top-down laws. In *Unfinished Empire*, John Darwin talks about how 'the "command and control" of this empire was always ramshackle and quite often chaotic. To suppose that an order uttered in London was obeyed round the world by zealous proconsuls is an historical fantasy (although a popular one). For this was an empire that depended on the co-operation of local elites, on the loyalty of settlers and the (often grudging) acquiescence of British officials, impatient of Whitehall's demands. None of these could be tested too far.' And reading about the origins of empire, you cannot help but be struck by the incredible variety in the motivations behind imperial expansion. *The Penguin Historical Atlas of the British Empire* claims that 'From the 1560s there was a growing support in England for colonization as a source of wealth and important commodities, national prestige and strategic security, partly through the spread of Protestantism in a Roman Catholic world.' But for Richard Hakluyt, known for promoting the English colonization of North America through his travel compendiums *Divers Voyages Touching the Discoverie of America* (1582) and *The Principall Navigations, Voiages, Traffiques and Discoueries of the English Nation* (1589–1600), the empire expanded because 'no greater glory can be handed down than to conquer the barbarian, to recall the savage and the pagan to civility, to draw the ignorant within the orbit of reason'. When Queen Elizabeth signed the charter of the East India Company on the last day of 1600, she did so, according to the History Channel, 'hoping to break the Dutch monopoly of the spice trade in what is now Indonesia'. Other explanations include exploration for the sake of exploration, the desire to participate in the profitable trade of slavery, the desire to emigrate, opportunism, idealism. Sometimes it expanded because the territory was necessary to defend trade, to protect missionaries and settlers, to save the 'natives' from their foolish and dangerous ways, or because the land might be valuable one day – or just because they could. As Jan Morris puts it, 'many a stroke of imperial history depended originally upon a quirk of individual character, or the mood of a moment' and 'it was all bits and pieces. There was no system.'

And this isn't just hindsight. Back in 1914, H. G. Wells stated that the empire had 'no economic, no military, no racial, no religious unity. Its only conceivable unity is a unity of language and purpose and outlook.' The single most famous description of this chaos came from Sir John Seeley, the founding father of British imperial history, who asserted in *The Expansion of England* that 'the British empire was acquired in a fit of absence of mind', arguing, as many have since, that empire was a bunch of accidents, errors and unintentional consequences, and responses to accidents, errors and unintentional consequences.★ Some have taken this idea to its logical extreme by questioning whether the British empire ever happened, chief among them our old pal Enoch Powell. In a twist that makes David Icke's journey from Coventry City goalie to conspiracy theorist feel unremarkable, this imperialist whose life was shaped by the colonial

---

★ It's an assertion that the literary imperial anti-hero Flashman challenges in George MacDonald Fraser's novel *Flashman and the Mountain of Light* (1990) when he describes the phrase as 'one of those smart Oscarish squibs that sounds well but is thoroughly fat-headed. Presence of mind, if you like – and countless other things, such as greed and Christianity, decency and villainy, policy and lunacy, deep design and blind chance, pride and trade, blunder and curiosity, passion, ignorance, chivalry and expediency, honest pursuit of right, and determination to keep the bloody Frogs out.'

mission, started to claim from the 1960s onwards that British empire had been 'a myth', 'a deception' and an 'invention, all along'. That people had ever believed in it was 'one of the most extraordinary paradoxes in political history'. He also insisted that 'England underwent no organic change as the mistress of a world empire.'[12]

Why did he say this? You'll find analysis putting it down to denial, explaining it as a coping mechanism or as nationalist logic – if British empire never happened, then Britain can't be said to have declined. It's impossible to know really, but I'm not surprised by the existence of the argument. In my experience, if you study anything for long enough, you'll discover someone denying it even existed. During my literature degree we had several weeks discussing Roland Barthes' theory about the Death of the Author, debating whether the existence of writers really mattered. When I was researching schizophrenia for my family memoir, I came across scientists arguing that the condition didn't really exist. And it serves to illustrate an important point that Simon Schama has made in relation to the removal of colonial statues: 'History is argument.' And so is interpreting what are the legacies of history. To say that anything happened at any particular time in history for any particular reason is almost always a matter of opinion. There will always be someone out there arguing the opposite point.

Furthermore, just because something happened in 1787 and in 2019 doesn't *prove* that the former caused the latter. Things happen spontaneously, patterns randomly emerge, the lines between coincidences, patterns, echoes and correlations are fine and subjective, and in picking out modern legacies of empire you're always at risk of resembling an imperial version of Mr 'Everything Comes from India' from the BBC sketch show *Goodness Gracious Me* – a man who insists that just about everything comes from India or was invented by Indians, including William Shakespeare, Cliff Richard and the British royal family, often to the vexation of his more knowledgeable son. At its hardest, identifying legacies of imperialism can feel like you're attempting the historical equivalent of demonstrating that a baked cake contains eggs: they're probably in there, but it's hard to prove, and there's no getting over the awkward fact that some perfectly delicious cakes don't actually contain any egg whatsoever.

In fact, the question of how much British empire shaped Britain itself is yet another area of heated debate among imperial historians – so entrenched that the dispute has its own name, 'the Porter–MacKenzie debate', and its own Wikipedia page. The controversy focuses on the extent to which colonialism was an important influence on British culture during the nineteenth and twentieth centuries. It began as a disagreement between the academic historians Bernard Porter and John MacKenzie, Porter arguing in *The Absent-Minded Imperialists* that even in the high imperial period of the nineteenth century the presence of empire was 'uneven, complex and changeable', making Britain 'a less imperial society than is often assumed', and MacKenzie arguing in books including *Propaganda and Empire* that colonialism dominated British popular culture for much of the period. Among the many points of contention is the idea that the famed social reforms of the 1905–14 Liberal governments, such as free school meals for poor children, state pensions, compulsory school medical services and a new Mental Health Act of 1913, are an imperial legacy. Porter contended they did not come about, as others have argued, because:

> imperialism required a fitter, 'manlier', and more loyal 'race' to sustain it . . . It is tempting to explain these entirely in terms of the demands of the empire. In this way the empire can be seen to have impacted on British domestic life immensely. But this kind of interpretation is too easy, and too reductionist. Some of these reforms pre-dated the 'new imperialism' . . . A tangible link can be traced back to the Committee on Physical Deterioration that had been set up in the wake of the [Boer] war to find out why so many volunteers had to be rejected . . . [but] that . . . is nowhere near the whole picture.

You'd be forgiven if, encountering these vociferous academic disputes for the first time as an amateur, you decided to run for the hills. It's one of the reasons empire, and the influence of it upon us, remains so poorly understood: participating can sometimes feel like joining a knife fight with only your bare hands as weapons. Or perhaps, given the esoteric nature of some of the arguments, it is better to say it is like joining a medieval jousting match with only your bare hands as weapons. But read books like MacKenzie's *Propaganda and Empire* and Porter's *The Absent-Minded Imperialists* closely enough and you'll discover good reasons to persist. Certainly, in Porter's intellectual openness, which sees him admit that he might be wrong and claim that he is 'genuinely open to persuasion on many points', he highlights an important one: that while there is little certainty in imperial studies, anyone can make an argument. Indeed, Seeley, the founder of imperial history, not only was himself, in MacKenzie's words, 'the great simplifier *par excellence*' but he also didn't do his own original historical research.[13] Too many people run scared of this vital history, which defines us. Given that some imperial legacies are easier to isolate than others, however, it makes sense to begin with one of the most tangible: the mounds of items stolen in such quantities from empire that the Hindi word for 'spoils of war' – *lut* – had by the 1850s entered the English language in the form of 'loot'.

4. Emotional Loot

Britain's invasion of Tibet in 1903 is rarely more than a footnote in the grand histories of British empire, but it is nevertheless gripping.[1] Not least there was the sheer romance of the enterprise: at the time, little was known about Tibet, the only Himalayan state untouched by the British. One of the last unmapped spots on the planet, it was, after the discovery of the sources of the Nile, the ultimate goal for explorers, its mystery the equivalent, perhaps, of modern-day North Korea. Since 1792 it had blocked Europeans from entering, and only one Englishman, Thomas Manning, had managed to infiltrate its capital, Lhasa.

Then there were the extraordinary characters involved – chief among them Colonel Sir Francis Younghusband, the head of mission, admired by Bertrand Russell, H. G. Wells and John Buchan. A charismatic leader, who was so precious and volatile that he spent the mission threatening to quit and writing to influential friends and relatives to lobby against senior colleagues, he was elected the youngest fellow of the Royal Geographical Society in his mid-twenties, held the world record for the 300-yard dash and was a great believer in British empire, writing to his friend Henry Newbolt that 'The empire must grow: we can't help it.' Nevertheless, on leaving Lhasa, he had a bizarre spiritual experience on a mountainside that he attributed to 'a great world-force energizing through nature' and ended up taking to religion, devoting many of his later years to a 'crusade for a universal world faith'.

Accompanying him, along with some 18,000 others, was the mission's Principal Medical Officer and official archaeologist, Dr Laurence Waddell, a man who is still regularly described as a real-life Indiana Jones (the latest such reference being in the *Indian Express* in May 2019), was loathed by Younghusband (who in a letter described him as a 'miserable old woman') and was considered a leading British authority on

Tibetan culture, even attempting in 1892 to reach Lhasa in disguise (his blue eyes gave him away). He ended up on the raid after he telegraphed the government asking to be involved, explaining that the mission offered a 'unique opportunity . . . for procuring from that closed land those manuscripts and books so greatly required by Western scholars'. This interest in Tibetan culture did not apparently extend to any kind of respect for it – Waddell characterizing Tibetan Buddhism as a 'parasitic disease . . . a cloak to the worst forms of oppressive devil-worship' and describing the people as 'sunk in the lowest depths of savagery' and 'more like hideous gnomes than human beings'.

Most intriguing of all were the motives for the mission, described by the historian Charles Allen as 'almost entirely bogus'. Apparently, Lord Curzon, the then Viceroy of India, didn't actually intend to annex Tibet into the British empire, but nervous about Russian intentions in the area, and aware of Tibet's potential military and commercial importance as a gateway to China, he wanted to end Tibet's isolation, for Tibet to accept British guidance in matters of security and thereby to protect India. And in this sense the mission failed. British forces, which included significant numbers of Sikh and Gurkha infantry, stormed into Tibet after its leaders refused to talk, having found a tenuous excuse to engage them in battle, and crushed them utterly with superior technology and tactics: in some sixteen engagements, the Tibetans lost up to 3,000 men as against just a few dozen deaths on the British side, with Waddell justifying one 'battle' where 625 Tibetans were killed with the claim that the Tibetans were enemies 'not only of ourselves, but in some sense, by reason of their savagery and superstition, of the human race'.

Such racialized arrogance was routine, with one account describing how an officer, finding grain hidden in a monastery, took the abbot 'by the nape of his lubberly neck, drove him down on his knees and rubbed his nose in it', and a certain Lieutenant Arthur Hadow remarking after one engagement that 'I got so sick of the slaughter that I ceased fire, though the General's order was to make as big a bag as possible.' The Dalai Lama, the spiritual leader, fled to safety and in his absence, on reaching Lhasa, Younghusband forced Tibetan officials to sign the hugely unequal Treaty of Lhasa, which attempted to impose a special trading relationship upon Tibet, obliged Tibet to pay vast indemnities for having the temerity to compel the British into launching such an expedition, and insisted that Tibet have no relations with any other foreign power. But the settlement proved ineffective: it harmed relations with Russia in ways neither Curzon nor the government wanted; its provisions were mainly superseded by a subsequent treaty; and Britain conceded that it still accepted Chinese claims of authority over Tibet. The mission created a political vacuum which China filled, the effects of which are arguably still felt today. Younghusband was effectively punished in 1904 by an award of an honour that a supporter described as 'shabby and inadequate'.

There was, however, one way the mission was a success: in terms of the material it accumulated and the academic curiosity it satisfied. Britain was, as a result of the invasion, flooded with examples of Tibetan gilt and brass Buddhas, painted scrolls, *thankas*, thigh-bone trumpets and aprons, brass bowls, prayer wheels, lamas' robes, brass trays, amber, diamonds, gold- and jewel-encrusted artworks, golden crowns, earrings, necklaces and tiger skins. And the way this material ended up in British collections provides an insight into how the considerable loot of empire furnished Britain during the imperial project. The official line on the mission was that looting was not actually permitted. In a letter home to his wife, a serviceman called George Preston wrote that he wished he could send her some loot 'but there are very strict orders about it', adding that two Mounted Infantry sepoys had been court-martialled after they were caught with gilt images looted from a nunnery. Dr Waddell ordered the stolen treasures to be returned, the men were handed prison sentences and the troops were reminded that looting was strictly forbidden. But elsewhere Lieutenant Thomas Carey complained that Waddell was in no position to lecture, considering that he was 'also noted for his looting propensities'. Carey went on to confess his envy of the Mounted Infantry because they 'get all the fun and have a fight nearly every day of their lives, and the pick of the loot. Some of the M.I. officers have very valuable loot, we only get the dregs and the same of curios. Of course, there are stringent orders against looting monasteries, unless they fire or make resistance.'

In Waddell's defence, most of what he collected was done through what was considered legitimate means, taking place under precedents established in the reign of George III, when a series of Parliamentary laws set out the rules for the spoils of land warfare. To keep armies motivated, plunder was seen as the reward for victory – basically, if the 'natives' resisted the British, then their goods were fair game. A committee would catalogue the loot and arrange for its sale at public auction before issuing a prize roll indicating what proportion of the proceeds would be given to each rank in the force. And so, given that the Tibetan troops at places like Gyantse Jong had initially resisted the British, what was found there was considered legitimate booty and doled out. Furthermore, everywhere the empire went, so did cartographers, archaeologists, botanists, linguists and museum acquisitions professionals, institutions sending representatives on such missions to bid for items. And the British Indian government had given Waddell 10,000 rupees to secure artefacts and texts, with the results intended to be divided between formal collections in India and Britain, and he had a private commission to acquire Chinese porcelain for the imperial legend Lord Kitchener.* He accumulated over

---

* In the twenty-first century, Kitchener is most famous for two things: his gimlet-eyed portrait on the Great War recruiting poster proclaiming 'Your country needs you', and his extraordinary moustache. And such extravagant moustaches, also sported by Younghusband and Waddell, are arguably another legacy of empire. The historian Piers Brendon has argued that the moustache became an 'emblem of empire' in the nineteenth century. Apparently, clean-shaven British soldiers in imperial India found themselves being glanced at with 'amazement and contempt' by their bearded Indian counterparts because of their '(unmanly) countenances emasculated by the razor'. As they 'could not afford to appear less masculine and aggressive than their Indian comrades in the Army' they 'had to assert the supremacy of the imperial race. So began what became known as "the moustache movement".' Soon the moustache was the sacred emblem of the imperialist. Back in Britain, the Edwardians saw the moustache as the preserve of the upper echelons of society – servants who tried to grow one were given short shrift – and Brendon goes as far as asserting there is a correlation between the prevalence of moustaches in public life and the vigour of empire, observing that the British commanding officer who in 1942 lost to the Japanese at Singapore, General Percival, 'had a miserable apology of a moustache'.

2,000 objects – over 400 mule-loads – such as porcelain, manuscripts, weapons, armour and paintings, many of which were rare and valuable. Considering Waddell's 10,000-rupee budget, this indicates that he bought the items for an average of just five rupees each – a succession of extraordinary bargains which suggests that he was not trading entirely fairly. Nonetheless, an exhibition was put on in the Indian Museum in Calcutta prior to the collection being shared out between the British Museum, the Bodleian Library in Oxford and the India Office Library (now the Oriental and India Office Collection of the British Library).

There is also evidence, however, that Waddell took items without offering any compensation at all, and that other officers and soldiers did so routinely too. The academic Michael Carrington describes how Younghusband and a colleague decided to 'do a bit of looting on their own before anyone else arrived', while two other figures broke into three buildings and helped themselves to loot. Following the fall of Gyantse Jong, other monasteries were plundered, such as those at Palkor Chode and Dongte, and within a matter of weeks Tibetan artefacts were being offered for sale at London auction houses and beyond. In May 1905, for example, Major Iggulden sold 169 artefacts to the British Museum. Some of the items were kept as trophies: a man called Newman helped himself to a luxurious scarlet gown which almost certainly belonged to a Tibetan official, and wore it as a dressing-gown for the rest of the campaign, while Lieutenant Carey of the Royal Fusiliers recorded in his diary that he had 'snaffled' some items which he hoped to send home to his parents. The lust for loot even led to the death of three sepoys, who came across a promising-looking box and tried to break the lock by whacking it with a stone: the stone sparked and the box turned out to be full of gunpowder.

There had been many precedents for such plunder and theft, for reasons of greed, souvenir-hunting and academic curiosity, during the long history of British empire. Personal enrichment through unofficial looting was such a routine part of life in the East India Company that years before he became the first de facto Governor-General of India, Warren Hastings expressed dismay at how the Company was looting Bengal, writing in 1762 of 'the oppression carried out under the sanction of the English name' which he had observed in his travels. 'This evil I am well assured is not confined to our dependants alone, but is practised all over the country by people assuming the habit of our sepoys or calling themselves our managers . . . A party of sepoys who were on the march before us, afforded sufficient proof of the rapacious and insolent spirit of those people when they are left to their own discretion . . . Every man who wears a hat, as soon as he gets free from Calcutta becomes a sovereign prince.' Looting was routine in war, an accepted part of soldiers' pay, the extent to which people collected souvenirs varying according to regimental culture and individual morals. And there was no limit, seemingly, to what soldiers were willing to collect during war as curiosities. Simon J. Harrison tells us how in the nineteenth century British soldiers serving in the colonies sometimes even collected enemy body parts: when Hintsa, a chief of the Xhosa in the Sixth Frontier War of 1834–6 was killed, his ears were cut off as souvenirs, a military surgeon was seen trying to extract some of his teeth and someone even tried to cut out 'the emblems of [Hintsa's] manhood'. Throughout the 1846–7 Xhosa War, 'native' heads were taken and traded as trophies,[2] with one Stephen Lakeman, leader of a regiment of irregulars, in the early 1850s admitting to a campaign of annihilation in the Waterkloof and Kat River valleys which involved one of his men carrying a broken sickle to slice the throats of the women and children captured on night patrols:

> Doctor A—of the 60th had asked my men to procure him a few native skulls of both sexes. This was a task easily accomplished. One morning they brought back to camp about two dozen heads of various ages. As these were not supposed to be in a presentable state for the doctor's acceptance, the next night they turned my vat into a cauldron for the removal of superfluous flesh. And there these men sat, gravely smoking their pipes during the live-long night, and stirring round and round the heads in that seething boiler, as though they were cooking black-apple dumplings.

After Western troops in 1860 had pillaged and burned China's Imperial Summer Palace, to the north-west of Peking, in retaliation for the murder of some their envoys by the Chinese, James Hope Grant issued a general order calling for all loot, with the exception of pieces purchased from the French, to be handed over to a prize committee. The items, put on display and auctioned off immediately for the 'general benefit', included furs, precious stones and jewellery, gold statues and lapis lazuli carvings, to say nothing of reams of yellow silk, a colour that Chinese law decreed was to be used only by his Imperial Majesty, and the Emperor's own seal of state. A Pekingese dog found there was taken to be sent back as a gift to Queen Victoria, and was christened 'Looty'.[3] The auction raised £26,000 (equivalent to £18.9 million today), which was divvied up between officers and men, although Hope Grant and his two generals of division forwent their shares. When Tipu Sultan, the ruler of Mysore in South India from 1782 to 1799, was finally defeated by the East India Company after an assault on Seringapatam, the city was ravaged by unbridled looting, rape and killing, with Arthur Wellesley, later the first Duke of Wellington and one of the leading military and political figures of nineteenth-century Britain who was to serve twice as Prime Minister, writing in a letter to his mother that 'scarcely a house in the town was left unplundered, and I understand that in camp jewels of the greatest value, bars of gold etc etc have been offered for sale in the bazaars of the army'. When the prize committee assembled what remained of Tipu's belongings, they found large amounts of gold plate, jewellery, palanquins, arms and armour, silks and shawls, the Sultan's solid-gold throne and an almost life-sized wooden semi-automaton, depicting a European soldier lying on his back being mauled by a tiger.

This item became known as 'Tipu's Tiger' and was shipped to London, where it was displayed in the Company's India Museum. It has since, for decades, been a centrepiece at the Victoria and Albert Museum (V&A), and the myriad ways in which such loot found its way into Britain, through institutions and individuals, through official and unofficial means, for reason of sincere intellectual curiosity and cynical financial gain, is reflected in the ways I encounter items from the Younghusband exhibition 115 years after it happened. The first time, it is by accident: I have the BBC antiques show *Flog It* on in the background while reading a newspaper when a member of the public turns up with an old brass-and-silver teapot. What I know about antiques could be etched on to the bottom of a Clarice Cliff pot, but as soon as the man mentions that it came from his grandfather, a captain in the Indian Army who was seconded to the Younghusband expedition to Tibet, I recognize it. He claims his relative 'came across' the teapot 'in the Himalayas, wrapped in paper in the snow', and when the expert patronizes the item to death, describing it as 'crude', 'primitive' but nevertheless 'charming', and values it at £120, I suspect she is wildly off the mark. And sure enough, after the voiceover has informed us that it was photos from that expedition which allowed the British public to see Everest for the very first time, the man brings along for auction a whole load of items from the same expedition (the producers don't explain how he came in possession of them all: they can't all surely have been spotted wrapped in paper in the snow), they sell for a record amount for the show: £140,000. The programme's obsession with the price achieved sits awkwardly with the fact that up to 3,000 Tibetans were killed on the expedition, that one private described the Tibetans being 'knocked over like skittles' by the British Maxim guns, and that a monk who tried to avenge the killing of a brother was hanged, his body left strung up for twenty-four hours as 'a warning to others'.

The second time I come across items from the Younghusband raid, they're in a small glass cabinet in room 33 of the British Museum. They include a pair of boots, belonging to a Tibetan oracle, that look surprisingly fashionable – you could imagine seeing them in a twenty-first-century Gucci store – a lacquered hat, 'part of the dress of a monastic official', and two stunning glass-and-turquoise ornaments. The labelling is frank, veering away from the euphemisms of empire by describing them as from 'the Younghusband military expedition', and saying that 'although some objects were paid for, many were forcibly taken by military officers from monasteries and the homes of Tibetans, especially in Gyantse. British machine guns killed over 600 Tibetans, armed only with bayonets and wearing gau, during a battle in Guru in March 1904.' I'd been uncertain what 'gau' might look like, knowing only they were worn in Tibet to protect against misfortune. It is startling to discover that the device thousands of murdered Tibetans hoped would protect them from machine-gun fire was just a kind of amulet box. Nothing more than a piece of jewellery. This is reflective of a people whose Buddhism inclined them to avoid violence and who placed their faith in their religion, rather than weapons, to protect them from invaders. Waddell described it as a 'bitter irony of fate' that 'many at Guru received their death-wounds through their charm-boxes' – but you could also call it criminal.

Of course, museums existed before empire became a significant enterprise for Britain: in 1498, the Tower Armouries opened to select visitors, and following Charles II's restoration in 1660 it put on a display celebrating the might and pomp of the English monarchy.[4] Most early museums were not enterprises of the state: they began as the private collections of wealthy individuals, families or institutions of art, with Sir Hans Sloane's personal collection of curios famously providing the initial foundation for the British Museum's collection. But even with personal collections there were often imperial connections: Hans Sloane was married to a Jamaica heiress and drew revenue from her plantations, worked by slaves. Imperialists were often collectors: in an echo of Lord Kitchener's order for Tibetan items, Lord Curzon himself was an enthusiastic antiquarian who once wrote that 'It is in my judgment . . . our duty to dig and discover, to classify, reproduce and describe, to copy and decipher, and to cherish and conserve.'[5] Public museums grew as empire grew, the practice of collecting, in the words of Michael Carrington, being 'institutionalized and symptomatic of the British imperial state's desire for artefacts with which to provide information about "exotic" societies. There was literally a "scramble" for information out of which, it was hoped, an ordered and systematic scheme of knowledge would realize the dream of an "imperial archive" in which fantasy became reality and ultimate knowledge became ultimate power.'

The East India Company incorporated a museum in its London offices, on Leadenhall Street, and after the Company had effectively been nationalized, its collection was, after a period in Whitehall, divided between the British Museum, the Natural History Museum, the Royal Botanical Gardens and the South Kensington Museum, which went on to become the V&A.[6] Between the 1880s and 1960s something called the Imperial Institute stood in South Kensington, which originated out of a plan to build a permanent empire museum or exhibition in London, and which was still being advertised on tube posters in 1927 with the slogan 'The Empire Under One Roof'. And there have been numerous other idiosyncratic colonial collections, such as the British Empire and Commonwealth Museum which existed in Bristol between 2002 and 2008 but eventually sold its premises and gave up its collections on account of 'post-imperial angst', according to the chairman of the museum's board of trustees. There is also the British in India Museum in Lancashire, which started life as the private collection of Henry Nelson, who had served in India in the 1940s, and displays various swords, kukris, commemorative boxes and plates, models carved in ivory, photographs and paintings.

This particular institution may be described online as 'one of the top five least visited museums in Britain', but its unpopularity is by no means typical: our largest museums, packed with imperial loot and free to enter, sit at the very heart of British cultural life. According to the Association of Leading Visitor Attractions, the British Museum had 6.2 million visits in 2019, an increase of 7 per cent on the year, the Natural History Museum had 5.4 million, an increase of 4 per cent, and the V&A had 4 million, an increase of 1 per cent. According to a survey by Statista, in 2018/19 half of all Britons had attended a museum or a gallery at least once in the previous year. According to the Museums Association, eight of the UK's top ten visitor attractions are museums and three British museums are among the top ten most visited museums worldwide. Meanwhile, the Nation Brands Index asked respondents from twenty countries around the world to select cultural products they would associate with the UK and half of respondents associated the UK with 'museums'.

A new generation of activists, however, feels about these museums the way other generations felt about zoos, and are campaigning for them to be decolonized. They include enterprises like the India Pride Project, which describes itself as 'a global effort to track and reinstate India's stolen heritage' and encourages supporters to photograph cartoon speech balloons or 'agony shrieks' erupting from the mouths of questionable museum artefacts, so that social networks are flooded with statues asking to be rescued. There is Craig Ritchie, head of the Australian Institute of Aboriginal and Torres Strait Islander Studies, which has identified more than 100,000 items of Indigenous Australian heritage in global institutions, around a third of which are in Britain. There was a campaign that emerged briefly on Twitter to change the name of the British Museum to 'the Museum of Empire, Colonialism and Migration' (a rather overambitious aim given that no serious person has ever claimed that *everything* in these museums is imperial loot). And there is the activist and critic Alice Procter who puts on 'Uncomfortable Art Tours', or guided walks, at all sorts of venues, from the National Gallery to the National Portrait Gallery, focusing on 'how major institutions came into being against a backdrop of imperialism' and intending to 'unravel the role colonialism played in shaping and funding' major national collections.

I join Procter on one of her evening tours of the British Museum. We begin at Hoa Hakananai'a, a stone figure weighing some 4 tons and standing some 8 feet high in a gallery near an entrance, its blocky face reminiscent of 1980s comedy turn Max Headroom, and its brooding brow like that of Liam Gallagher. Sporting a badge proclaiming 'display it like you stole it', Procter challenges the use of the word 'donated' in the museum description, arguing that 'the label doesn't say how it was taken and why . . . the Rapa Nui people see it as stolen and as a living ancestor.' Then there is the Kayung totem pole, a 12-metre pole made by the Haida people of the American Pacific North-West, on display in the Great Court: Procter takes issue with its indoor location – 'it is divided from its original context' – and with the fact that the museum signage doesn't make clear that the village it was taken from had been abandoned because 'the population was decimated by successive smallpox epidemics in the late 1800s, introduced by colonizers.' Then, in a cabinet, there is the Gweagal Shield, an artefact many believe tells the story of Captain James Cook's arrival in Australia, which featured in the book and radio series *A History of the World in 100 Objects* compiled by the former Director of the British Museum Neil MacGregor. Procter alleges that the gallery label doesn't convey how murderous and deadly the encounter probably was for its owner and claims that the lack of specificity in the gallery, with its herding together of disparate cultures, illustrates how First Nations people are improperly represented across the whole museum.

Procter makes a series of powerful arguments for the restitution of imperial artefacts, but omits what I feel is the strongest single point in her argument's favour: that what happened with imperial loot was, in many cases, bitterly condemned at the time. It is routinely remarked in debates on empire that we shouldn't judge the past by modern moral standards, but when the British authorities became aware of what had happened in Tibet, for example, there was outrage. The raid occurred at the height of British empire, when jingoism about colonialism was fading and international law was altering the way colonialism could be pursued, with the Hague Convention of 1899, one of the first multilateral treaties to address the conduct of warfare and a forerunner of the Geneva Convention, declaring in Article 46 that 'Private property cannot be confiscated' and in Article 47 that 'Pillage is formally prohibited.' Indian newspapers published rumours of looting in Gyantse, and the British press followed them up. Lord Kitchener defended the mission, but issued renewed orders against further looting. At other times there was uproar when the public became aware of the colonial practice of collecting human remains. And it wasn't just the masses who found body snatching repugnant: at the end of the 1881–99 Mahdist War, which culminated in the establishment of effective British control over Sudan, the Mahdi's tomb had been raided and his 'unusually large and shapely' skull removed and presented to Kitchener. After 'toying with mounting it in silver or gold for use as an ink stand or drinking cup', Kitchener decided instead to give it as an exhibit to the College of Surgeons, and when all this was revealed it played badly with the army, with the press and even with Queen Victoria who thought the whole business 'savoured too much of the Middle Ages'.[7] There was outrage over what had happened in China and the looting and burning of the Summer Palace. There was perhaps an even better illustration of how looting was condemned during the enterprise of empire with the 1868 British incursion into Ethiopia.[8]

The episode had numerous parallels to Tibet, not least insofar as that euphemism of the 'British expedition to Abyssinia' – like the 'Tibet Frontier Commission', the 'Younghusband mission to Tibet' and the 'Younghusband raid' – rather disguises the fact that it was essentially an invasion. Another parallel: the exploits occurred in a part of the world that was romantic for the British. The country had not been invaded for centuries, partly due to the precipitous terrain, and Ethiopian Christianity was of intense fascination to British scholars. Also, as with Tibet, the invading forces were accompanied by a team of experts with explicit interest in gathering cultural material, in this case Clements Markham, the official 'geographer' to the expedition, and Richard R. Holmes, assistant in the Department of Manuscripts in the British Museum, who was sent as official 'archaeologist' with £1,000 (£638,000 today) 'to cover the cost of excavations or collections'. The ostensible trigger for the mission was, however, less tenuous than it would be with Tibet: from the beginning it was a clear attempt to restore the honour of the British nation after Emperor Tewodros II of Ethiopia had imprisoned several British missionaries. And unlike with the unsuspecting monks, there was no question that the Emperor was a nasty piece of work: a highly unstable character, he had captured the missionaries in order to grab the attention of the British government, who had denied his requests for military aid; during the ordeal, the servants of the missionaries were beaten to death and British diplomats who went in to negotiate their release were also taken hostage. Leading the retaliatory force was Lieutenant-General Sir Robert Napier, a veteran of key empire events such as the surrender of the Sikh Army during the Anglo-Sikh Wars and the entry into Peking in 1860. His Ethiopia mission, described by the historian Harold Marcus as 'one of the most expensive affairs of honour in history', involved 13,000 soldiers, both British and Indian, along with 26,000 camp followers and 40,000 animals, including forty-four trained Indian elephants to carry the artillery.

Preparations included 20 miles of rail track laid across the coastal plain, complete with train, and the construction of piers, lighthouses and warehouses. Once the party had set off, it took them three months to traverse 400 miles of treacherous mountain ranges to reach the Emperor's terrain. As you'd expect with such a force, the British comprehensively crushed their enemy. In one early clash, Tewodros' men were fighting with no more than spears while the British blasted them with rockets from the Naval Brigade, mountain gun artillery and rifle fire. Just one ninety-minute skirmish left between 700 and 800 Ethiopian fighters dead and 1,200 to 1,500 wounded, while the British suffered only twenty dead and twenty wounded. When Napier's troops reached the Emperor's fortress town of Maqdala (also called Magdala or Makdala), they swiftly defeated the last 9,000 of Tewodros' men, losing only two British soldiers in the process and leading Marcus to observe in 1995: 'For a total cost of about £9,000,000 Napier set out to defeat a man who could muster only a few thousand troops and had long ago ceased to be Ethiopia's leader in anything but title.'

Even so, Tewodros did not surrender, instead releasing European hostages one by one over the course of several days. When the British eventually reached the Emperor, they found him dead, having committed suicide with a pistol that had originally been a gift from Queen Victoria. Tewodros' body was cremated, and priests were permitted to inter his ashes inside a local church. At that point, the looting began. It is impossible to know who took what for whom and how, but, as was conventional, soldiers were asked to return what they had found to the centre of the camp after the shooting was over and an auction was held upon Dahonte Dalanta plateau. The journalist Henry Morton Stanley observed how during the auction 'Mr. Holmes, as the worthy representative of the British Museum, was in his full glory. Armed with ample funds, he outdid all in most things but Colonel Frazer ran him hard because he was buying for a wealthy regimental mess . . . and when anything belonging personally to Theodore [Tewodros] was offered for sale, there were private gentlemen who outbid both . . .' The haul was so vast that fifteen elephants and almost 200 mules were needed to transport it home. All treasures were put on display at the South Kensington Museum in 1868, and they subsequently ended up in all kinds of places, from the collection of the press baron William Randolph Hearst to being loaned out to the South Staffordshire Exhibition in Wolverhampton in 1869, to the British Museum, to the Bodleian Library and to the V&A, which has since 1872 displayed the famous Maqdala Crown, an intricate work of African craftsmanship commissioned by the Ethiopian Empress Mentewab in the 1740s.

The discomfort in Britain was acute. William Gladstone, the Prime Minister, told the House of Commons that he 'deeply lamented, for the sake of the country, and for the sake of all concerned, that these articles . . . were thought fit to be brought away by a British army'. He urged that they 'be held only until they could be restored'. When, in the summer of 1902, the Ethiopian Prince Ras Makonnen came to England for the coronation of King Edward VII and saw some of the manuscripts owned by Lady Meux, who resided at Theobald's Park, he, according to *The Times*, knelt down and prayed for the souls of the ancestors who had once owned them and burst into tears. It affected Lady Meux so much that she reportedly remarked to the man who had obtained them for her, Dr Budge, Keeper of the Egyptian and Assyrian Antiquities at the British Museum: 'What a beastly thing it is for your horrid people to go about the world stealing these books! What's the good of them?'[9] This was a little odd as she had bought them, but she presented Ras Makonnen with a whole set of the magnificently printed, translated editions, which the Prince received with much gratitude. Then, in her will, dated 23 January 1910, she bequeathed all her Ethiopian manuscripts to the Emperor Menelik or his successor.

There's an assumption in most discussions on repatriation that we're talking about the return of items of academic curiosity, which have always flowed between communities, in and out of warfare. But, as the examples of Tibet and Ethiopia illustrate, people wanting repatriation are often talking about essential national and religious material, which they require for reasons of basic self-esteem and dignity. Some of this material is human remains, with Procter arguing powerfully in her book *The Whole Picture* that it cannot be right that 'museums have been known to drag their heels over the repatriation of remains even in cases where grave robbing is clearly involved'. She gives the example of the remains of two Beothuk people, Nonosbawsut and Demasduit, which were removed from their graves in the

1820s and ended up in the National Museum of Scotland; the museum only agreed to send back their skulls, after nearly 200 years, in 2019. She is also right to point out in relation to indigenous attempts to reclaim the Gweagal Shield that 'the shield's potential "healing power" for Indigenous Australians', who paid such a massive price for colonization, 'far outweigh[s] its possible value to the British Museum's collection'. The idea that the shield might briefly visit Australia, as the British Museum has conceded, is insulting. And when I think of everything that was taken by the British from Maharajah Ranjit Singh's treasury, it is not the heaps of gold, jewellery, antiques, textiles, paintings and sculptures – or even the Koh-i-noor diamond – that sting, but the rare religious artefacts, which were said to include Guru Gobind Singh's *kalgi*, a jewel worn on the front of a turban, and relics of the Prophet Muhammad. There is a temple in my father's village in India which owes its fame to the fact that it holds some of the clothes belonging to the fifth Guru of the Sikhs, Shri Guru Arjan Dev Ji. Guru Gobind Singh's *kalgi*, so much part of his identity in pictorial representations, would mean even more to Sikhs, a minority faith with a paucity of historical heritage. Both items have, heartbreakingly, gone missing, but the idea that the British Museum might have held on to them because it happened to inherit them as a result of some military shenanigans is painful. Or to put it another way: imagine how the British would feel if the French had won the Napoleonic Wars, occupied Britain and transferred Stonehenge to Lille. Some things don't matter because of their monetary worth or academic value, they matter because they tell people who they are.

Unfortunately, the museum establishment remains unmoved by such arguments. Tristram Hunt, head of the V&A, penned a long piece for the *Observer* acknowledging anxieties about items in his museum's collections, but concluded that 'we need to tread carefully along a path of total restitution, dictated by a political timetable. There remains something essentially valuable about the ability of museums to position objects beyond particular cultural or ethnic identities, curate them within a broader intellectual or aesthetic lineage, and situate them within a wider, richer framework of relationships while allowing free and open access, physically and digitally.' Jeremy

Wright, in his brief stint as Culture Secretary, ruled out the permanent return of artefacts and said that discussions should be focused on lending. In September 2020, Oliver Dowden, the Culture Secretary, was revealed, in a leaked letter, to have warned museums and galleries to cease removing controversial artefacts or risk losing funding.* Some museum directors have even questioned the wisdom of long-term loans.

In short, things have moved on little since the days when, in response to claims made by Greece for the Elgin Marbles and by Nigeria for the Benin Bronzes, museums would simply state that repatriation was illegal under the 1963 British Museum Act, or when David Cameron remarked in 2010 about India's demand for the return of the Koh-i-Noor diamond: 'If you say yes to one, you suddenly find the British Museum would be empty. It is going to have to stay put.' The disingenuousness of this argument was exposed by a BBC investigation which found that a whopping 99 per cent of the British Museum's collection was in storage in 2009 and 2010. Similarly, only 5 per cent of the Natural History Museum's specimen collections had been on display at the same time. The National Maritime Museum, which owns around 4,000 paintings and 70,000 prints and drawings, had 93 per cent of its collection in storage. Olivia Grange, Jamaica's Culture Minister, emphasized this point when in 2019 she publicly requested that the British Museum return precious carvings by Taíno peoples, found in a cave in the Caribbean in 1792, and not on display in the UK.[10] The desire to hold on to things even when you don't value them enough to show them is surely an attitude that goes back to empire. In 1860, Sir Anthony Panizzi, the British Museum's Principal Librarian, was asked by a Parliamentary committee to explain why the museum focused so heavily on artefacts from the cradles of European civilization – Rome, Greece, Egypt and Mesopotamia – while consigning colonial objects to 'five paltry cases' (for China and

* The letter said: 'As publicly funded bodies, you should not be taking actions motivated by activism or politics. The significant support that you receive from the taxpayer is an acknowledgement of the important cultural role you play for the entire country' (https://www.dailymail.co.uk/news/article-8777415/Oliver-Dowden-issues-statue-warning-museums-galleries.html).

Japan), labelling them 'ethnological' and 'curiosities' or simply just keeping them in storage. He replied: 'I don't think it is any great loss that they are not better placed than they are.'[11]

While our museums are as central to British culture as ever, we have been slow to confront the nature of our ownership. This relative tardiness is demonstrated by the restitution that is already happening elsewhere. Some of this is driven by individuals – such as Dr Mark Walker, a British citizen who in 2014 returned to Nigeria two bronze artworks inherited from his great-grandfather, who had participated in the looting of Benin, and an eighteenth-century Ethiopian crown repatriated after being surrendered by a refugee who had kept it in his apartment in the Netherlands for twenty years having discovered it in the luggage of one of his visitors. Some of it is being driven by the decisions of individual institutions around the world: the German Lost Art Foundation, established to recover Nazi loot, has extended its remit to include colonial objects. Some of it is being driven by the establishment of new museums in the developing world, such as the Museum of Black Civilization in Senegal, which can house recovered artefacts and so expose the racism inherent in routine claims that developing countries cannot look after artefacts as well as the British do. Some of it is being driven by the fact that hundreds of smaller institutions are not bound by the same restrictions as large institutions, with *The Times* recently finding that about 85 per cent of requests for the correction of 'past wrongs' in the last five years were accepted by universities. Then there is the legislation that actually allows large institutions to return artefacts in certain circumstances – if, for instance, they're human remains, or if they were pillaged in relatively recent wars, or if they're shown to be Nazi loot. Following the appointment of a provenance expert, the V&A intends to return eighty artworks stolen by the Nazis, and the British Museum has identified about 4,500 Egyptian antiquities believed to have been illicitly traded.

In 2017, President Macron pledged that France would repatriate any items his country had taken from Africa and commissioned a report on the Restitution of African Cultural Heritage by the Senegalese academic and writer Felwine Sarr and the French art historian

Bénédicte Savoy, which formulated measures for restitutions of collections in France to their countries of origin. Germany too has agreed to make a concerted effort to repatriate items taken during colonialization. And in July 2019 a prominent trustee of the British Museum, the Egyptian novelist Ahdaf Soueif, publicly quit her position, citing as her reason the museum's lack of action on restitution. This new spirit is perhaps best encapsulated by a viral tweet from a user calling themselves @Rehune which asked, 'How come some ppl have no problem telling some ppl to "go back home" but ask them to repatriate one little thing from the British Museum and it's all "This priceless inanimate object from someone else's culture BELONGS HERE."' It is also echoed in a scene from the blockbuster *Black Panther*, where a black character at a thinly disguised British Museum informs a director that he will take certain African artefacts off her hands, is told the items are not for sale and then asks: 'How do you think your ancestors got these? Do you think they paid a fair price? Or did they take it . . . like they took everything else?'

5. We Are Here Because You Were There

I'm no fan of the British seaside. I don't need to work on my tan, I can barely swim, I grew up in the beach-free West Midlands and my heritage can be traced back in its entirety to the landlocked state of the Punjab. Frankly, the kindest thing I can bring myself to say about Brighton on this bitterly cold February afternoon is that if you close your eyes, the sea sounds a little like the M6 on a busy day – a sound which, having grown up near junction 10, I will always regard as comforting. And the only solace when I open them is that I'm not, at least, standing on the beachfront, shielding my fish and chips from marauding seagulls. Instead I'm somewhere marginally more cheerful: the graveyard at St Nicholas Church. It is located in one of the oldest parts of the city, its cornerstone dating from the Saxon period, the church being cited in the Domesday Book of 1086, though the grave I have come to lay flowers at is not as ancient, belonging to one Sake Dean Mahomed. He lived between 1759 and 1851 and is a figure so fascinating that I spent a significant chunk of time while writing this book wanting instead to turn it into a novel about him.

How was he remarkable? Well, for one thing he was, as the title of a biography by Michael Fisher conveys, 'The First Indian Author in English'. Centuries before V. S. Naipaul got cracking on *A House for Mr Biswas*, before Salman Rushdie was put on to the English Literature Tripos at Cambridge University, Mahomed was, in the late eighteenth century at the age of thirty-four, taking out a series of adverts proposing to publish a book about his life called *Travels*, making personal visits to potential subscribers throughout southern Ireland and then publishing it from Cork. The book conveyed how Mahomed had been born into the politically turbulent city of Patna, where the English, French and Dutch each had a presence and families had to choose with whom they wanted to align themselves: the waning Mughal Emperor, their local Muslim community or one of the increasingly powerful European East India Companies. How, in 1769, while still a child, Mahomed plumped for working for the English Company's Bengal Army as a camp follower and then as a subaltern officer was taken under the wing of one Godfrey Baker, who became his patron and 'best friend'. How when he was discharged Baker persuaded him to accompany him back to Ireland, where Mahomed found himself, among other things, working for the Anglo-Irish elite as a manager – a rather nebulous position that was not quite a servant but equally not an independent gentleman.

Unfortunately, he was no Naipaul or Rushdie or Kureishi. Presented 'as a series of letters to a friend', a fashionable literary device at the time, *Travels* is not an easy read. The prose is laboured, full of allusions and rhetorical flourishes that illustrate his erudition but reveal little about what we actually want to know. So we don't learn enough about what must have been the profound emotional struggle of leaving his family to live on the other side of the world. About what exactly his intense 'friendship' with Baker involved. About how he felt when Baker was dishonourably discharged from the East India Company for embezzling funds. About what it felt like to become a sepoy at the age of just twelve. About what it felt like, as an Indian, to be employed to do the dirty work of the East India Company, coercing money from Indian villagers. About how it felt experiencing Europe, encountering poor white people for the first time in Cork, and about whether integration was difficult. Still, he got there first! As his biographer says, 'up to this point, no Indian had ever written and published a book in English, either in India or in Britain,' and it surely counts for something that Mahomed managed to write and publish a book at a time when white supporters of slavery assumed that black people were unable to write for themselves: he was the Neil Armstrong of my field.

Another remarkable thing about the man: in 1786, more than a hundred years before the British were being cautioned against the 'sexual pollution' and racial degeneration that would come with relationships with Muslim men,* centuries before actors Joan Hooley and

---

* In *The Infidel Within: Muslims in Britain since 1800*, Humayun Ansari observes that sexual relations between Muslims and white women were taboo because they

John White made history with one of the first interracial kisses on British television in a 1964 episode of the British soap opera *Emergency Ward 10*, even longer before I was making an almighty fuss in my memoir agonizing about defying my family's expectations to marry a good Sikh girl, Mahomed was just going ahead and doing it. In 1786, in his mid-twenties, the year his Anglo-Irish patron died, Mahomed eloped with the teenager Jane Daly. There is a high degree of uncertainty about what happened, but it seems he renounced his faith to do it, and while his biographer says that 'Jane's family does not seem to have supported the young couple – they lived in a world where a range of generally unflattering images of Indians and Muslims abounded,' the newlyweds appear to have been accepted by Cork society.

Jane was evidently an intrepid woman. In 1807, when Mahomed was approaching fifty, the pair left Ireland and moved to London with their children. They settled near fashionable Portman Square and Mahomed began work for a Scottish nobleman, Basil Cochrane. That brings us to another remarkable thing about Mahomed. In London, in 1809, he opened the first curry house in Britain. It was called the Hindostanee Coffee House but, as Fisher explains, it didn't actually proffer coffee – it was instead an 'eating house' where Mahomed prepared 'a range of meat and vegetable dishes with Indian spices served with seasoned rice', which customers would consume while reclining on bamboo-cane sofas and chairs, under paintings of Indian landscapes. It was a unique offering in London at the time, aimed at the British who had come back from the subcontinent, and initially did so well that it expanded into a neighbouring house. Unfortunately, for ultimately unfathomable reasons, he headed into bankruptcy in

---

challenged notions of British racial superiority essential to maintain empire. 'Social distance was necessary to sustain the charisma of British character and its resulting prestige and authority in the minds of subjugated people, which familiarity would dissipate.' It was generally believed that Muslims lusted after white women, would lose control around them, and that white women were 'therefore in need of protection from them . . . At the turn of the twentieth century Indian students, who were coming to Britain in growing numbers, were described as "raw youths" who were in "no way fitted to encounter the temptations to which many of them succumb".'

1812, but this failure gave rise to a final extraordinary chapter in this extraordinary man's life.

Not unlike certain prominent identity-shifting British Asian politicians, having spent the early years of his European residency trying to become as Western as possible, Mahomed realized his real value lay in emphasizing his Indian identity. So he moved to Brighton with his family and set up as a bathhouse keeper, flogging an Indian service dubbed 'shampooing' and which nowadays might be dubbed a kind of Turkish bath or thalassotherapy. A surprising development, perhaps, to the people who knew him best, because he had previously been dismissive about the practice in print, describing it as immoral and emasculating, but at the time Brighton was a fashionable seaside spa, with bathing machines transporting people down to the sea, and taking an 'Indian Medicated Vapour bath' seemed to fit into many people's idea of an outing. Mahomed threw himself into self-promotion, took out ads calling himself a 'Shampooing Surgeon', claimed the baths cured all ailments, 'giving full relief when everything fails; particularly Rheumatic and paralytic, gout, stiff joints, old sprains . . . aches and pains in the joints', and became a self-proclaimed expert, lying about his medical credentials, and writing a quasi-medical textbook. He had form when it came to this kind of bullshitting: he called himself everything from 'Deen' to 'Dean' to 'William Dean' and 'Sake [Sheikh] Dean Mahomed', he plagiarized a significant portion of the material in his book from other travel narratives, such as John Henry Grose's *Voyage to the East Indies*, he frequently edited his biography to suit him – claiming, for instance, that he went straight to London from India, omitting the twenty-five years he spent in Ireland, increasing his official age by up to a decade. And there were awkward mistakes, not least the member of his team who snapped a man's arm during a massage, resulting in it being amputated, and the elderly customer who died while having a shower on his premises. But at a time when George IV was building the orientally inspired Marine Pavilion as an expression of England's rapidly expanding Eastern empire, with India as its crown jewel, Mahomed's Indian baths were in tune with the zeitgeist. Both George IV and William IV partook of his vapour baths and Mahomed was awarded a Royal Warrant. He was delighted, put up pictures of royalty in his bathhouse in a gesture that would be echoed by the curry-house owners of the future and was so successful that hospitals referred patients to him.

Unfortunately, Mahomed became less of a novelty over time, the death of a silent business partner created financial problems, he lost his premises to a rival and his last years were lived in relative obscurity, which maybe explains why his grave is difficult to locate in the rain and at dusk centuries later. I had imagined a sentimental scene, getting down on my knees at his grave and giving him the good news: that he had achieved more than the stiffs in the grand tombs nearby, and that his legacy is very much alive in the twenty-first century. But the gravestone is behind a locked wire fence and I end up throwing my bouquet of petrol-station flowers over it, which promptly blow back into my face, attracting the mockery of a nearby daytime drinker. Still, I manage to find a moment to reflect on Dean Mahomed's many achievements from a bench nearby. After all, this was a man who introduced curry houses to Britain (and thereby played a role in transforming our national cuisine), laid the literary ground for the likes of Naipaul and Rushdie (who in turn revolutionized English literature), helped popularize massage and the word 'shampoo', from the Hindu *champi* for 'massage', and was a pioneer in his personal life. But for me the most remarkable thing about him was simply that he was a brown man from the empire living and working in the British Isles hundreds of years ago, and he thereby demonstrates a simple and profound fact about Britain: it is a multicultural, racially diverse society because it once had a multicultural, racially diverse empire. Or as the Sri Lankan writer Ambalavaner Sivanandan once famously put it: 'we are here because you were there.'*

British empire was why, even before Dean Mahomed arrived, a number of Indigenous Americans journeyed from their homes to England, including, in 1730, the Cherokee Beloved Man Adgalgala

* A sentiment echoed by the historian David Olusoga who, in response to a racist remark, tweeted: 'If you don't want Nigerians in the UK all you need to do is go back to the 19th century and persuade the Victorians not to invade Nigeria.'

and his compatriots: they came on a diplomatic mission to solidify links with imperial Britain and in the process made public appearances at Windsor, at Sadler's Wells, at the Royal Hospital at Greenwich, at fairs at Croydon and Tottenham Court, and at Bedlam Hospital among other places.[1] London was teeming with Asian seamen, thanks to empire: known as Lascars and recruited by the East India Company from ports such as Singapore, Calcutta and Shanghai, the men were considered to be harder working and cleaner living – and less expensive – than English sailors. Once on British soil, some couldn't afford the journey home and eventually settled here, often marrying white women and establishing multiracial households. Communities could be found around the docklands of London, Liverpool, Cardiff, Glasgow, Hull and South Shields.[2] Another inadvertent new community, a by-product of empire, were the *ayahs* – hundreds of Indian (and Chinese) women who were transported to Britain to provide childcare and domestic help for well-off white families on their long voyage home. However, on their arrival in Britain, these jobs often came to an abrupt end and many women were left stranded, with no means of getting home. Some managed to find other employment; others ended up destitute. Lodging houses for these women appeared in the capital and the charitable Ayahs Home was established in the nineteenth century – its building still stands in East London. Landing cards suggest that the vast majority of these women were treated as if they were the property of their employers, being given the names of the families (for example, 'Ayah Smith'), but there is also evidence that some refused to be victims. One *ayah* is known to have taken her exploitative employers to court and won, while another is registered as having travelled between Britain and the subcontinent fifty-four times, having made a profession out of such specialized childcare.[3]

Empire was why Indians found themselves employed by the East India Company within British educational institutes, such as Haileybury College, founded by the East India Company to train administrators, and Addiscombe Military Seminary for cadets. At Haileybury, the master of Persian orthography, Sheth Ghoolam Hyder, had a salary of £350 per year. At Addiscombe, one Meer

Hassan Ali penned a book, *Grammar of the Hindoostanie Language*, in 1812. Empire was the reason some former slaves, known as Black Loyalists, ended up in Britain, having been offered their freedom for fighting for the British during the American War of Independence. The fact that slavery was such an essential element of imperial trade is the reason black slavery was imported into Britain: Lord Chief Justice Holt's declaration in 1760 that 'No man can have property in another . . . there is no such thing as a slave by the laws of England' is often used to give the impression that there were never black slaves on this island, but the publication of advertisements appealing for the return of runaway slaves shows that, in practice, laws were evaded and black slavery was a feature of British life.★ Numerous academics have discovered proof of black slaves in Britain, including a team at the University of Glasgow who have launched a digital database of fugitive slave adverts from eighteenth-century UK newspapers, based on more than 800 advertisements placed by masters and owners offering rewards for the capture and return of 'runaways', and David Olusoga, who has explained how the captains of slave ships were frequently allowed to bring a few enslaved people back home to Britain and sell them. 'Many were young boys who were sold as exotic servants: fashion accessories,' he wrote in the *Guardian* soon after the statue of Colston was hurled into a dock in Bristol.

> They appear as commodities for sale in advertisements in 18th-century Bristol newspapers, publications that also carried notices offering rewards for the recapture of enslaved people who had absconded from the grand homes of the city's elite. Metres from where Colston's statue now rests [it has now been fished out and

★ For example, this from the *Liverpool General Advertiser* on 5 May 1780: 'RUN AWAY, on the 18th April last, from Prescot, a BLACK MAN SLAVE, named George Germain Foney, aged 20 years, about 5 feet 7, rather handsome, had on a green coat, red waistcoat, and blue breeches, with a plain pair of silver shoe buckles, he speaks English pretty well. – Any person who will bring the Black to his master, Capt. Thomas Ralph, at the Talbot Inn, in Liverpool, or inform the master where the black is, shall be handsomely rewarded. – All persons are cautioned not to harbour the black. N.B. The black is not only the slave but the apprentice of Captain Ralph.'

might be heading to a museum] runs Pero's Bridge, named after Pero Jones, one of those enslaved people who lived and died in Bristol. A man who may well have taken his first steps on British soil on the docks from which Colston's statue was hurled.

Hundreds of years ago, empire was the reason brown people could be found practising in Britain as doctors (such as Soojee Comar Chuckerbutty, who trained as a medic in 1845, converted to Christianity and became a member of the Royal College of Surgeons), law students (Cornelia Sorabji, a single woman from a Parsi Christian family, in 1892 became the first woman to study law at Oxford University, after her application was supported by notables including Florence Nightingale. On graduation she returned to India and became the country's first practising female lawyer, specializing in advising 'purdah-nashins', confined women), actors (Ira Aldridge, Britain's first classical black actor, was a huge star in the mid-nineteenth century, collecting armfuls of awards as well as an official honour in Germany), nurses (Mary Seacole, the African-Caribbean businesswoman and carer who was instrumental in the war effort in Crimea) and sportsmen (one of the most famous athletes of the early nineteenth century was Thomas Molineaux, an African American bare-knuckle boxer who had possibly been a slave). Empire is the reason Hindus from the Gujarat region of India, Muslims from the Pakistan region of Punjab and Bangladesh and Sikhs from the Indian Punjab (including my parents and grandparents) came to live here after the Second World War. Empire is the reason Brixton is a largely black neighbourhood: it was here, in an emergency hostel, that the immigrants on SS *Empire Windrush* spent their first night after landing in Britain in 1948, and many of them subsequently made it their home.[4] Empire is why in the 1970s, as my siblings grew up, Britain wrestled with the question of what to do about the 60,000 Ugandan Asians expelled by President Idi Amin and what to do about the 23,000 Kenyan Asians driven out due to trading bans on Asian citizens. Empire is why thousands of Somalis, Palestinians, Kurds, Iraqis, Tanzanians, Nigerians settled here and empire is largely why according to the 2011 Census people from Asian ethnic groups make up 7.5 per cent of the population, black ethnic groups make up 3.3 per cent, why, according to a study from the University of Manchester, white Britons are now a minority in Leicester, Luton and Slough and why, according to some estimates, ethnic minorities could account for almost a third of the population by 2050.[5]

I am as much evidence of the fact that Britain once had an empire as the Maqdala Crown in the V&A, and if I have rather over-emphasized my point here, it's because it needs to be. Britain has long struggled to accept the imperial explanation for its racial diversity. The idea that black and brown people are aliens who arrived without permission, and with no link to Britain, to abuse British hospitality is the defining political narrative of my lifetime. It was famously pro-pounded, of course, by our local MP, Enoch Powell, who regularly called for the repatriation of immigrants, but it was also taken up by the far-right groups who were so keen to etch graffiti on to Wolver-hampton homes telling us to 'fuck off home' and has been spread for decades in press coverage painting brown immigrants as spongers. In the twenty-first century it has continued to be perpetuated in the way public figures of colour are still told to 'go home' on a daily basis on social networks, in endless talk of 'second-generation immigrants' (how can you be an immigrant if you were born here?), in the fact that Shamima Begum, one of three schoolgirls who left London to join the Islamic State group in Syria in 2015, could have her British citizenship casually removed by politicians and in the recent *Wind-rush* scandal which saw British subjects who had arrived before 1973, in particular those of Caribbean origin, refused benefits, legal rights and medical care before facing deportation.

Many historians have remarked upon this imperial amnesia. Writing in their introduction to *At Home with the Empire: Metropolitan Culture and the Imperial World*, Catherine Hall and Sonya Rose observe, for instance, that in mid-twentieth-century Britain 'empire had gone and was best forgotten. The West Indians and South Asians who were arriving were thought of as postwar migrants rather than imperial subjects with a long history connecting them to Britain.' Laura Tabili has argued that a long history of migration to and from the colonies has been essentially rubbed out, with workers from the British col-onies being portrayed as 'an alarming anomaly'. I'd go further and say that imperial history is routinely omitted in every racial controversy Britain ever suffers: governments not acknowledging centuries of slavery, exploitation, state racism, cultural connections and economic ties when facing up to everything from the murder of Stephen Lawrence to the *Windrush* scandal.

Indeed, the narrative that brown people imposed themselves on Britain is so powerful that I absorbed it myself, as a young brown Briton. My parents never really explained why they came here beyond the fact that my grandparents had already arrived and they were entitled to call over dependants to join them, and they essentially corroborated Powell's politics with their behaviour: never packing away the suitcases they had arrived with, resisting getting British passports in case they had to go back to India, and telling me that you voted Labour if you wanted brown immigrants to stay and Conservative if you wanted immigrants to go 'home'. At school, my education taught me nothing about the history which would have explained why there were so many brown people in Wolverhampton and the only politician I ever remember visiting my school was Powell's successor, Nicholas Budgen, once described as 'Powell's vicar on earth' and every bit as anti-immigrant as the man he replaced.

A survey of friends suggests that other 'second-generation immigrants' didn't grow up quite so clueless. When I recently asked them on Facebook to tell me why their parents came to Britain, they generally responded with a version of the same thing, 'to do the jobs no one else wanted or was around to do', with the replies including 'They needed the labour'; 'I remember my father telling me that they needed teachers and the UK were giving out "vouchers" for entry'; and 'NHS needed doctors in the 60s.' And this is true. Following the Second World War, it became clear that restarting the British economy would need a great surge of overseas labour, and word quickly spread to the Caribbean, India and beyond. In April 1947, it was announced by the Ministry of Labour that 4,000 overseas workers a week would be introduced to Britain. Soon, the newly formed NHS, as well as companies such as London Transport, would advertise for workers in former imperial territories, sometimes offering sweeteners in the form of loans for travel fares. The Minister of Health at this time, driving the NHS overseas recruitment scheme? None other than that familiar paradox ... Enoch Powell. There is no escaping the guy. Health workers in Britain's former empire answered this appeal to such a degree that in 2003 it was claimed that in the Rhondda Valley, in Wales, nearly three-quarters of all GPs had South Asian origins.[6]

But actually even the point that our parents were invited, that they helped to rebuild post-war Britain, is just part of the story. As Robert Winder explains, the fact is that black and Asian immigrants didn't always have jobs to come to: the arrivals on the SS *Windrush* were nothing to do with Britain's recruitment drive. Rather, the troopship docked at Kingston, Jamaica, in order to transport British service-men home, and because it was only half full for the journey the skipper put out a call for more passengers, at £28 a berth. Hundreds set sail for a new unspecific life in an unknown country – and it was not until the voyage was well underway that the British government was told about the shipload of migrants heading to Tilbury Docks. In short, some black and Asian people were simply allowed to come to Britain – as was their legal right at the time as British citizens. In 1948, with the country still shell-shocked by the war, it was felt that any legislation with a whiff of the Nazi's racist ideologies – such as discriminating against 'coloured' immigrants – would be unpopular. The government also believed that racial discrimination might be damaging to Britain's plans for the imperial project. As Sir David Hunt, Winston Churchill's Private Secretary, put it later: 'The min-ute we said we've got to keep these black chaps out, the whole Commonwealth lark would have blown up.' Accordingly, Parlia-ment passed a law which, in subsequent years, would gradually be undone: the 1948 Nationality Act, which enacted what had been true for decades, that anyone born in the empire had the rights of a British citizen. David Maxwell Fyfe (for the Conservative opposition) spelled out the 'historic principle' behind the legislation in the House of Commons. 'We are proud', he said, 'that we impose no colour bar restrictions ... We must maintain our great metropolitan tradition of hospitality to everyone from every part of our empire.'

So it's not only true that many came to fill labour shortages, and help rebuild Britain after the war, but many also came because centuries of imperialism had tied them to Britain and ultimately made them citizens. The ties were deep, and if we acknowledged this simple fact as a nation it would transform all conversations about multiculturalism, which is forever deemed to be in a state of crisis. In 2005 a report from the right-wing think-tank Civitas claimed that multiculturalism is divisive, encourages racial hatred and may have helped to produce the 7 July suicide bombers of 2005. In 2018, a You-Gov poll of 5,200 people commissioned by the anti-fascist group Hope Not Hate found that more than two-thirds of Conservative Leave voters believed multiculturalism wasn't working. Meanwhile, every Prime Minister of recent times has expressed reservations, with David Cameron asserting in 2011 that 'state multiculturalism has failed' and that the UK needed a stronger 'national identity' to prevent people turning inwards. But what if this 'national identity' embraced a simple truth: that black and Asian people had been made citizens through the imperial project? What if we accepted that, ultimately, multiculturalism is, in the words of the Jamaican poet, actor and broadcaster Louise Bennett, just 'colonizin' . . . in reverse'? The 'debate' would be instantly transformed.

As it happens, I'm no fanatical supporter of pure multiculturalism. I don't think communities should be left alone to become isolated and myopic. I know from my own family's experience that the people who suffer most if they don't integrate, if they don't learn English, if they live in ghettos, if they insist on practices such as FGM and forced marriages, are immigrants themselves. Too much of my energy as a young adult was expended on getting my family to accept that I wanted to be more British, to change more quickly than they were. But they have accepted it, and they have changed, and my experience is that all communities eventually do, if you give them space, time and resources, and that multiculturalism of the kind the British Sikh communities have achieved can be extremely successful. There are Sikhs now in the Commons, in the Lords, on TV, in print, in banks, and the whole process would have been significantly less agonizing if, during my lifetime, Britain had not acted like we were aliens and interlopers but were here because of long-standing historical ties. In the 'debate' about multiculturalism, almost all the pressure is put on immigrant communities, to integrate, to pass citizenship tests, to learn English and to accept certain national values. But the 'host' society has responsibilities too. Chief among them, in the case of Britain, is surely to acknowledge that brown people are here because Britain, at best, had close relationships with its colonies for centuries, which included millions of the colonized putting their lives on the line for Britain during two world wars, or because Britain, at worst, violently repressed and exploited its colonies for centuries.

Furthermore, the multicultural 'debate' and the way we view brown communities in Britain would be transformed if we accepted an adjacent fact also demonstrated by the likes of Dean Mahomed: that brown people have lived in Britain for centuries. Discovering him offered the same level of excitement I felt when I saw my first Sikh on TV – when a man in a turban dressed up as Elvis and was grinding away to celebrate the glory of Walkers Poppadum Crisps had me yelping at everyone in the house to hurry downstairs to witness the incredible revelation on the telly. Mahomed's very existence challenged the idea that has been hammered into me my entire life: that brown people are relatively recent interlopers. It's a narrative propounded in multiple ways: through the complete absence of ethnic figures in my history education (the closest thing we got to anyone with a tan was the Tollund Man), through the elision of ethnic figures in my extended literary education (aside from *Othello* and Man Friday in *Robinson Crusoe*, a brown character didn't appear in any of my literary studies, until I was allowed, for one term during the final year of my Literature degree, to study fiction published after 1970), through the consistent whiteness of museum and art gallery exhibitions (I was so excited when the V&A did an exhibition on the Sikhs in 1999 that I visited three times and bought the book and poster), through our absence in local history books (as Shirin Hirsch puts it: 'In nostalgic histories such as *Wolverhampton Memories* the photographs show only white residents. When immigration is mentioned at all it is in relation to a "Latin love and romance" between an Italian migrant and a Wolverhampton local . . . the absence of black people is neither noted nor explained'), through the perpetuation of the idea that British history is intrinsically white (David Starkey, addressing a teachers' conference in 2011, opined that 'Britain is a white mono-culture and schools should focus on our own history'), through the regular accusations of 'wokeness' whenever a brown person is featured in a period drama (most recently when Dev Patel starred in a new adaptation of *David Copperfield*) and through the repetition of the idea that brown immigration only started with the arrival of black immigrants on the *Empire Windrush* (propounded in the opening ceremony of the London 2012 Olympics, which featured a giant model of the *Empire Windrush*, which docked at Tilbury in June 1948).

Not only had there been Africans in the royal courts since the reign of Henry VII – as well as in the households of notables such as Sir Walter Raleigh, William Cecil and Sir Francis Drake – but by 1596 Elizabeth I had had enough, writing to the Lord Mayor of London that 'there are late divers black moores brought into this realme, of which kinde of people there are already here to manie' and adding that 'those kinde of people should be sente forth of the land'. The first known record of an Indian youth being baptized in England is a Bengali boy who was christened 'Peter Pope' in London in 1616.[7] The presence of 'many of the hundreds of Africans in Tudor England' was recorded in single-line references in parish registers, such as one in Hackney which noted, in 1630, the burial record for one 'Anthony a pore ould Negro aged 105'. A black Londoner named Mingo appears in Samuel Pepys' diary in 1661.* There were visits from brown foreign diplomats, with John Evelyn detailing one such mission in his diary in 1682, saying the visitors resembled 'in countenance some sort of monkeys'.† In

* 'To the Dolphin to a dinner of Mr. Harris's, where Sir Williams both and my Lady Batten, and her two daughters, and other company, where a great deal of mirth, and there staid till 11 o'clock at night . . . At last we made Mingo, Sir W. Batten's black, and Jack [a black servant working for Sir William Penn] . . . dance, and it was strange how the first did dance with a great deal of seeming skill.'

† 'I went to the entertainment to contemplate the exotic guests. They were both very hard-favoured, and much resembling in countenance some sort of monkeys. Their garments were rich Indian silks . . . they wore poisoned daggers at their bosoms . . . they sate croosed-legged like Turks, and sometimes in the posture of apes and monkeys . . . They eat their pilaw . . . without spoons . . . Taking up their pottage in the hollow of their fingers, and very dexterously flung it into their mouths without spilling a drop.'

1723, the *Daily Journal* complained: 'A great number of Blacks come daily into this city, so that 'tis thought in a short time, if they be not suppressed, the city will swarm with them.' In 1764, there was a report of a party exclusively for Africans – an 'all black hop' – held at a Fleet Street pub, and in the same year the *Gentleman's Magazine* claimed that in the capital alone there were 20,000 'negroe servants', though this is likely an exaggeration: most historians agree that by the late eighteenth century there were about 10,000 black people in the whole country. By the early eighteenth century, it is possible to locate references to black Britons within newspapers and the Old Bailey records, with one Anne Duck in 1743 being put on trial for 'violent theft' – a witness at the time claiming they had seen Duck stealing from a man because 'I took Notice of her, because she is a black Woman, and so the more remarkable.' A mosque opened in Woking in 1899. One eighteenth-century African Briton and former slave was included in the first *Dictionary of National Biography* in 1885: Ignatius Sancho, who became renowned variously as a writer, composer, abolitionist, shopkeeper and social reformer. The eighteenth century saw the rise of a number of black communities in London centred around Wapping, Limehouse and St Paul's, while up in Liverpool a road was unofficially renamed Negro Street. Dickens, visiting the city in 1861, reported finding the pubs in the slum area full of black people.[8]

If I had to guess when the first black activists became famous in Britain, I would have said it was the 1960s, with the rise of the black power movement and individuals like Darcus Howe. But William Cuffay was prominent more than a century beforehand. A militant Chartist leader, so infamous during his life that the press nicknamed the movement 'the Black man and his party', he was fully grown at only 4 foot 11 inches as a result of spine deformities and was the off-spring of a relationship between a white woman and a freed slave man from St Kitts, who had been a cook on a naval ship and was one of the rare West Indians who entered England as a free man. William trained as a tailor and built up a career in London, lost his job in 1834 after joining a strike for better conditions and as a result of blacklisting went into working-class activism, publicly supporting the People's Charter of 1838, which demanded, principally, universal

male suffrage, and by 1848 he had become leader of the London Char-
tists. If I had to guess when the first Indian MP was elected, I would
have said the 1980s, and that the person was someone like Keith Vaz,
but the first British Indian MP was actually elected in 1892. Dadabhai
Naoroji was a professor of mathematics and natural philosophy and
entrepreneur before he stood for election to Parliament several times
as a Liberal, winning the marginal seat of Finsbury Central in 1892
and holding on to it for three years before losing to the Conservatives
in 1895.

If I had been taught about these amazing characters, instead of endlessly being fed the idea that my family and I were some kind of novel
social experiment, interlopers in a white country, it would have made
a huge difference to my sense of belonging. Having said that, it is
worth noting that not *all* these and other black and brown Britons
ended up here because of British empire. There is evidence that Roman
Britain included many people from Africa, the most famous visitor
being Emperor Septimius Severus, who was born in what is now
Libya and ruled from AD 193 to 211. Surviving Roman inscriptions
often mention residents with African backgrounds, and a skeleton discovered in Greyfriars monastery in Ipswich is believed to be that of a
slave brought to Britain from Tunis during the Crusades in 1272.[9]
DNA tests on a rather more ancient skeleton, the Mesolithic Cheddar
Man, so called because it was discovered in Cheddar Gorge in Somerset in 1903, have revealed that the 10,000-year-old man probably had
dark skin. 'So dark', observes Angela Saini in *Superior*, 'that by today's
standards he would be considered black ... Scientists had already
known for a few years, from analysing the skeletons of other hunter-
gatherer bones found in western Europe, that dark skin pigmentation
could well have been common back then. After all, light skin was
likely an evolutionary adaptation, one that helped people living in
northern climates absorb more vitamin D when there wasn't enough
sunshine.' The first significant waves of black immigration came with
the Spanish court of Catherine of Aragon in the 1500s. Most likely,
it was the fact that she brought her entourage with her to England
that explains why two images of a black trumpeter called John
Blanke appear in a 60-foot-long vellum manuscript known as the

Westminster Tournament Roll – the only identifiable portrait of an African in Tudor England.[10]

It hasn't just been immigration from empire which has created Britain's multiculturalism. Poles, for example, have been coming here for longer than you might think: the Polish government-in-exile, formed in the aftermath of the invasion of Poland of September 1939, was based in London from 1940, and Poles were an important part of the post-war migrant labour movement: in 1960, the number of Polish people arriving in Britain was equal to the number from the Caribbean. In fact, after the war, the appeal for foreign workers was targeted primarily at white Europeans, as well as refugees from the Soviet Union and other Communist states – after the failed 1956 revolution in Hungary, some 14,000 of its people came to Britain – and even some German prisoners of war. And if there is one book I could wish on to the national curriculum, it would be *Bloody Foreigners* by Robert Winder. It not only highlights the imperial context of post-war migration but articulates how 'Britain has absorbed migrants at a thousand points and times. Its history is the sum of countless muddled and contradictory experiences.' He tells us how in the twelfth century there were French Jews in London, Lincoln, York and Norwich; that in 1500 some 6 per cent of the civic population of London – around 3,000 people – were foreigners; that in Henry VIII's day a Londoner complained that 'Tottenham has turned French.' He reminds us that many of Britain's monarchs were foreign, and that in the seventeenth century Huguenot refugees from France were responsible for creating vital commercial industries. Other incomers included Greek Christians fleeing persecution from the Turks; Italians; Germans; Dutch immigrants; and, not least, Jews: perhaps 150,000 Jewish refugees fled the Tsarist pogroms in Russia in the 1890s. Ford Madox Ford echoed the argument in *The Spirit of the People: An Analysis of the English Mind*: 'In the case of a people descended from Romans, from Britons, from Anglo-Saxons, from Danes, from Normans, from Poitevins, from Scotch, from Huguenots, from Irish, from Gaels, from modern Germans and from Jews, a people so mixed that there is in it hardly a man who can point to seven generations of purely English blood, it is almost absurd to use the almost obsolescent word "race".'

It is also important to bear in mind that not all immigration from the empire was coloured. The nineteenth century saw a dramatic increase in the Irish population in Britain – up to 1.5 million by the 1880s. Of course, the fact that the Irish were British subjects in that century meant that they were, formally, not immigrants, but looking closely at what happened to them in Britain explains why many regard them as having been colonial subjects. Like black and Asian immigrants more than a century later, many Irish arrived unable to speak English (despite concerted efforts to spread English in the 1830s through Ireland's national school system), they had a different religion (Catholicism), they did the dirty, tough work that the British shied from (laying roads and railways, digging canals, working in factories/mines), they settled in ghettos (by 1871 nearly one in five of the population of Wolverhampton was Irish, and the city was nicknamed 'Little Rome' due to the number of Catholics living there, in the way that a ghetto in Wolverhampton inhabited by a subsequent wave of black and Asian immigrants became labelled 'Caribee Island'), they often lived in slums (a predominantly Irish district in Wolverhampton was dismissed in a 1849 report as an 'open gutter', while Sikhs complained out loud in the 1960s that they could only buy slum housing) and they were regarded with suspicion by the police (foreshadowing the attitudes towards brown Wulfrunians a century later, local police records reveal that the Irish were viewed as an inescapably suspect community and 1848 saw a violent clash in the slum district between the police and a 2,000-strong crowd of Irish residents. Thirteen arrests were made, and one Irishman claimed he had been beaten by the police: however, the police replied that his wounds were self-inflicted, and the man received a two-month prison sentence for his trouble).[11] In the late 1960s, just a few months after my parents had arrived in Wolverhampton, and a few weeks after Enoch Powell had made his Rivers of Blood speech addressing the problem of immigration in his constituency, the *Observer* sent a reporter to see what locals thought of the new arrivals. The litany of abuse he noted down and paraphrased over three hours was much the same as would have been directed at the Irish a century beforehand, and, let's face it, at European and Middle Eastern immigrants in the twenty-first century: 'they smell, they're violent, they take our jobs, they take our houses, they breed like rabbits, they live off the country, they cause disease, they don't want to mix, they've more rights than us, they want their teeth kicking in, they're ignorant, they're useless but some of our best friends are coloured.'[12]

We all know that the Irish story, with its roots in the bitter tragedy of the Irish Potato Famine, ended well for Britain. The immigrants integrated, they produced individuals like Oscar Wilde, Bernard Shaw and Thomas Barnardo (the founder of the charity) who shaped national culture, and the intensity of their work is reflected in a report in the *Irish Times* in 1862 that, over the course of fourteen years, Irish workers in Britain had sent over £12 million home to their families (£8.5 billion today). 'What a tale of industry, thrift and love of kith and kin is here!' Post-war imperial emigration has already proved to be just as successful, a result of just as much toil by migrants from the Caribbean and South Asia. It is hard to imagine modern Britain functioning without its thousands of Indian restaurants and shops, its millions of brown railway and other transport workers, its hundreds of black and Asian entrepreneurs who created employment for thousands and businesses from nothing, and talents such as Sir Lenny Henry, Mo Farah and Meera Syal. And as a nation I do feel that we have moments of insight, often in times of crisis, that brown and Asian people really do belong here as much as anyone else. It happened around the time of Stephen Lawrence's death, when the Metropolitan Police was declared institutionally racist, and the establishment had a dark night of the soul. It happened around the *Windrush* scandal of 2018, when there was widespread outrage that black Britons were being deported from a country that had been their home for decades, and to which some had come as citizens. And it happened in 2020 around the Black Lives Matter movement, and around the coronavirus crisis when the public suddenly seemed to appreciate that BAME staff not only accounted for a disproportionate segment of NHS medical staff (44 per cent, when the 2011 Census puts the BAME population in England and Wales at 14 per cent) but were dying at seven times the rate of white colleagues.

I met some relatives of black and Asian doctors who had died of

Covid-19 for *Channel 4 News* and *The Times*. It was emotional. Medicine runs in many immigrant families, and some of the bereaved were themselves doctors, going back to work to face the virus that had killed their loved ones. Many of the deceased had experienced racism even as they built the NHS: studies confirm that not only are BAME doctors routinely racially abused, but they're also pushed towards 'Cinderella' specialities such as geriatric medicine rather than the higher-status disciplines. Some were paying an NHS surcharge, introduced for all recent immigrant workers, which meant they were paying to use the service they were sustaining, which was, in turn, sustaining the nation. While I was writing about the subject, I felt optimistic about the possibility that Britain was finally beginning to appreciate multiculturalism and to understand the deep historical reasons for it. But the response online was generally negative: 'they came here to make money'; 'my consultant drives a Mercedes'; 'why the constant race stories?'; 'why can't we train our own?'; 'strange how prison population demographics or crime demographics aren't reported in the same way'; 'why does race matter? Seems you only care for your own'; and so on.

If the history and facts of British empire were more embedded within our national consciousness, would these doctors and nurses be regarded as not 'our own'? If everyone knew that the hospital porter and bus driver they encounter was the child or grandchild of a British citizen invited to rebuild Britain after the war, would I still receive messages about the prison population? I'd like to think I wouldn't. The idea that black and Asian families had served this nation due to a historical connection, let alone that we owed them something after empire had colonized their countries, was absent from the conversation. Indeed, in all my research, I came across only one article in one newspaper that mentioned the imperial connection, and that was in the *New York Times*, which found time even amid America's own savage coronavirus outbreak to report on how doctors who had 'moved to Britain from different corners of its former empire' faced a 'devastating toll'. I guess it's true that sometimes outsiders see us more clearly than we can see ourselves.

6. Home and Away

There were warning signs, I suppose, in the name. I booked into the Imperial Hotel in Delhi on the advice of a colleague, who informed me that New Delhi's first luxurious grand hotel, opened in 1936 and designed by an associate of Edwin Lutyens, who in turn designed what became the capital city of the British Raj, was a great place to recuperate after filming my documentary before returning home. But when obsequious waiters weren't repeatedly enquiring during each meal how I was enjoying my food, I was being namaste'd by a member of staff who referred to himself as 'boy', or I was encountering sycophantic portraits of British royalty in parts of the hotel with names like 'The Spice Route' and '1911', or I was sitting in a lobby decorated with prints of Sikhs being defeated by the British in the Anglo-Sikh Wars.

There are tens of such colonial hotels around the world according to the historian Maurizio Peleggi, places where Sikhs are traditionally employed as uniformed doormen, 'exploiting the symbolic capital Sikhs derived from their conspicuous presence in the colonial police', hotels which are nowadays wilfully marketed as 'heritage sites of sorts, where the colonial past is represented as a stage set for tourist consumption', and which in my experience are popular with Britons. They include the Taj Mahal Palace Hotel in Mumbai which has 560 rooms and 44 suites and employs some 1,600 people, and which according to the myth was built by Jamsetji Tata in 1903 after he had been refused entry into the nearby Watson's Hotel as it was whites only.[1] There is Raffles in Singapore – named after the British statesman Sir Thomas Stamford Raffles, founder of Singapore – featuring the Long Bar where the Singapore Sling was invented, and the Writers Bar, where no writer this side of Stephen King could surely afford the drinks and where, at the start of the Japanese occupation of Singapore in 1942, it is said that the Japanese soldiers encountered the guests dancing one final waltz. Then there is the Great Eastern Hotel in Kolkata – established in the 1840s at a time when Calcutta was the base of the East India Company – which in its heyday was known as the 'Savoy of the East' and about which it was said in 1883 that 'a man could walk in at one end, buy a complete outfit, a wedding present, or seeds for the garden, have an excellent meal, a burra peg (double) and if the barmaid was agreeable, walk out at the other end engaged to be married'.[2]

If the stiff colonial vibe at the Imperial made me feel as if the Indian staff or I were at risk of being flogged if we broke a rule, it may have been because, as Peleggi explains, these sorts of places, which include Shepheard's in Cairo, the Casino Palace at Port Said and the Grand Oriental Hotel in Colombo, were historically venues where the racism of empire played out. We know that these hotels rarely excluded people for their race given occasional visits by Asian royalty, but they would segregate brown people from white people in quieter ways. Apparently, one George Peet's English host at the Europe Hotel in Singapore told him: 'If stengahs★ (Eurasians) come in here . . . they are not actually refused admittance, but they are put off somewhere in a corner of the dining room, given slow service and cold food, and generally made to feel that they are not wanted. So they don't come again.' Meanwhile, there were reports of Eurasians being excluded from the ballroom at Raffles. In the twenty-first century, one is confronted by another imperial legacy in the foyers of these luxury hotels, so often packed with Britons: the intense way British people travel and live abroad.

The numbers involved are staggering. At the start of the seventeenth century there was an exodus of almost 40,000 people from the British Isles to the New World, otherwise known as America.[3] These people crowded aboard packed ships and risked their lives for fresh opportunity abroad, leaving behind a country that was experiencing religious turmoil and even a mini ice age. This emigration set a precedent for the next 350 years. In the early seventeenth century, the British Isles had a population of less than 7 million, but 350 years later

★ Coming from the Malay *sa tengah*, meaning 'one-half', 'stengah' was also used by colonizers to refer to mixed drinks such as Scotch and soda.

there were 140 million of their descendants living overseas.[4] Some 9.7 million people migrated from Britain between 1853 and 1920, 2.3 million going to Canada, 1.7 million to Australia and New Zealand, and 671,500 heading to South Africa.[5] More than 5 per cent of the population permanently left Britain between 1900 and 1914.[6] The compilers of the Census of 1861 remarked that 'the people of these islands are more movable than other nations, and large numbers of them are always abroad'. So many Cornish miners migrated to South Africa that they accounted for a quarter of the white mine workforce on the Rand by the mid-1890s, by the 1900s every mail was bringing £20,000–£30,000 (£8 million–£12 million today) for the families back home, and South Africa was referred to as 'Greater Cornwall' and Johannesburg 'a suburb of the Duchy'.[7] In 1938, a US Census demonstrated that 40 million US citizens declared 'some degree of ancestry' from England, 43.7 million from Ireland, 14.2 million from Scotland and 2.5 million from Wales. Meanwhile, Niall Ferguson has asserted that 'no other country in the world came close to exporting so many of its inhabitants', and Eric Richards has claimed that Britain 'pioneered mass migration, sustained the outward flows for two centuries . . . [and] helped to repopulate other continents': the British 'have been phenomenal people exporters'.

Just as empire turned us into a multicultural society, it has also made the world more British, spreading millions of our citizens all around the planet. And this desire to emigrate and travel has continued into the post-imperial age. Until 1984, twentieth-century Britain was a net exporter of people – as Robert Winder points out, 'between 1961 and 1981, usually thought of as a time of energetic immigration, we ran up a deficit of over a million people.' A recent report found that the UK has the largest number of expatriates within the Organization for Economic Co-operation and Development.[8] Samir Puri argues in *The Great Imperial Hangover* that as well as ensuring that Britain is an attractive place for foreigners to visit, its history having made it one of the fixtures of global life, empire has also rendered its people globally minded. 'Each year the Queen's Christmas speech to the nation thanks those Britons working in international development, and in response to emergencies and conflicts around the world . . . Britain is hardly a country that sits on its hands, when there is profit to be made and problems to be solved around the world – and this industriousness is one of its great imperial legacies.' And Boris Johnson picked up on the theme in his 2016 Conservative Party Conference speech, which must class as the single most imperial pronouncement by any British politician in my lifetime. In it, he boasted – among other rodomontades, some of which we will discuss later – that:

> of the Brits now alive and born in this country fully one in ten is now living abroad . . . we are talking 5 or 6 million people – a population the size of Scotland. No other rich country – according to the World Bank – has a diaspora on that scale. No other country is such a formidable exporter of human talent, business people, lawyers, teachers, prospectors, adventurers, poets, painters, whisky-sellers, French knicker sellers to France. No other country is turned so tangibly outwards and into the world.

We Britons remain persistent and dedicated tourists too, travel for leisure itself arguably being another legacy of empire. Thomas Cook, which was established by a cabinetmaker in his thirties, may have closed for business, but the company pioneered Western tourism, in parallel with the expansion of British empire, the historian F. Robert Hunter writing that 'the tourist enterprise accompanied British armies to Egypt and the Sudan in the 1880s and 1890s. Tourism was inseparable from the West's conquest of the Middle East.' Nearly two centuries after the company's foundation and more than 150 years after the opening of the Suez Canal, which permitted wealthy Britons to visit Asia in comfort and style, the British are the world's fourth most enthusiastic tourists, spending $71.4 billion on tourism every year, behind Germany, the USA and China, but ahead of France, Canada and Korea.[9] More than three-quarters of residents in England and Wales hold passports, according to the last Census in 2011, compared to just 40 per cent in the USA.[10] In 2018, when global pandemics were merely the stuff of dystopian fiction, the British took over 71.7 million trips abroad and in the month of August 2019 alone[11] British travellers made 9.4 million trips abroad.[12] Five per cent of these trips were to America, which has remained a popular destination for the British since the colonies were settled in the early seventeenth century.[13]

But it's not just our predilection for travel and relocation that has been shaped by our imperial history – the *way* we travel and live abroad has been influenced by it too. Many of the details of imperial travel and relocation feel remarkably familiar when you read about them in the twenty-first century. We all know, for instance, that expats generally earn more abroad than they do at home, one recent survey finding that moving abroad boosts the average worker's income by $21,000, with workers in India even getting a 'hardship allowance', a generous sum that takes into account the difficulty of living on the subcontinent; as we will see later, imperial life could be similarly enriching.[14] Tourists and expats have long documented their travels in photographic form, just as the employees of the East India Company often had themselves painted in imperial scenes. Modern British travellers and imperial Brits are/were known for dressing badly abroad: a recent survey of 15,000 European hoteliers, from the travel company Expedia, found that as a nation we are regarded as second only to the Americans as terrible holiday dressers, way behind the chic French and Italians; while Jan Morris observes that for the Victorians 'to be smart was to be dressed just as you would be at home in England, even though the temperature might be 109 degrees in the shade.' Another proud British imperial tradition is getting violently sick abroad. Cehat, the Spanish hotel and apartment trade body, recently estimated that the British cost them €100 million in food-poisoning claims over the past three years (while the sums from German and French tourists were negligible), and while there is a difference between Delhi Belly and dropping dead, it reflects the legendary and grim sickliness of Britons who ventured into empire. Tragically, over 20,000 of the total settlers in Virginia did not survive and, in an even more extreme case, of the 150,000 who emigrated to Barbados only 20,000 lived to form a community.[15] Meanwhile, in his book *The British in India*, David Gilmour reports on the extraordinary mortality rate on the Indian subcontinent in the early days of empire, where, at the end of the seventeenth century the British had a saying: 'Two monsoons are the age of man.' In 1692, the British population of Bombay actually decreased thanks to a heavy death toll among the expatriates in the city.

Some imperial traditions deserve dwelling upon longer than others, chief among them surely being the proprietorial air with which we Britons swan about the planet. We're rather used to getting wherever we want as a result of holding the world's seventh most travel-friendly passport, in joint position with the United States and Norway,[16] rather used to getting what we want when we get there, and we tend to assume we can relocate wherever we fancy. Such privileges were noted by the Indian national Ritwik Deo in an entertaining *Guardian* column in 2012, where he marvelled at the ease with which Britons travelled while he had 'protracted arguments with customs, who jabbed at my documents every time I tried to nip over to Ireland or France' – 'you would think there are no British immigrants anywhere in the world . . . instead, there are only legions upon legions of expats.' More recently this sense of privilege and entitlement was inadvertently dramatized by a Brexiteer commenting on social media: he had campaigned to liberate the UK from the EU but when he found himself being forced to wait in an immigration queue at an EU airport in Amsterdam, he complained out loud that 'this isn't the Brexit I voted for'. And such cockiness surely goes back to a time when the British ruled a quarter of the planet, when, as Jan Morris has observed, 'The Englishman expected the best seat, throughout his quarter of the world,' and when Enoch Powell, who according to his biographer never dressed appropriately for the weather, even sporting 'his full military uniform – tunic, collar, tie, Sam Browne' in extreme heat, travelled to Australia by flying-boat and was hit by an 'immense revelation'. 'It was a living geography and imperial lesson . . . the extraordinary sense of the inevitability – an apparently strange word to use – of British power was very strongly borne in upon me. It seemed to me that the combination of sea power and air power which Britain still exhibited, gave to the structure of a British empire an inherent strength which I was later to learn it didn't possess.'

Then we have our tendency as travellers and expats to remain aloof. Boris Johnson claimed that our predilection for relocation revealed a nation turned 'tangibly outwards', but there is an argument to be made that we are not necessarily open-minded once we get out into the world. According to a 2014 study by the international relocation company Robinsons, which questioned 1,000 UK expats about their life overseas, 'a quarter of Britons living overseas socialise mainly with fellow expats, and have no friends from their adopted country,' with expats living in Africa and the United Arab Emirates being the least integrated. This contrasts sharply not only with the attitude of foreigners who relocate to Britain for work (according to the latest HSBC Expat Explorer survey, the UK is the top location for expats to socialize with locals over fellow expats), but it also contrasts with what we expect of immigrants to this country, who are endlessly instructed to integrate. Such aloofness, if not hypocrisy, arguably goes back to empire when the British in Hong Kong were, in the words of Jan Morris again, almost 'psychotically aloof from the swarming Chinese who were their workforce', and when the colour bar in India was upheld at all costs. After the Uprising of 1857, the British created for themselves a cohesive imperial community that was entirely separate from Indian people and Indian culture – a culture the British saw as a threat to their carefully cultivated routines, traditions and sensibilities. They thus forged their own world in India, impenetrable to Indian people. According to David Gilmour, the distance was not only physical, but moral, emotional and theoretical: evenings were spent either on one's terrace or, commonly for men, at the social clubs which became popular in the nineteenth century. Clubs like the Bengal, the Madras and the Byculla of Bombay, established in 1827, 1831 and 1833, around the same time as many of the most famous London clubs along Pall Mall, were an environment in which one could eat, drink, relax, play sport, socialize and, most importantly, social-climb, away from the 'natives'. On occasion, the Indian elite were accepted within British social circles, but this was rare, particularly after the Uprising of 1857 when even Indians educated in Britain were snubbed.

Another imperial habit of both British expats and tourists is habitual drunkenness. If you've ever peered into Wetherspoon's at Gatwick airport at 7am before a flight, or into the Writers Bar at Raffles at gin-and-tonic time, you won't need the proof, but a recent survey for Alcohol Concern found that half of British holidaymakers drink alcohol each day of their summer break, about a third down at least four alcoholic drinks each day and about a fifth admit to having a 'regrettable experience' as a consequence of being under the influence of alcohol. This is the sort of bad behaviour that imperial Britons pioneered abroad. Abu'l-Fath Jalal-ud-din Muhammad Akbar, better known as Akbar the Great, the third Mughal Emperor, who reigned from 1556 to 1605, banned the sale of booze in his empire, but allowed the English to partake in Surat because, he said, 'they are born in the element of wine, as fish are produced in that of water and to prohibit them the use of it is to deprive them of life.' When the East India Company began making headway in India, its soldiers became renowned for drunkenness, with one of Clive of India's men attempting single-handedly to take the fort of Baj-baj near Calcutta on his own after too much arak.[17] Meanwhile, in Volume 6 of the 1914 *Oxford Survey of the British Empire*, the very first ailment to be discussed in a chapter on 'problems of health and acclimatization in the British dominions beyond the seas' was alcoholism, ahead of tuberculosis, diphtheria, cholera and bubonic plague.* Indeed, as Henry Jeffreys observes in his entertaining book *Empire of Booze*, 'alcohol oiled the transactions between Europeans and African slavers' (John Atkins, a Royal Naval surgeon, noted that African slavers 'never care to trade with dry lips'), while the misplaced belief that 'large quantities of alcohol helped acclimatise Europeans to the tropical humidity' routinely led to excessive drinking, and alcoholic innovations were, like the English language, railways and organized sports, regarded as

---

* It continues: 'The inhabitants of northern climates have always been addicted to strong drink as well as to a strong meat diet, but although educated people have learnt the power of self-control and do not become intoxicated, many still consume more than is physiologically good for them. Our coloured brethren, who seem to have been intended by Nature for a more vegetarian diet, seldom enlivened by alcohol, take to strong drinks with avidity, lose their higher control at once, and yield without a struggle to the poisonous effects of alcohol. For these, as for all children and for intemperate northerners, only one doctrine can be preached – absolute teetotalism.'

'lasting gifts to the world'. These included the development of India pale ale (the long journey to India having been found to have a winning effect on 'stock' beer, as we've seen), the opening of the first brewery in India in 1830 (by Edward Abraham Dyer, father of Brigadier Reginald Dyer of the Jallianwala Bagh massacre), the establishment of the institution of the sundowner (the alcoholic drink taken after completing the day's work) and the popularization of gin and tonic (the quinine in which helped ward off malaria).

Then we have the famous and, it turns out, historical British resistance to foreign food. The sight of a British tourist tucking into a full English or fish and chips in a foreign location, literally not even doing as the Romans do when they're in Rome, is a routine feature of modern tourism, with a recent study conducted by the flight-comparison site Jetcost confirming my worst suspicions. Apparently, almost half of Britons don't try the local cuisine when on holiday, two-thirds of Brits will go looking for a takeaway from a brand they recognize, and one in ten British people admit to spending most of their holiday in a pub, with just 10 per cent eating local food every day.[18] This was a common aversion during empire, with traditional British food being consumed in India – fried breakfasts remained a staple in any British diet – and residents of Calcutta boasting that they could get anything that was stocked in Fortnum & Mason.[19] Lizzie Collingham observes how the British abroad glorified produce from home, even if these provisions were as humdrum as tinned mushrooms, bottled peas and Carr's Captain's Thins. These relatively simple foodstuffs morphed into precious representations of life away from empire – the cracker or the tinned food becoming emblematic of 'home' even when the foods were in actual fact Scandinavian reindeer tongues or soup made from West Indian turtles. It also led to terrible imported British food developing social cachet in the colonies. In an echo of my experience as the child of immigrants – we would instantly reject my mother's beautifully prepared fresh curries for a sniff of a frozen pizza – the indigenous middle classes of British Honduras began denigrating local 'bush' foods and favouring the consumption of European produce. 'As a result, they eschewed game and freshly caught shellfish in favour of tinned Australian rabbit and cans of

American lobster. The ultimate absurdity was their purchase of "English" boxes of imported tapioca (cassava granules) to make "shape", a bland and archetypical colonial dessert, when cassava grew in the colony in abundance.'

Another imperial tradition which lives on among British expats is the desire to educate children in British schools. Just as British food was seen as the best, and just as David Gilmour reports that colonialists fetishized other British items like Vaseline, Pears Soap and Anadin,[20] there was a feeling among imperial Britons that British was best when it came to education. The feeling is echoed today, with Yvonne McNulty, an expat academic specializing in expatriation research, remarking in 2017 that school choices abroad are often a consequence of parental emotion ('There's a lot of guilt linked to moving abroad so [parents] want to make it up to their children'), just as it is echoed in the advice issued by the Council of International Schools to the *Daily Telegraph* in 2012 that 'sticking with the British national curriculum will make any move back to the UK less problematic . . . A child may feel more secure in their home environment, so a UK boarding school is worth considering.' The fact that so many public schools, from Repton to Epsom and Dulwich College, now have international outposts means that a boarding school in Britain is no longer the only option for expats, but it was a common choice in the days of empire. Even as late as 1939, the Colonial Service's 'General Conditions of Employment' handbook was recommending that children be sent away (for example, 'Infants and children up to three or four years of age and adolescents are generally unaffected by the climate but children of school age should not remain in Aden'), while in India children were frequently plucked from the sides of their *ayahs* as young as three and sent to England. Gilmour explains that the general consensus among expatriate parents was that a combination of climate, disease and culture made it necessary, with concern about Indian culture weighing particularly heavily. An expat in India called Sheila Fraser broached the idea of educating her children in India to her husband, Indian Civil Service officer Sir Denholm. He retorted that they would 'end up speaking chee-chee'. The concern about Indian influence on young children ranged from the fear that opium would be administered to babies to stop them crying to the danger of children being sexually corrupted by Indian culture. The resulting separation anxiety was huge. The trauma of exiled children is depicted by Charles Dickens in *Dombey and Son* (1846) when Master Bitherstone asks Florence Dombey for directions to Bengal, desperate to return to the only home he knows, in India. George Orwell hated being sent away from Burma so much he recalled his experiences in his essay 'Such, Such Were the Joys'. Meanwhile, the literary agent Gillon Aitken, born in Calcutta in 1939, remembers being sent away, first to a boarding school in Darjeeling and then to a school in Britain at the age of seven – he thought his parents were dead.[21]

Yet another experience shared by modern expats and imperial Britons is the stress of reintegration on repatriation. In the twenty-first century, this is enough of a challenge to be the subject of self-help books (Craig Storti's book *The Art of Coming Home* is considered a classic) and newspaper articles (the *Wall Street Journal* published an article in March 2009 bearing the headline 'Combating the Repatriation Blues', in which Storti was quoted saying, 'Most people find coming home to be a more difficult transition than going abroad'). That imperial Britons faced similar problems is reflected in the fact that colonial repatriates had self-help books too, with titles like *How to Live in England on a Pension*. And if such titles were produced in significant quantities, it's because empire was a phenomenon not only of immigration and emigration, but of repatriation too. In *The Empire Strikes Back?* Andrew Thompson estimates that as many as 40 per cent of migrants returned, 1.1 million people coming back from Australia between 1901 and 1915 and nearly 1 million from New Zealand between 1853 and 1920. When India gained independence in 1947, some 5,000 British expatriates were shipped back to England at the rate of 1,000 per month.[22] Many of them were thrilled to be coming home, to experience real Christmas with holly and mistletoe, or eat fish and chips from a 'fish and tatty shop', but others, like their modern counterparts, felt the departure as a loss. Lots of them moved into areas that were known repatriate communities; much like in India, people formed cohesive communities of mutual understanding, isolated from the outside and from those who could not identify, in areas like Bayswater, Mayfair, South Kensington, Cheltenham Spa, Bedford, Eastbourne and Dublin. They often struggled with the British weather and lack of servants. In India, families were accustomed to as many as thirty servants, yet on their return to Britain they would have to make do with four at the most. This was problematic for many as they had lost any knowledge of how to do even the most basic of household tasks, such as lighting a fire. The sense of domestic inadequacy extended into the professional sphere. Men who had held powerful positions in India were now powerless and commanded less authority and respect. This only added to the nostalgia for life in India. In his novel *Coming Up for Air*, George Orwell describes a 'poverty-stricken officer class' who were reduced to existing in 'little dark houses' in the back streets of Ealing. These people were obsessed with their own reduced circumstances and talked constantly of the Raj, surrounded by their 'teak furniture' and photographs of 'chaps in helmets'.[23]

You might wonder, given all these challenges, the pain of departure and repatriation, the dislocation, the desperate efforts to hold on to a sense of identity in foreign climes, the risk of illness and death, why Britons continued to emigrate and travel to empire in huge numbers. In attempting to answer the question, you'll discover various explanations which are in themselves, I would argue, imperial precedents for modern British behaviour. Take, for instance, the way the desire for adventure drove emigration. I'm writing this in the middle of a coronavirus lockdown, and while some people are predicting that we will never travel as we used to again, I don't believe a word of it. The first thing we will do the moment we can is see the world beyond our homes. Frankly, I want to go to the island of Run more than ever: if Britons could get there in the seventeenth century, I can get there in the twenty-first. There is no shortage on Instagram of people who confuse travelling with having a personality, there is evidence that millennials are travelling more than other recent generations, and this desire for adventure was present, and perhaps even more intense, in the imperial age. Empire provided an opportunity for adventure for many young men, raised on adventure books by the likes of G. A. Henty, Robert Louis Stevenson and Kipling – *Robinson Crusoe* being seen to glamorize colonialism so much that James Joyce once described it as a 'prophecy of empire'.[24] Boyhood dreams of imperial adventure were also fostered within the Boy Scouts and within the public-school environment, while parents encouraged their sons to pursue a career overseas in a bid to make them more 'manly' – the idea being that physicality, endurance and toughness of empire would remove any concern of 'softness', according to the historian John Tosh.[25] It was not only young men or boys who were attracted to empire for this reason. It was not uncommon to find men with a stammer working in administrative roles in the Indian Civil Service – to have a position in empire instantly gave a man kudos, and a speech impediment might be overlooked for 'empire served as proof for masculinity'. At its darkest, empire served as an opportunity for men to play out fantasies of violence, the imperial arena providing ample opportunity to demonstrate strength and power over people, over animals and in battle. Tosh argues that such violence often went unpunished and men were able to exercise aggression with no consequence. More prosaically, empire provided many men with an escape from the tedium of normality. Andrew Thompson writes about a school of imperial history which maintains that 'the drawbacks of domesticity' were 'acutely felt' by the 1880s and that 'the empire offered freedom and adventure, the domestic sphere routine, conventionality and constraint'. And the 1874 painting *North West Passage* by John Everett Millais takes up the theme: a seaman sits next to a map, looking distracted, while a woman, possibly his daughter, sits at his knee, draped over his feet and absorbed by a book. You can read what you want into it, but for many it conveys a man's desire to escape the supposed comfort of domesticity.[26] For some, though, the appeal of empire was just being somewhere else for the sake of it – a sentiment many of us can relate to in lockdown and which Somerset Maugham touched upon when he remarked: 'I never felt entirely myself till I had put at least the Channel between my native country and me.'

Another all too familiar reason imperial Britons continued to emigrate and travel in huge numbers in spite of all the evident risks and challenges was propaganda. Social networks are not, of course, the only place where travel is obsessed over in the twenty-first century:

if you've ever spent any time working at home like I do, you're doubt-less all too aware of how modern wanderlust is fuelled by endless escapist daytime TV shows like *Escape to the Continent*, *A Place in the Sun*, *A New Life in the Sun*, *Sun, Sea and Selling Houses*, *Property Down Under*. Given the onslaught, it's a wonder there is anyone left in Brit-ain to watch daytime TV, and many Britons ended up abroad during the days of empire as a result of similar hype about immigrant prospects – spread through a tsunami of chapbooks, plays, pamphlets, maps and sometimes lectures extolling the virtues and profits of overseas settlement, with the poet John Donne even being hired in 1622 to give one for the Virginia Company.[27] In *Propaganda and Empire*, John MacKenzie describes all the forms this hype took at the height of imperialism: schemes were put in place to promote emi-gration as a means to create a sustainable and affluent community overseas; societies were also formed to sell the dream of emigration, wrapping it up as an elitist, fashionable club that people should endeavour to be a part of. Emigration effectively became a mark of social status, which in turn exuded literary paraphernalia, from handbooks and specifically designed journals to advertising via consumable goods. Meanwhile Andrew Thompson reports how shipping companies and colonies employed 'emigration agents', many of them 'newspaper editors, emigrants, first-generation colonials, war veterans or career civil servants', to spread the word. Between the 1840s and 1920s these agents travelled Britain, dishing out leaflets, plastering posters on to walls, making lectures, arranging displays at markets and even attempting to bribe people with discounts on travel. 'Migration was, of course, a business and they were frequently accused of peddling false impressions and making fraudulent promises. Yet reasonable limits usually prevailed. Indeed, a leading historian in this field accords professional agents a vital role in the migration process, laying particular emphasis on the importance of their personal contact with migrants.'

There was an additional reason Brits kept on drifting out to the colonies which feels remarkably familiar in the twenty-first century: they had nothing to lose. The acronym Filth ('failed in London, try Hong Kong') is well established in City and legal circles nowadays, and Jeremy Clarkson expanded on the notion in 2009 when he wrote in the *Sunday Times* that 'every single person who ever moves to another country – with the exception of America, where you go to grow – is a failure. Seriously, no one has ever woken up and said: "I am completely happy. I have a lovely family, many friends, a great job and plenty of savings. So I shall move to Australia." '[28] He was being deliberately provocative but the sentiment was common during empire. Here we have E. B. Fitton writing in 1856 that 'no person who has ever enjoyed a life in England would, I think, profess to prefer a colonial life.' Here is Robert Louis Stevenson remarking, when sailing on an emigrant ship from Glasgow in the summer of 1879, that he was aboard a 'shipful of failures, the broken men of England, whom any casual observer might well have assumed were all absconding from the law'. More prosaically, the East India Company for some time offered a way out for minor gentry feeling the squeeze: imperial trade and administration being the only way they could hope to survive while retaining respectability. And, of course, alongside disasters such as famine in Ireland, depression in England, civil war, rebellion, brutal repression, cattle plague, crop failure, unemployment, inflation, poor harvests associated with the climatic downturn of the little ice age, malnutrition and the 'Black Winter' of 1771–2, criminal conviction was a major driver in imperial emigration. As Eric Richards tells us, the authorities were keen to send 'prostitutes, paupers, and criminals' to the colonies, threatening them with hanging if they dared to return. Between 1661 and 1700 around 4,500 English felons were transported, and when Britain lost its American colonies in 1776 the nation quickly found an alternative dumping ground in New South Wales. Meanwhile, 'organised children's emigration', or 'philanthropic abduction' as one critic has put it,[29] raged between the late nineteenth and early twentieth centuries, with Dr Barnardo's transporting 28,000 children to Canada between 1870 and 1914.[30]

Finally, there is the motivating factor of sex. Its role in modern travel comes in such different forms that it feels crass to group them together: from the 'sun, sex and sand' casually suggested and hoped for in package holidays to the abuse inherent in sex tourism, to expat workers using their wealth and power to obtain it in the Far East (one British investment banker recently writing anonymously for *The Times* talked about how 'people who may not be the most handsome catch back home' can suddenly transform themselves as expats in Hong Kong 'into serious philanderers, all owing to being white and well-off. Asian girls flock to you, seemingly charmed by your Western looks, but really more intrigued by your wallet'). And sex keeps arising, in similarly varying forms, as a motivating factor in my reading on empire. It comes up when Raleigh recounts that during his 1595 expedition to Guiana the 'most pleasing thing' he encountered in the Orinoco was a 'native' woman – 'In all my life I have never seene a better favoured woman: she was of good stature, with blacke eyes, fat of body, of an excellent countenance . . . I have seene a Lady in England so like to her, as but for the difference of colour, I would have sworne might have been the same.' It comes up when Edward Long arrives in Jamaica in 1757 and is mortified to discover that 'fellow-planters routinely took sexual partners from among their slaves . . . Many are the men, of every rank, quality and degree here, who would much rather riot in these goatish embraces, than share the pure and lawful bliss derived from matrimonial, mutual love.' It comes up when Samuel Snead observes in *Home Letters Written from India* (1830s) that 'those who have lived with a native woman for any length of time never marry a European . . . so amusingly playful, so anxious to oblige and please [are they] . . .' It comes up when the aforementioned academic study of colonial hotels notes that 'one can assume homoerotic intimacy and sexual encounters between male tourists and local youth, particularly servants in hotels and boarding houses, to have also been not infrequent,' when every book on empire mentions that British men (before it became more common for wives to join their husbands in India) had relationships with mistresses known as *bibis*, when David Gilmour reports that use of prostitutes was so widespread in the 1880s that in parts of Bengal almost half of the British troops stationed had some kind of sexually transmitted infection, and then tells us about one British officer in India who made it his business to 'sample different forms of sex with different kinds of sexual partner'. His experiments included 'horrible orgies' with his brother officers, a three-night orgy in Bombay which involved sex with a Greek, a Pole and a Japanese, and physical experiments with boys, animals and fruit, including a papaya, which proved more satisfying than a melon, 'being the nearest approach to the human vagina'.

The historian Ronald Hyam takes up the theme in his fascinating *Empire and Sexuality: The British Experience*, beginning with the reflection that, when he began research into the British empire in 1960, 'to write about its sexual aspects seemed so chimerical a project that I then put aside such evidence I came across . . . There was almost nothing in the way of secondary sources . . . historians writing about empire remain extremely shy about putting sex on to their agenda.' Hyam more than makes up for it, pointing out, over the course of more than 200 startling pages, how sex shaped the imperial mission in myriad ways. For example, there was the case of Colonel James Skinner (1778–1841), who it is believed had a harem of fourteen wives – a figure denied by his family who claimed there were only seven – and as a result Skinner produced eighty children. There was Valentine Baker, who in 1875 sexually assaulted a woman in a railway carriage: as a result, Baker destroyed his career in the military and was forced to seek employment in the Turkish Army instead. General Sir Eyre Coote, previously an MP and Lieutenant-Governor of Jamaica, was caught fondling and even flogging six teenage boys, aged fourteen and fifteen. The boys were members of the Christ's Hospital School to which Coote made regular Saturday-morning visits for his own sexual gratification. In 1922, Lewis Harcourt, or 'Loulou', the ex-Colonial Secretary, exposed himself to a young Etonian boy, Edward James. Shocked at the sight of the 'hideous and horrible old man', James complained to his mother, and the story leaked into London circles. The scandal possibly took its toll on Harcourt, who was found dead in his dressing room after an overdose of Bromidia. In the 1820s, a missionary, the Rev. Thomas Kendall, was discovered to have been living in New Zealand's Bay of Islands with a young daughter of a Maori chief: Kendall admitted that he had a sexual relationship with the girl, but claimed that it was nothing serious. In his autobiography *Paidikion*, Kenneth Searight (rumoured to have inspired E. M. Forster's novel *Maurice*, after Forster met him in 1912 on a voyage to India) recounts a series of erotic and sometimes sadistic encounters with young boys in India between 1897 and 1917 – at least 129 of them, with an average age of fifteen, eleven of them ten or younger. Hyam's bibliography also leads me to the case of the intrepid canoeist and celebrated explorer Major Rowland Raven Hart OBE, who gained fame for his arduous adventures on the Irrawaddy River in Burma. It was on these adventures that he found young Burmese boys to accompany him, including one called 'Ma Tu, with a radiant smile, [who] gives Raven Hart a relaxing massage'.[31]

In the nineteenth century, cities such as Singapore and Macao were melting pots for sexual liaisons between 'natives' and Europeans new to empire. By the twentieth century, there was even a new generation of mixed-race children such as in Rangoon, Burma, where a school was specifically built in order to educate children fathered by whites. It was particularly in Burma that the trend for taking a 'native' mistress took off, with around 90 per cent of expats estimated by one 'investigator' to have had sexual encounters with local women. In his book Hyam concludes, variously, that 'Sexual consciousness was heightened among soldiers and traders alike. Sexual relationships soldered together the invisible bonds of Victorian empire'; 'there seems every reason to take seriously the allegations of the anonymous contributor to the *Pall Mall Gazette* in 1887 who argued that empire was inconsistent with morality'; 'sexual dynamics crucially underpinned the whole operation of British empire and Victorian expansion. Without the easy range of sexual opportunities which imperial systems provided, the long-term administration and exploitation of tropical territories, in nineteenth-century conditions, might well have been impossible'; 'Britain has spread venereal disease around the globe along with its racecourses and botanical gardens, barracks and jails, steam engines and law books.'

Crucially, however, Hyman also presents several caveats, not least that the formation of British empire cannot be *explained* by sex drives, stating that it would be 'nonsense' to imply that any more than a few men went abroad for sex. This select group may have included explorers, but for most men there were plenty of sexual opportunities in nineteenth-century Britain. Nevertheless, he explains, even if sex does not count as a significant motive for imperial expansion, it may 'explain how such enterprises were sustained'. He also points out that alongside all this sex and, let's be frank, paedophilia and rape, the British also exported 'official prudery' – introducing inhibitions, repression, guilt and notions of sexual purity where they didn't previously exist, and doing so to such a degree that after 1914, he asserts, 'outside the fighting services, almost no sexual interaction between rulers and ruled occurred'.

Reading about this I am alerted to yet another possible modern imperial parallel, if not legacy, remembering a 2015 survey conducted by Lastminute.com which found that almost a third of British people felt offended by topless sunbathing, with the UK having the highest proportion of people (40 per cent), out of a selection of European countries, who said they thought it was a no-no for women to wear a thong on the beach, and 20 per cent of Britons saying they liked to be covered up with a towel or t-shirt on the beach, when only 4 per cent of Italians and Spaniards did the same. This brings us back to the bewildering complexity of British empire. There are legacies, patterns, correlations and echoes, but we have also inherited some of the contradictions of the enterprise. Empire might have made us permanently internationally minded, but it may have also made us insular and closed-minded once we get abroad. Sure, as I argued earlier, many Britons were in the days of empire, as they are now, dismissive of international cuisine when travelling. But at the same time the improvement in modern British cuisine in recent decades has been due to the increase in budget travel across the world, and this, in turn, is echoed in the fact that some servants of the East India Company pined for Indian food when they returned to Britain in the eighteenth century, with the diarist Thomas Turner complaining in 1763 that imperial groceries were too much in fashion, and Britain's growth as an imperial nation was to blame. Even tea, he demanded, should be abandoned as a non-British commodity. Through its 'frequent and continuous use', along with that of other imperial foods, 'we increase our expenses, bring on idleness and render ourselves less capable to struggle with the world and above all hurt our health and . . . entail a weakness upon our progeny.'[32]

Meanwhile, some imperial travel habits and motivations have clearly gone into reverse in the modern age. British missionaries once headed out in droves to spread Christianity across the empire, but nowadays the average unbelieving Briton is more likely to be on the receiving end of such zeal, *The Times* reporting in March 2016 that 'Christians from converted countries are now engaging in "reverse mission" to reintroduce God to an increasingly secular Britain. The growth of Pentecostal churches in Britain has been driven by migration from around the world, including from Nigeria, Ghana, the Caribbean and Protestant communities in South America.' Britons may nowadays be notoriously bad at languages, with a recent survey published by the European Commission naming us as the worst language-learners in Europe – just 38 per cent of Britons speak at least one foreign language, compared to the European Union average of 56 per cent – but there was a time when we seemed to be very good at them. The East India Company set up a college, Haileybury, to teach serious courses in 'oriental languages' before you headed off to the subcontinent, Enoch Powell casually mastered Urdu while he was in India, and one Charles Bell of the Indian Civil Service became so good at Tibetan that he published an English–Tibetan dictionary. Then we have the awkward fact that the thirst for travel inspired by empire has not necessarily made us tolerant of immigrants who themselves came from the empire, a tendency that podcaster Helen Zaltzman picked up on when she tweeted: 'Britain is hostile to people arriving in boats because Britain knows what happened when Britain arrived in other countries in boats.' The legacies of empire run deep and are sometimes contradictory. The pulling down of statues may have created the popular idea that one can erase or retain the values of empire by pulling monuments down or keeping them up, but imperialism exists within us in much more complicated ways.

7. World-Beating Politics

Multiculturalism has been inspiring regular controversies and crises in British politics for as long as it has been a thing. In 1964 there was the general election where the Conservative candidate in Smethwick reportedly told his voters, 'If you want a nigger for a neighbour, vote Labour.' In 1968 we had Enoch Powell's Rivers of Blood speech. In the 1970s we had the dilemma of what to do about 60,000 Ugandan Asians and 23,000 Kenyan Asians, in the 1980s we had 'race riots' which were more often than not inspired by white aggression directed at ethnic communities, while, more recently, we have had the murder of Stephen Lawrence and the *Windrush* scandal. And the historian Anna Marie Smith was on to something when she observed that as a nation we work through 'decolonisation trauma' by making 'the black immigrant . . . the postcolonial symptom . . . the most visible symptom of the destruction of the British way of life'.[1] Paul Gilroy put it even more forcefully in *After Empire* when he suggested the possibility that:

> many people in Britain have actually come to need 'race' and perhaps to welcome its certainties as one sure way to keep their bearings in a world they experience as increasingly confusing. For them, there can be no working through this problem because the melancholic pattern has become the mechanism that sustains the unstable edifice of increasingly brittle and empty national identity. The nation's intermittent racial tragedies become part of an eventful history. They punctuate the boredom of chronic national decline with a functional anguish.

I wouldn't go as far as Gilroy. I don't think British national identity is brittle and empty. There are times in my life, not least during the London 2012 Olympics, when it has meant a great deal. Nor do I accept Britain's national decline as a fact: our multicultural society has achieved great things, not least the development and sustaining of the NHS. I do agree, however, that our repressed and confused feelings about empire keep emerging in our repeated crises about multiculturalism and, more generally, overlay many key political events of the twentieth and twenty-first centuries. Not least there has been the significant political energy expended on the task of letting so much of our empire go its own way: the Balfour Declaration of 1926 granting Canada, Australia, New Zealand and South Africa their independence, for instance, India and Pakistan becoming free in 1947, Sudan in 1956, Ghana in 1957, Zambia in 1964, Hong Kong, which had been a Crown colony since 1841, being handed over to China in 1997, and so endlessly on. Then there are the two significant moments of the Suez Crisis of 1956, when Israel, the UK and France invaded Egypt with the ostensible aim of regaining Western control of the Suez Canal, and the Falklands War of 1982. The former proved rather more humiliating and traumatic than the latter, Suez being generally accepted as one of the key moments in the shaping of Britain's post-war psychology, Samir Puri arguing that the 'debacle' in 1956 was 'the moment that Britain's status as a global superpower was revealed as fiction', and other analysts even arguing that it marked the true end of British empire.

In contrast, the Falklands War, the single event which first made me aware as a young child of something called 'the news', was a success for Britain, having played out like imperial events from other eras.[2] The ten-week war, sparked when the Argentinians invaded the Falkland Islands, British territory in the South Atlantic, was reported by the press with the kind of jingoistic enthusiasm the popular press had reserved for Queen Victoria's empire (on the first day of the crisis, the *Sun* had a front-page splash declaring 'WE'LL SMASH 'EM', printed over pictures of Winston Churchill and a bulldog); the fleet of warships sent on the 8,000-mile journey to the region was compared by commentators to the Armada; the campaign was depicted by some as a moral enterprise – 'a purifying fire', according to one clergyman at San Carlos, a settlement in north-western East Falkland – just as similar campaigns were in the late nineteenth century; and Prime Minister Margaret Thatcher adopted a distinctly colonial tone in a speech she made in 1982 to a Conservative Party rally. 'When we started out, there were the waverers and the faint-hearts,' she declared.

> The people who thought that Britain could no longer seize the initiative for herself. The people who thought we could no longer do the great things which we once did. Those who believed that our decline was irreversible – that we could never again be what we were. There were those who would not admit it – even perhaps some here today – people who would have strenuously denied the suggestion but – in their heart of hearts – they too had their secret fears that it was true: that Britain was no longer the nation that had built an empire and ruled a quarter of the world. Well they were wrong. The lesson of the Falklands is that Britain has not changed and that this nation still has those sterling qualities which shine through our history.[3]

There have since been other wars which have been deemed imperial by various analysts. In *The Colonial Present*, the geographer Derek Gregory sees the influence of empire in Western escapades in Afghanistan, Iraq and elsewhere, arguing that the war on terror is a 'violent return of the colonial past, with its split geographies of "us" and "them," "civilization" and "barbarism," "Good" and "Evil" ', reminding us that Britain embarked on numerous Afghan wars in the nineteenth and early twentieth centuries in order to keep Tsarist Russia from its doorstep in India, and highlighting the remarks of journalists who have expressed distinctly imperial sentiments about contemporary wars. They include Max Boot, an editor on the *Wall Street Journal*, claiming not long after 9/11 that Afghanistan was 'crying out for the sort of enlightened foreign administration once provided by self-confident English men in jodhpurs and pith helmets', and Britain's Philip Hensher pronouncing in the *Independent* in October 2001, after the Prime Minister had made a series of speeches on that country, that what Afghanistan needed was a British viceroy.

> The British believed from the start that their rule in India represented an improvement in the lot of ordinary Indians, and, on the whole, I think they were right. It might even be argued that the current state of affairs in Afghanistan arises from their success over the years in

fighting colonisers off; if they had been subjugated as India was, investment and the exchange of ideas might have produced a tradition of parliamentary democracy and some kind of substantial infrastructure. The Prime Minister is within an ace of saying that life, for the ordinary Afghan, would be better under our rule than it is under the Taliban, and who could disagree with that?

The Iraqi capital, Baghdad, fell to Britain in 1917 during the First World War, and Lieutenant-General Sir Stanley Maude issued a proclamation to its citizens which sounded eerily like many more recent statements made by contemporary British politicians. 'Our armies do not come into your cities and lands as conquerors or enemies, but as liberators,' he said. '[Through history] your city and your lands have been subject to the tyranny of strangers, your palaces have fallen into ruins, your gardens have sunk in desolation, and your forefathers and yourselves have groaned in bondage. Your sons have been carried off to wars not of your seeking, your wealth has been stripped from you by unjust men and squandered in distant places.' Robert Gildea reminds us in *Empires of the Mind* that while imperial parallels may have been lost on many in Britain at the time of the Iraq War, they were not lost on people on the ground. He quotes a man called Sadiq who described a family wedding in 1920 that turned into a bloodbath when 'a two-winged plane suddenly came over the horizon and dropped a fireball among the celebrations'. In 2003, he said:

> It's the British again. They have been bombing my family for over eighty years now. Four generations have lived and died with these unwanted visitors from Britain who come to pour explosives on us from the skies . . . I often wonder how they would feel if we had been bombing them in England every now and again from one generation to the next, if we changed their governments when it suited us. They say that their imperial era is over now. It does not feel that way when you hear the staccato crack of fireballs from the air. It is then that you dream of real freedom – in shaa' allah – freedom from the RAF.

Samir Puri has argued that the influence of empire on these wars is not as neat as some imply, writing that 'historical acts from different eras do not connect to each other with such straight lines, but the past bears down on the present by imbuing it with certain meanings rather than others.' Others, such as Jeremy Paxman, have observed more generally that Britain's prime ministers cannot resist adopting an imperial tone of voice nor can they 'resist the temptation to lecture other governments'. It's an attitude that has found numerous manifestations, from Tony Blair's arguments in favour of the Iraq War to David Cameron's arguments in favour of intervention in Libya, to Robin Cook's notorious 'ethical foreign policy'. Cook was derided when he announced it after the Labour government had been in power for just two weeks in 1997, but the former Foreign Secretary Lord Carrington acknowledged that such a policy was hardly a novelty when he remarked shortly afterwards in a BBC documentary that 'we've always had an ethical foreign policy,' even if it hadn't been stated. It's an impulse that surely goes back to the nineteenth century, when, according to Robert Tombs, 'British politicians often felt moral pressure to intervene where states were failing or non-existent, most extensively in India and Africa.' He adds: 'inaction was seen as a shameful dereliction of duty . . . it was strongly felt to be an obligation to provide leadership and assist the forces of progress, preferably by peaceful means, but by force if necessary against "barbarity".'

The influence of empire can also be felt in recurring crises about the status of Gibraltar, in the way Scottish nationalists talk about gaining independence from their English 'colonizers' and in the use of the monarchy as a lobbying force in national and international affairs. The royal family are wheeled out routinely to cement relations for Britain, whether it is inviting Donald Trump over for a state visit or the Queen visiting Ireland to seal the ultimate success of the peace process, much as they did during empire. Queen Victoria may not have visited her treasured possessions, but her grandson King George V visited all Britain's main territories, some 14,000 people with 600 elephants escorting him on a hunting trip in India in 1906, when in one day his party slaughtered eighteen lions, thirty-nine tigers and four bears, and the heir to the throne, the Prince of Wales, went on a series of imperial tours, being greeted by a banner at Aden in 1921 which declared: 'TELL DADDY WE ARE ALL HAPPY

UNDER BRITISH RULE'.[4] 'A martial spirit still pervades the royal regime,' Jan Morris has observed. 'It is restrained nowadays, in the interests of diplomacy and political correctness, but it is still present in the thump and discipline of public sessions, the massed bands and the gun-salutes, the barking of sergeant-majors, the languid elegance of cavalry officers and the old military marches. For the ethos of empire is still ingrained in the national psyche.'

If our appetites for war or foreign intervention have been dulled by our recent experiences in Iraq, Afghanistan and Libya, the effect of nostalgia for empire is perhaps even more deeply entrenched in the British psychology. For when it comes to the question of how our politics has been shaped and influenced by empire, there is one issue that dominates all else – a political event which has been compared to Suez by many, and which also happens to be the most divisive and contentious political issue of our lifetime: Brexit. Difficult as it has been confronting the subject of empire in the middle of a global pandemic, I have consoled myself during these challenging months that I have at least been offered respite from the enervating question of our relationship to Europe. There turns out, however, to be no escape, with the argument that our departure from the European Union has been ultimately inspired by our experience of empire being one of the most common criticisms of Brexit. And when another outsider who is very perceptive about Britain, the Irish journalist Fintan O'Toole, published an entire book on the theme, *Heroic Failure: Brexit and the Politics of Pain*, I rushed to buy it as if it was a new release from Bros, and I was a Brosette.

It did not disappoint. As well as demarcating the colonial inspiration of Brexiteers such as Boris Johnson, who spent a significant portion of his brief time as Foreign Secretary telling us we needed to create a 'Global Britain', and Liam Fox, who spent a significant portion of his time as International Trade Secretary wanting to renew trading relationships with the Commonwealth (dubbed by Whitehall officials 'Empire 2.0'), he also highlights the curious habit among Brexiteers of describing our past and future relationship with the EU in colonial terms. So we have Alex Downer arguing in the *Daily Telegraph* that 'it's astonishing that Great Britain risks ending up an EU colony after Brexit', Jacob Rees-Mogg telling the BBC in 2017 the UK must not become a 'colony' of the EU during the two-year transition period after Britain's withdrawal, Daniel Hannan tweeting in May 2018 that 'leaving the EU while remaining in the customs union would be far worse than staying where we are. We'd be an EU colony, subject to taxation without representation,' and Nigel Farage talking about 'an independent United Kingdom' in his 4am Brexit victory speech, before adding: 'We'll have done it without having to fight, without a single bullet being fired.' Describing this Brexiteer mentality as 'the ironic reversal of zombie imperialism', O'Toole contends that the 'crucial idea here is the vertiginous fall from "heart of empire" to "occupied colony". In the imperial imagination, there are only two states: dominant and submissive, colonizer and colonized. This dualism lingers. If England is not an imperial power, it must be the only other thing it can be: a colony.'

It's a compelling argument. But it is also an interpretation Brexiteers reject. The leading Brexiteer Daniel Hannan has tweeted 'a rule of thumb' that 'if someone you meet keeps banging on about the British empire, you're talking to a Remainer' (itself a response to a *Financial Times* story reporting that the EU's Donald Tusk had claimed that Brexiteers were 'longing for the empire'). Boris Johnson explicitly rejected the accusation of imperial nostalgia when resigning as Foreign Secretary in 2018, saying the inspiration for Brexit was 'not to build a new empire, heaven forfend . . . It meant taking the referendum and using it as an opportunity to rediscover some of the dynamism of . . . bearded Victorians.' Jacob Rees-Mogg ruled out empire nostalgia in a similar way ('I am not suggesting that we have some neo-imperial vision and are going to become a superpower'), and maintained he was inspired by Britain's nineteenth-century success in free trade. Other Brexiteers have emphasized the same thing, whether it is Liam Fox waxing lyrical about 'our proud trading history', Priti Patel, then International Development Secretary, claiming the Commonwealth was an 'exemplar' of 'free markets, private enterprise and liberal economies', Grant Shapps encouraging Britain to re-establish its position as 'the world's greatest trading nation', Brexit Secretary David Davis remarking in a documentary that 'our history is a trading, buccaneering history – back to Drake and beyond', and Dominic Raab, another former Brexit Secretary, encouraging Britain to resume its 'historic role' as 'buccaneering free traders'.

This defence is one you could swallow, I suppose, if you had only a superficial understanding of imperial history. After all, when Britain abandoned its mercantile economy – a system based on protectionism, imposing high tariffs on foreign trade and offering incentives for colonies to buy only British goods and to export their own products to Britain only – for free trade, it transformed the nation. Food became cheaper and more abundant. Also, this free-trade ideology was at the time seen as intrinsically unimperial. The free-traders' world was not one of colonies; they believed countries should trade with Britain out of self-interest, not because of political bonds. Some free-traders also supported the eradication of the slave trade, allying themselves with anti-slavery Whigs in Parliament, because they thought only a universal ban would ensure that other countries couldn't gain an advantage over Britain due to lower labour costs. The free-trader Richard Cobden, who worked to repeal the Corn Laws, which applied tariffs to protect Britain from foreign competition and gave preferential treatment to Britain's overseas empire, was particularly outspoken against empire, describing Britain's role in India as 'a career of spoliation and wrong', opposing the annexing of Burma in 1852 and writing in 1853 that Britain would ultimately be punished for its 'imperial crimes'. It would be a happy day, he stated in 1856, 'when England has not an acre of territory in Continental Asia'.

Overall, the prevailing view in the first half of the nineteenth century was that empire should take a new direction, centred on internationalism and freedom. Britain managed to have influence in areas such as Ottoman Turkey and South America without colonization, and in the mid-nineteenth century Lord Palmerston, who served twice as Prime Minister in that period and set the tone for British imperialism, actively rejected opportunities for accumulating new colonies. He said of Abyssinia: 'All we want is trade and land is not necessary for trade; we can carry on commerce very well on ground belonging to other people.' Meanwhile, he said of Egypt: 'We want to trade with Egypt and to travel through Egypt but we do not want the burden of governing Egypt . . . Let us try to improve all these countries by the general influence of our commerce, but let us abstain from a crusade of conquest.'

The problem, however, with this Brexiteer defence is that, as much as some free-traders saw commerce as theoretically separate from the quest for empire, in practice . . . it wasn't. In another illustration of the complexity of empire, even as Britain embraced free-trade ideology *it still had a massive empire*, and it was *still expanding its empire*. As John Gallagher and Ronald Robinson point out in their essay 'The Imperialism of Free Trade', 'between 1841 and 1851 Britain occupied or annexed New Zealand, the Gold Coast, Labuan, Natal, the Punjab, Sind and Hong Kong. In the next twenty years British control was asserted over Berar, Oduh, Lower Burma and Kowloon, over Lagos and the neighbourhood of Sierra Leone, over Basutoland, Griqualand and the Transvaal: and new colonies were established in Queensland and British Columbia.' When the commerce of empire was threatened by other countries' annexations, Britain joined the tussle for parts of sub-Saharan Africa. Even Lord Palmerston annexed Aden in 1839 and Lagos in 1861.

Moreover, the popularity of the free-trade ideology eventually morphed, for some, into the notion of 'free-trade imperialism'. It may feel as paradoxical as the ghost of Cecil Rhodes featuring in a Benetton advert, but this involved the British government using force to achieve its 'free-trade' goals, resorting to what the shipping magnate Macgregor Laird described as 'the moral power of the 24 pounder' to cajole weaker countries into engaging in 'free trade'. Applying military pressure to encourage smaller nations to sign free-trade treaties led Palmerston to remark famously that 'these half-civilized governments such as those of China, Portugal, Spanish America, require a dressing every eight to ten years to keep them in order.' And to the dismay of free-traders like Richard Cobden, empire continued to find new violent expressions throughout the age of glorious free trade. When the Neapolitans refused to reduce tariffs, Lord Palmerston sent gunboats to the Bay of Naples to force the government to compensate British merchants for commercial losses.[5] When the Chinese government confiscated and destroyed 1,000 tons of opium that the British were sending into the country from India, Britain decided that it was the time to try and force China to open up to them fully, and a series of clashes escalated into three years of fighting on the coast in the form of the Opium Wars.[*]

It was also Britain's fanatical commitment to free trade that made our response to the Irish Potato Famine so calamitous. Queen Victoria initially ordered some aid to be sent – at the peak of the crisis, soup kitchens were installed in Ireland for a pitifully short period of six months – but the 'laissez-faire' free-trade ideology of the Whig government, led by Prime Minister Lord John Russell, meant that trade did not stop. The island was still required to export produce like butter, grain and livestock to England, despite the food being desperately needed by its own people. As a consequence, around 1 million people died, and millions more lost their homes or emigrated. There is an argument that Britain's failure to step up could also have had something to do with fiscal problems which restricted borrowing, but there's no doubt that had Ireland not been compelled to export its food, many thousands of lives, and livelihoods, could have been saved. India suffered in a similar way, for similar reasons. Lizzie Collingham estimates that as many as 16 million Indians died in famines between 1875 and 1914. 'The colonial government did very little to alleviate the misery, insisting that this was nature's way of keeping a check on the burgeoning Indian population,' she writes.

> But famines were not a natural consequence of poor harvests. They were the result of the unchecked functioning of the free market, which allowed merchants to continue to sell their wheat to the highest international bidders while inflation priced the poor out of their

* The East India Company recognized the immorality of its trade, its directors in London writing in 1781 that 'Under any circumstances it is beneath the Company to be engaged in such a clandestine trade; we therefore, hereby positively prohibit any more opium being sent to China on the Company's account.' The Company in India replied that the nature of the trade meant it was 'not a matter of choice but necessity' – the Chinese would not buy anything else.

ability to buy food. Some administrators argued that famines were good for India's agricultural sector, as they forced unproductive and indebted smallholders off the land. In fact, every famine had the effect of pauperising an ever-greater proportion of the Indian population. And yet in 1900, one fifth of Britain's wheat imports came from India.

In summary, even if you give Brexiteers the benefit of the doubt, concede that their historical wistfulness is more about nostalgia for nineteenth-century free-trading prowess rather than nostalgia about empire per se, you ignore the fact that free trade at that time was actually imperial. You also ignore that some of the deadliest calamities in Britain's history of empire, some leaving millions dead, happened in the name of free trade. It has admittedly become a cliché to think that Brexit is an exercise in empire nostalgia, but clichés often exist for a reason. I'll concede that Brexit imperial nostalgia is more a feeling than an intellectual phenomenon, not being thought through as a coherent manifesto, and it intermingles with nostalgia for all sorts of other historical moments, including the Reformation and free trade and Victorian ingenuity, but it is a thing. Furthermore, the Brexiteer obsession with replacing EU membership with new 'Anglosphere' alliances with Canada, Australia and New Zealand in itself harks back to a time during empire when people preferred their bond with these nations – Lord Curzon, the Viceroy of India, complaining in 1909 that 'when Englishmen speak or think of the British empire, they are apt to leave India out of sight, and to think only of the colonies that were founded and largely peopled by the men and women of our own race.'[6]

It's not difficult to tease out the basic logic behind this imperial nostalgia: when Britain joined the EEC in 1973 it had just emerged from the defining experience of ruling over an empire on which the sun never set, and membership felt like demotion. At its most extreme, it felt like colonization, because colonization was the prism through which Britain had viewed the world for centuries. Furthermore, Britain's interests had historically been outside Europe. So, as our relationship with Europe deepened and inevitably became more complicated, Brexiteers started pining, consciously and unconsciously, for some sort of rebirth of the empire. And in Boris Johnson Brexit has had a leader who has, more than any other modern politician, sought imperial inspiration, writing hagiographic books on the colonialist Winston Churchill in which he challenges 'those who despise the empire' to decide whether they hate it more than 'slavery or female genital mutilation', somehow finding time in the middle of a global pandemic to write a column and send a series of tweets declaring that he would fight 'with every breath' in his body any attempt to remove the statue of his political hero from Parliament Square, saying at another time that the problem with Africa is 'not that we were once in charge, but that we are not in charge any more', writing of 'flag-waving piccaninnies', referring to the 'watermelon smiles' of Africans, being prevented only by wiser souls from reciting Rudyard Kipling's 'Mandalay' at a Buddhist temple in Myanmar, observing that 'we used to run the biggest empire the world has ever seen' before asking 'Are we really unable to do trade deals?', and suggesting that Barack Obama removed a bust of Winston Churchill from the Oval Office because 'it was a symbol of the part-Kenyan President Obama's ancestral dislike of the British empire.'

Then there was that party conference speech of 2016 again, its intense imperialism being tangible even though it ostensibly focused on how 'Global Britain is a soft-power superpower' and not *hard* power, and featured the caveat that the end of empire was 'a profoundly good thing'. Among other sentiments, it featured Johnson claiming that London is 'the greatest city on earth' where 'we lead in . . . creative and cultural sectors', and the assertions that 'we have the best universities', 'that Britain is ranked among the top three most innovative societies on earth', that 'we are still the fastest-growing European economy, according to the OECD', that 'we were instrumental not just in ending the civil war, but in wiping out Ebola' in Sierra Leone, that 'we initiated a bold programme to tackle the pirates that plagued the coast' of Somalia ('British ships took them on, with all the courage and decisiveness of our nineteenth-century forebears'), that we are 'the leading military player in western Europe for the foreseeable future' and that we 'invented or codified just about every sport or game known to humanity'.[7]

You might be tempted to see a party-political divide when it comes to such imperial nostalgia. After all, Conservative politicians have tended to be defenders of empire while Labour politicians have seemingly generally felt the need to apologize for British empire – Tony Blair formally apologizing to the Irish people for the Great Potato Famine and condemning Britain's role in the slave trade as 'one of the most inhuman enterprises in history', Gordon Brown apologizing for the shameful Home Children scheme in which, between the 1860s and 1960s, more than 130,000 children from poor families were sent to Australia and Canada on the promise of a better life, Jeremy Corbyn in 2019 pledging (I touched upon this earlier) to make schools teach students about the injustice of British empire, and Tony Benn making anti-colonial pronouncements throughout his life. Visiting Jallianwala Bagh in 2013 David Cameron didn't make himself wildly popular with Indians by claiming that 'there's an enormous amount to be proud of in what the British empire did and was responsible for', while Johnson has wilfully gloried in Britain's imperial past. But things aren't that neat. In 2005 Gordon Brown, as Chancellor, used a visit to one of Britain's former East African colonies to argue that Britain should stop apologizing for its colonial past and recognize that it has produced some of the 'greatest ideas' in history. Meanwhile, the aforementioned 2001 *Independent* column by Philip Hensher which called for a viceroy to be installed in Afghanistan was inspired by Tony Blair's speeches. 'Listening to the Prime Minister's remarkable speeches on the subject of Afghanistan, one reflected that imperialism has, perhaps, been buried somewhat prematurely,' he opined. 'The political will to set things right in faraway places (Rwanda?) was in his conference speech in abundance. All that was missing, which would have followed the Prime Minister's line of thought quite naturally, was a commitment to move in and rule there.'

Indeed, now that Brexit has happened, it's becoming clear how it fits into a wider pattern of British imperial exceptionalism which has afflicted politicians of all hues – the idea that we are different, better than everyone else and therefore don't necessarily have to obey the same rules, has seduced all our leaders. Britain's unceasing obsession with its much vaunted 'special relationship' with the superpower of the United States reflects a deep longing among many of us, if not for a period where Britain's American colonies were part of its empire, then at least for a time when we had influence as a superpower too. It is reflected in the global vision of our increasingly stretched armed forces, with Britain spending about the same proportion of national wealth on its military now as it did in the nineteenth century (2 to 3 per cent, according to Robert Tombs),[8] the Royal Navy website citing 'deploying globally' as one of it missions – 'Our versatility gives us the freedom to deploy anywhere in the world' – and the army asserting, despite its modest size, that 'we are persistently engaged around the world to help shape the environment and prevent conflict in the future.' It is a feeling that is flattered by Britain's permanent seat on the UN Security Council: despite boasting only a fraction of China's population, a mere portion of Russia's surface area, a slice of the USA's economic might and a smidgen of France's culinary capabilities, we sit alongside these nations, with Theresa May in a speech at the UN General Assembly in 2017 talking about the 'special responsibilities' that the UK holds within the United Nations.

And then there is the coronavirus crisis. Boris Johnson's announcement at the beginning of the pandemic that thousands might die, led to one *FT* reader remarking online that his tone was defined by the 'Etonian mindset that caused famines across the empire' – 'these lords and masters are trained to shrug it off with the certainty that they are the stewards of society, born and raised to make tough decisions.'[9] Furthermore, every stage of the crisis has been characterized by the idea that Britain is a special case. Initially, when the world was beginning to take the crisis very seriously, Johnson played it down, telling Britons they should 'be going about their business as usual' and even boasting about shaking hands with people at a hospital that was treating coronavirus patients. While the rest of Europe went into lockdown, Johnson delayed introducing containment measures, at the same time trumpeting a controversial 'herd immunity' strategy. There is evidence that we refused to subscribe to European efforts to source ventilators, going our own way, only to face a serious shortage. As Google and Apple combined to develop a global tracing app, we went it alone to develop our own NHS app, with disappointing results. When the world's nations rushed to quarantine foreign visitors arriving in their airports, we let them in, and then when Covid seemed to become less of a threat to the world after its initial onslaught, our advice switched to quarantine. Our politicians gloated endlessly about how we were leading the world in efforts to find a vaccine, while the Health Secretary boasted in June, amid disastrous mortality figures, that 'British science is among the best in the world.' Johnson talked about how we needed a 'world-beating' testing regime when just getting a world-equalling one would have been progress. Later he promised a 'world-beating' track-and-trace system to stop a second coronavirus peak, which Britain's newspapers then revealed was a failure.★ Even when Johnson contracted Covid-19 himself, there was a view among his supporters that he was somehow immune to an illness that had killed thousands just because he was a British leader, with Toby Young confessing in the *Spectator* to 'a kind of mystical belief in Britain's greatness and her ability to occasionally bring forth remarkable individuals . . . who can serve her at critical junctures. I've always thought of Boris as one of those people – not just suspected it, but known it in my bones.' It's quite possibly a view that Johnson has had of himself, with Martin Hammond, one of his masters at Eton, writing to his father in 1982: 'I think he honestly

---

★ As I write, the exceptionalism continues, with the Chancellor talking about how 'we're introducing a world-leading £1.57 billion rescue package to help cultural, arts and heritage institutions weather the impact of coronavirus,' the government announcing plans for 'the world's most effective and secure border', Education Secretary Gavin Williamson insisting he will be 'delivering the world's best education system' even as a fiasco with exam results leads to the normally supportive *Daily Mail* describing his actions on its front page as 'ANOTHER FINE MESS', and Boris Johnson responding to a question in Parliament about why our infection rate is worse than Germany's and Italy's with: 'actually, there is an important difference between our country and many other countries around the world and that is that our country is a freedom-loving country, Mr Speaker, and if you look at the history of this country over the last 300 years virtually every advance, from free speech to democracy, has come from this country.' The Opposition leader Keir Starmer has also succumbed, tweeting in July that he was off to meet local business owners and workers in Falmouth and 'it's absolutely crucial we protect and support jobs in the UK's world-leading tourist industry.'

believes that it is churlish of us not to regard him as an exception, one who should be free of the network of obligation which binds everyone else.'

After his recovery, even as we drifted towards the worst death toll in Europe, Johnson remarked that 'there will be many people looking now at our apparent success.' People *were* looking at us, just not for the reasons the Prime Minister claimed. In May the *Sydney Morning Herald* observed that, unlike Italy, the United Kingdom had had 'time to prepare for the coronavirus tsunami' but had failed to act, *Libération*, the French centre-left newspaper, reported 'breathtaking shortages', 'fiasco' and a nonchalant handling of the crisis by the Johnson government, the *New Yorker* said that despite its 'internationally respected public-health apparatus' Britain had taken an 'obvious misstep' in hesitating to implement a national lockdown, while in Turkey the Anadolu state news agency warned that the UK's death toll from the crisis could be worse than those of Italy or Spain and that Boris Johnson's crisis management of the pandemic should be questioned and examined in terms of this projected outcome.[10] The *Irish Times* put it most damningly of all, some days later: 'Another example of British exceptionalism backfiring in grand style, some might say, and a bad omen for Brexit, the UK's other social-distancing project.'

8. Dirty Money

Few areas of Britain feel more quintessentially English than the Cotswolds, with its thatched cottages, rolling hills, overpriced garden centres and pubs that present themselves as high-end restaurants. Meanwhile, there are few more quintessentially English things to do while you're in the Cotswolds than to visit a country house, with their Downton Abbey associations, Farrow & Ball paint schemes and cream teas. And as you pull up to Sezincote House,[1] set on high ground on a 4,500-acre estate, about a mile and a half from Moreton-in-Marsh, it feels as if you're about to have the archetypal experience of visiting a country house in the Cotswolds. But look beyond the men consulting ordnance survey maps on pathways, the Cotswold stone, the striped lawns, the ha-ha which stops the handsome herd of cows from wandering on to the cream driveway, and you'll discover something unusual.

Sure, the gardens, as with so many of the most famous English country-house gardens, were created with the help of Humphry Repton, but they also feature rockeries with an unusual foreign air, a large water feature overlooked by what resembles a Hindu god, and you get to the house over a bridge bearing models of Brahmin bulls. And yes, the house is essentially a Palladian villa, designed in 1805 by one Samuel Pepys Cockerell, the great-great-nephew of the renowned English diarist, fashioned from stone taken from a local quarry and featuring carvings of pineapples, a common symbol of wealth in the eighteenth century. But there are Indian lotus buds amid the carvings, a copper onion dome reminiscent of Wolverhampton's many Sikh temples dominates the roofline, what is thought to have been the original owner's main bedroom sits away from the main house and has been designed to resemble a nineteenth-century tent of the kind the imperial Britons would have been familiar with, and there is a rickshaw parked outside.

I consider myself an expert in modern British Indian homes, with their front gardens paved over to make space for Audis and porches graced with large shoe racks, but Sezincote, which has been described variously as 'the only Indian country house ever built in Britain', an example of 'Indian revival . . . a short but fascinating episode in the history of taste', 'the first high point of the Picturesque Style which flourished for a limited time around the year 1800', makes me wonder whether I actually know anything at all. My guide is the current owner, the genial Edward Peake, whose family purchased the estate in the twentieth century, and who asserts, while standing next to an Indian Ambassador motorcar that he purchased for his wife as a birthday present, that the idiosyncratic house stands as a celebration of a fruitful and mutually respectful relationship between the sub-continent and Britain. It's a relationship he marked recently by pouring water collected from the source of the Ganges into the spring that feeds the house and its fountains (which is itself one of the sources of the Thames), and which is reflected in the house's history and influence.

After the Prince Regent visited in 1807, Sezincote is said to have inspired the design of the Brighton Pavilion, which, in turn, has significance for British–Indian relations as being the place where, between 1914 and 1916, some 2,300 Indian soldiers who had been wounded on the battlefields of the Western Front were treated. Also, Jan Sibthorpe, writing a blog for 'The East India Company at Home' project, which examined the British country house in an imperial and global context, has speculated that while the 'house did not create a national style as a legacy', the lodges at one of the entrances, which have since been remodelled, might have been 'the first buildings in Britain to represent Indian vernacular architecture' – that is, they might have been the first 'bungalows' in Britain, the architecture and the word 'bungalow' both being imperial imports.*

* The *Hobson-Jobson* entry for 'bungalow': 'The most usual class of house occupied by Europeans in the interior of India; being on one story, and covered by a pyramidal roof, which in the normal bungalow is of thatch, but may be of tiles without impairing its title to be called a bungalow . . . The word has also been adopted by the French in the East, and by Europeans generally in Ceylon, China,

But Sezincote is also evidence of something darker: of the vast amounts of wealth Britons siphoned from India during empire. For the estate was bought in 1795 by one of the architect's brothers, Colonel John Cockerell, who worked for the East India Company and was a friend of Warren Hastings. He died soon afterwards, and it was yet another brother, and yet another servant of the East India Company – Sir Charles Cockerell, who like his late brother had amassed a fortune in private trade while on the subcontinent – who commissioned the eccentric house. Together, the men were members of a social elite known and mocked at the time as 'nabobs', a term derived from the Persian *nawab*, signifying officials in the Mughal court, but used in Britain to denote East India Company officials who had lived on the subcontinent, accumulated substantial fortunes and bought up English houses and seats in Parliament. Basil Cochrane, the nobleman Dean Mahomed worked for in London, was one of them, establishing a personal fortune through lucrative private trade, official positions and the exclusive contract to supply the Royal Navy with food and equipment. And as Tillman Nechtman explains in his authoritative survey of the phenomenon, in the eighteenth century these men became the subject of foreboding (Lord Chatham: 'The riches of Asia have been poured in upon us, and have brought with them, not only Asiatic Luxury, but, I fear, Asiatic principles of government. Without connections, without any natural interest in the soil, the importers of foreign gold have forced their way into Parliament by such a torrent of private corruption as no hereditary fortune could resist'), critical newspaper coverage (a letter to the *Gentleman's Magazine* in February 1772 fretted that 'Our Eastern nabobs possess the power of doing ill in a greater degree than perhaps was ever known in the annals of time'), plays (for example, Samuel Foote's *The Nabob* in 1772, Richard Sheridan's *The School for Scandal* in 1777) and official inquiries (Robert Clive, the first Governor of Bengal, being

---

Japan, and the coast of Africa . . . the probability is that when Europeans began to build houses of this character in Behar and Upper India, these were called Bangla or 'Bengal-fashion' houses; that the name was adopted by the Europeans themselves and their followers, and so was brought back to Bengal itself, as well as carried to other parts of India.'

forced to defend himself for three days in the Commons in May 1773 against the attacks levelled against him by the chairman of a committee examining his administration in India, and Warren Hastings, the first de facto Governor-General of India, being impeached before the House of Lords in 1788 and acquitted in 1795).

In turn, these nabobs illustrate a claim made routinely about British empire: that, just as our museums were built with its loot, it made Great Britain rich. Here, for instance, we have Shashi Tharoor protesting in 2017's *Inglorious Empire* that 'Britain's Industrial Revolution was built on the destruction of India's thriving manufacturing industries.' Here in 2005 we have Richard Drayton penning a column for the *Guardian* bearing the headline 'The wealth of the West was built on Africa's exploitation' and arguing that 'without Africa and its Caribbean plantation extensions, the modern world as we know it would not exist.' Here we have the Mayor of London Sadiq Khan remarking on his Instagram page as the statue of the slave trader Robert Milligan was removed from West India Quay that 'it's a sad truth that much of our city and nation's wealth was derived from the slave trade.' And here, in 1937, we have George Orwell writing in *The Road to Wigan Pier* that 'the high standard of life we enjoy in England depends upon our keeping a tight hold on the empire, particularly the tropical portions of it such as India and Africa. Under the capitalist system, in order that England may live in comparative comfort, a hundred million Indians must live on the verge of starvation – an evil state of affairs, but you acquiesce in it every time you step into a taxi or eat a plate of strawberries and cream.'

Imperial figures also observed this as a fact of empire, with General Charles Napier, who became Commander in Chief in India, declaring in 1844 that 'our object in conquering India, the object of all our cruelties, was money – lucre: a thousand millions sterling are said to have been squeezed out of India in the last sixty years. Every shilling of this has been picked out of blood, wiped, and put into the murderers' [East India Company's] pockets.' Meanwhile, Lord Salisbury, who would later become Prime Minister, declared in 1878 that 'If our ancestors had cared for the rights of other people, the British empire would not have been made.' He added: 'as India must be bled, the bleeding should be done judiciously.' And an illustration of what this 'bleeding' might have involved in practice can be provided by Clive of India, who is celebrated in a Grade II-listed bronze statue in Whitehall, and whose nickname rather detracts from the fact that he actually loathed India, writing at the end of his first year there, 'I have not enjoyed one happy day since I left my native country,' dismissing Indians as 'indolent, luxurious, ignorant and cowardly', and being blamed by many for the Great Bengal Famine of 1770 which is estimated to have killed up to 10 million people. This man, described as an 'unstable sociopath' by William Dalrymple, was the original nabob, who, over two stints in India, led the British to victory at the Battle of Plassey in 1757, defeated the Nawab of Bengal and his French allies, before being himself anointed Governor of Bengal, Bihar and Orissa in 1765, and became wildly rich through his endeavours. After the Battle of Plassey, which arguably marked the founding of British rule in India, Clive received what Dalrymple describes as 'one of the largest corporate windfalls in history', and ten years later he was worth, by his own calculation, £401,102 – equivalent to £702 million today.

He spent a large part of his fortune buying significant tracts of Shropshire. Having paid off the mortgage on his family estate and commissioned a new house there, between 1761 and 1771 he bought a further four grand Shropshire estates along with a handful of more modest properties. He also bought up 12,000 acres of County Clare and named the estate 'Plassey', after 'the place where we gained our great victory in India to which I owe all my good fortune'. In its final report, the Select Committee that had been set up to investigate East India Company abuses in India concluded that between 1757 and 1765 employees had benefited from 'presents' worth around £2 million (£4 billion today) from Bengal alone. This was on top of the £500,000 (£1 billion) a year made through 'private' trade. This prompted Clive to make his most famous speech, in which he complained of being treated like 'a common sheep-stealer'. After Plassey, he roared, 'a great prince was dependent on my pleasure, an opulent city lay at my mercy; its richest bankers bid against each other for my smiles; I walked through vaults which were thrown open to me alone, piled on either hand with gold and jewels! Mr Chairman, at this moment I stand amazed at my own moderation.' Not that there was any sign of this moderation in his spending: in his mid-thirties Clive continued to buy houses, including the Claremont estate from the Duchess of Newcastle, which he bought for £40,000 in 1768 (£80 million) and then spent a further £15,584 (£31.2 million) on hiring Capability Brown to rebuild it. The *Salisbury Journal*, meanwhile, claimed Lady Clive's pet ferret sported a diamond necklace worth over £2,500 (£5 million today).

Then there was Warren Hastings, the first Governor-General of British India and a man who had significantly more affection for the subcontinent, learning Bengali, Urdu and Persian and describing Indians as 'gentle', 'benevolent' and 'as exempt from the worst propensities of human nature as any people on earth', but who at the end of his career nevertheless stood accused of enriching himself. During his lengthy impeachment, which, rather like Brexit, enthralled the public as much as it bored them rigid, various newspapers valued his wealth at between £200,000 and £300,000 (up to £500 million), his adored wife Marian was reported by the *Lady Magazine* as having 'made an elaborate show of making gifts to the royal family during her reception at court in 1784', including 'a state bed of rich and very curious workmanship from India, which far exceeds anything of the kind for grandeur, ever seen in this kingdom'. And then in 1788 Hastings spent £11,434 (£19 million) on buying back his old family seat, the estate of Daylesford, which his great-grandfather had been forced to sell in 1715. This was a bold move, considering his fortune had been overestimated by reports and actually amounted to £75,000 (£125 million). Furthermore, he was set to be heavily penalized if found guilty of the twenty-two charges he faced in Parliament – as it turned out, it took until 1795 before he was acquitted. Nonetheless, over his first seven years of ownership, he spent a further £60,000 (£100 million) – a stunning sum – on doing up Daylesford.[2] This included commissioning Sezincote's eventual architect Samuel Pepys Cockerell (who had never, by the way, actually visited India himself) to design a new main house, which incorporated oriental features including a large Islamic-style dome over the central hallway, a conservatory with Eastern-style windows and a scattering of Hindu temples and other subcontinental follies in the garden.

Going to work in India was essentially the eighteenth-century equivalent of becoming a banker or getting a top job at Google: seen as a licence to print money. As we have already heard, though, there was always the distinct possibility that the enterprise would leave you dead, and as the example of Dean Mahomed's first boss in Ireland illustrates, it didn't always work out: Godfrey Baker was dishonourably discharged from the Company for embezzling funds. But it made lots of people very rich and you didn't always have to go to India to benefit: by 1773, there were nearly 3,000 shareholders in the East India Company, which paid a high annual dividend of at least 5 per cent.* Investors in such colonial stocks put their cash into all sorts of purchases and the 'trade' in India took all sorts of forms, one of the more glamorous examples of enrichment being Thomas Pitt, Governor of Madras, who in 1702 purchased a diamond said to be 'the finest jewel in the world and worth an immense sum' for the relatively bargainous price of £24,000 (about £48 million in modern terms), brought it to Britain and then sold it on to the French Regent, the Duc d'Orléans, for £135,000 – £337.5 million in today's money. Pitt bought an estate near Swallowfield and a Parliamentary seat, and, his dynasty now firmly ensconced in English society, went on to produce two prime ministers: his grandson, William Pitt, followed by *his* son, William Pitt 'the Younger'. This demonstrates how, together with the example of William Gladstone, whose father was one of the largest slave owners in the British empire,[3] the direction of British politics was altered by imperial wealth.

However, if you accumulated significant amounts of money, country houses were the favoured asset through which to launder colonial booty. They may nowadays be considered one of our most English institutions, but a recent internal audit for the National Trust, which is Europe's largest conservation charity, one of the largest

---

* Some time before this, in 1711, there was the establishment of the South Sea Trading Company, which invested in the slave trade and in plantations. Its shares rose rapidly in value, resulting in the so-called South Sea Bubble of 1720, the first 'boom and bust' in Britain.

landowners in the United Kingdom and, with more than 5.6 million members, our second-largest membership after the National Union of Students, found that almost a third of its 300 houses and gardens were tainted by wealth from slavery or have treasures plundered from overseas.* Stephanie Barczewski has shown in her fascinating study *Country Houses and the British Empire, 1700–1930* how the global history of empire is woven into the history of our most famous houses, with around 1,100 individual landed estates in Britain being purchased by men who 'made their money in the empire between 1700 and 1930', accounting, depending on whose numbers you choose and how you define imperial wealth, for between 6 and 16 per cent of all the country houses in Britain. While proffering these numbers, she illustrates the complex ways empire might have influenced such houses by using the example of the fictional house at the heart of the popular TV show *Downton Abbey*: the family patriarch is a Boer War veteran, as is his valet; the very first dish mentioned is the Anglo-Indian creation of kedgeree; the Dowager Countess of Grantham talks about a great-aunt who 'manned the guns at Lucknow' during the 'Indian Rebellion of 1857'; after Lord Grantham loses his wealth to a bad investment in the Canadian Grand Trunk Railway, his cousin and heir saves Downton by inheriting a fortune because the person ahead of him in line dies while tea-planting on the

---

* An interim report published in September 2020 named more than ninety National Trust properties with connections to slavery and colonialism. They included Winston Churchill's country estate Chartwell, on the grounds of his imperialism, Hare Hill in Cheshire, a country estate built by slave owner William Hibbert, and Speke Hall, Merseyside, owned by Richard Watt, who traded in slave-produced rum and sugar and purchased a slave ship in 1793 that sent 549 Africans to Jamaica. Ten slaves died on the journey. Twenty-nine National Trust properties were found to have links to successful compensation claims as a result of the abolition of slavery, including Glastonbury Tor in Somerset. A month later, the *Daily Telegraph* reported that the National Trust could face an official investigation by the charity regulator for veering from its 'clear, simple purpose' to preserve historic buildings and treasures. Baroness Stowell of Beeston, the Chair of the Charity Commission and a Conservative politician, was quoted saying it was 'important' that the National Trust did not 'lose sight' of what members expected and that it was right that it was facing questions.

subcontinent; money problems compel another character to flog his Scottish estate and become the Governor of Bombay.

The view of empire as an enterprise where colonies were systematically bled and looted for wealth in the way they were bled and looted for museum artefacts is echoed in the 'wealth drain theory' of India, popularized by one of the aforementioned pioneers of multi-culturalism: the nineteenth-century Indian nationalist Dadabhai Naoroji, the British Parsi scholar, trader and politician who was the first Indian to become a British MP. He claimed that between 1835 and 1872 Britain received approximately £13 million (£7.6 billion) worth of goods from India annually, with no corresponding return of money. The idea was taken up by Holden Furber, a twentieth-century expert on South Asia, who estimated that the annual 'drain' from India to Britain was around £1.3 million during the ten years from 1783 to 1793 (£1.8 billion); by Aditya Mukherjee, who in 2010 calculated that India was 'bled anything between 5 to 10 percent of her GDP annually for close to two centuries'; and by Utsa Patnaik, who recently drew on almost two centuries of data on tax and trade and calculated that Britain 'drained' a total of nearly $45 trillion (in today's money) from India during the period 1765 to 1938 – seventeen times more than the total annual gross domestic product of the United Kingdom today. In turn, this alerts us to other estimates made of the economic value of various aspects of British empire. Klas Rönnbäck of Gothenburg University has estimated that the triangular slave trade between England, Africa and the Caribbean peaked at 6 per cent of GDP, with total output dependent on slavery being double that and accounting for about the same proportion of GDP that professional and support services account for nowadays. This led the *Financial Times* to conclude recently that 'slavery was integral to the UK economy for more than a century, with proceeds enjoyed at home and misery parked offshore.'[4] Meanwhile, in August 1999, the African World Reparations and Repatriation Truth Commission suggested $777 trillion as a suitable sum for reparations paid as compensation for lives lost during the African slave trade and the gold, diamonds and other resources stolen from the continent during colonization.

Such large figures regularly get bandied about in arguments over the legacies of imperialism but there are several reasons why non-economists should approach them carefully, the first being that imperial economics, like every aspect of imperial history, is a field of intense argument. The common claim, for instance, that money 'drained' from India helped 'prime the pump of the Industrial Revolution' is disputed by a bunch of historians, with P. J. Marshall presenting a mound of evidence in *East Indian Fortunes: The British in Bengal in the Eighteenth Century*, to rebut the argument that 'money made in Bengal' had a meaningful role in financing our Industrial Revolution. There are even more intense arguments about the economics of the slave trade. For instance, in his influential 1944 work *Capitalism and Slavery* Eric Williams argued that slavery was an economic phenomenon, and that the slave economies of the British West Indies caused or contributed greatly to the British Industrial Revolution, with the author stating that 'the West Indian islands became the hub of the British empire, of immense importance to the grandeur and prosperity of England.' Williams also presented what has since been termed the 'decline theory of abolition': the idea that Britain gave up on slavery, not for moral reasons, but because the profits of the slave-based economy had entered into an irreversible decline. Various academics have corroborated his assertions with detailed research, but others have questioned his methodology, his estimates and his conclusions. Seymour Drescher, an American historian, for example argued in 1977 that the British slave trade had remained profitable until the end, and that abolition was primarily a result of growing public moral outrage, compelling the government to commit what he terms 'econocide': an action against Britain's own economic interests. Others have taken a more balanced approach to this question, arguing that it was the coincidence of growing popular support for the abolitionist movement and the growing economic influence of factory owners over sugar planters which set the stage for abolition in the early nineteenth century.[5]

Second, looking back at what happened during empire, it is impossible to establish for certain how much 'trade' was coerced and how much of it was legitimate or regular. The assumption behind some of the larger aforementioned estimates of the 'drain' is that British trade with India was mostly or entirely coerced, leaving little room for Indian agency in shaping that trade. But how do we know how many of the dealings were under duress? Even some of Clive's may have been legitimate trade with willing Indians. Put another way, if empire hadn't existed, is it reasonable to assume that Indian merchants would not have participated at all in the growing maritime trade of the era? Mukherjee's top estimate of 10 per cent of GDP implies that virtually all of the export sector, the services sector and the government sector were extractions which benefited only Britain. To translate, that would imply that all of the salaries of Indians working for the colonial government or the money made by Indian producers of exports and all of the services they consumed should be counted as a 'drain' to Britain. While some public expenditure – such as the excessively high salaries and pensions paid to British administrators – should clearly be classified that way, others are less straightforward.[6] At least some of the tax revenue collected went to Indian schools, for instance, and this spending can be linked with improvements in literacy, even if overall rates of schooling were low.

It is an unavoidable fact that imperialists relied on indigenous merchants and producers for the material they traded, and those merchants and producers undoubtedly gained from the trade. We have plenty of empirical evidence that there were improvements in income and living standards at least for some during the colonial period, though also often rising inequality. At the same time, worries in Whitehall about controlling the costs of empire shaped how colonies were governed, and the need for tax revenue meant that colonial governments had an interest in raising local incomes. And while coercion did occur – for instance, European settlers in Kenya and Southern Rhodesia (now Zimbabwe) were given ownership of huge landholdings with little attention paid to the rights of the people living there – colonial states were often too weak to use it widely. One reason for this was that in most colonies British officials were thin on the ground, in part because they cost a lot to employ. Even in the 1920s, there were fewer than 300 British administrators in Nigeria, Africa's largest country by population. In Sierra Leone, there were fewer than thirty.[7] Understaffed and under-resourced colonial governments relied on indigenous intermediaries to do much of the actual work of governing – enlisting African and Asian elites to collect taxes, enforcing rules, building infrastructure. They simply didn't have the staff to depend entirely on coercion.

A third reason why it is hard to come up with neat, reliable, unanimous estimates of colonial economic activity: the territories of empire were not routinely or uniformly profitable, for individuals or for the British government. The experiences of Clive of India and Thomas Pitt may give the impression that colonization was habitually lucrative, but it wasn't. Territories were annexed for all sorts of reasons which were not necessarily economic – strategic concerns, prestige, religious or ideological zeal, jingoism, or because the government had to clean up after missionaries or merchants who had intervened in local politics. It cost money to launch wars, these costs ate into profits, and the salaries of colonial administrators were often very high relative to local levels of income. These costs generated many a debate among British politicians at the time about the wisdom of acquiring an empire in the first place, with Disraeli remarking in a famous speech made in Crystal Palace in 1872 that, far from being an asset to Britain, 'it has been shown with precise, with mathematical demonstration, that there never was a jewel in the crown of England that was so costly as the possession of India'.

Fourth, historic calculations are difficult to make. Places like Wolverhampton, Clydebank, Tyneside and South Wales unarguably generated enormous wealth building the ships the empire needed to run, mining coal to power them, making guns to protect and expand imperial territory, the irons to keep slaves and producing goods for newly opened markets – but how much of what they did can be attributed to empire specifically? It is impossible to know, for example, how many of Wolverhampton's locks and chains were used in slavery, and how many were used in regular industry. It is an ambiguity that Matthew Lesh, Research Director at the Adam Smith Institute, seized upon recently when talking to the *FT* about the economic legacies of slavery, claiming that 'most of our prosperity is independent of slavery' and arguing that innovation drove the Industrial Revolution more than investment by former slave owners. One way that historians have tried to measure the benefits of empire to Britain is by comparing the returns on investments in colonies with investment in the rest of the world. While this seems like it should be straightforward, variable Victorian accounting practices along with limitations in the data that survives make even this very complicated. Investments outside the empire had higher returns, but also high risks. What investors preferred to do depended partly on their appetite for risk. As Avner Offer puts it, 'a different kind of society, with wealth in different hands, might have had other priorities.'[8] Imagining a world without empires gets very complicated very quickly, because it in effect involves imagining a completely different world.

The main thing to remember when encountering very large numbers about imperial economic activity is that such numbers put you in the realm of economics, and in economics, even more so than in history, everything is a matter of definitions, perspectives and debate. The most useful illustration of this is that while one academic can claim that the triangular slave trade alone between England, Africa and the Caribbean peaked at 6 per cent of GDP, *British Imperialism: 1688–2015* by P. J. Cain and A. G. Hopkins, an acclaimed book on imperial economics, barely mentions slavery at all, 'slavery' being cited in the index just a few times.* Individual economists discount all sorts of massive things for all sorts of reasons, make all sorts of

---

* I wrote to Hopkins and his witty explanation provides a succinct summary of the challenges of discussing the macroeconomics of British empire: 'We stand on the brink of a correspondence that will easily extend beyond my now limited life span. Here's the problem. Capitalism, we can all agree, is a many-humped beast. Anyone writing about it faces the problem that you need at least a chapter and preferably a book to deal with the definition. But to take that amount of space will kill readers . . . So you have to be selective and emphasise the features that pertain particularly to your own enquiry. My book with Peter Cain took a particular line of enquiry based on our concept of "gentlemanly capitalism", which emphasised the crucial part played in UK's modern development since 1688 by financial and commercial services. Consequently, the definition we summarised was chosen not to be comprehensive but just to ensure that the activities we were concerned with can properly be described as capitalist . . . I would advise you to steer clear of wrangles over definitions because . . . what seems like a contradiction . . . is really just a different view of the same phenomenon.'

massive assumptions for all sorts of reasons, a tendency encapsulated in the jokes economists often tell about themselves. Such as the one about the student sitting an economics exam who pointed out to a lecturer that the questions were the same as last year, to which he received the response: 'Yes, but the answers have changed.' Or as Dr Leigh Gardner at the London School of Economics, whose refreshingly accessible work, including *Taxing Colonial Africa: The Political Economy of British Imperialism*, focuses on the economic and financial history of sub-Saharan Africa during the nineteenth and twentieth centuries, and who patiently spent tens of hours explaining these issues to me, put it: 'Trying to come up with numbers is useful for asking questions about who the winners and losers were over such a long period of history. But it may never be possible to come up with an exact number for the economic impact of empire on Britain. There are too many unknowns and the answer you get depends on what assumptions you make. As a discipline it produces more questions than answers.'

She can say that again. I'd put it differently: for people who have some formal training in economics, who understand the terms and definitions being employed, the methodology and the massive numbers are useful. For the rest of us, it is more helpful to focus on the detail, rather than the macroeconomic picture, where you'll find much evidence that the wealth of empire, acquired through both moral and immoral means, officially and unofficially, made some individuals very rich and helped certain cities, institutions and businesses flourish. Not least, the economic importance of empire is reflected in the privileged position of the City of London as one of the world's major financial centres. Sure, London was already a fairly important player on international financial markets as early as the sixteenth century, and it really came into its own with the end of the Napoleonic Wars, which undermined some of London's rivals (for example, with the French invasion of Amsterdam). But why, despite the fact Britain mines very little gold itself, is London at the centre of the international bullion trade? As the relevant website explains: 'The roots of the London Bullion Market can be traced to the partnership between Moses Mocatta and the East India Company, who started shipping gold together towards the end of the 17th century.' More generally, why did the City become lined with the offices of clearing or high-street banks, merchant banks, overseas banks, insurance companies, shipbrokers, mining engineers and maritime insurance providers which are required by global finance? As John Darwin outlines in *Unfinished Empire*, the scale of it all was originally established by the fact of British imperialism: he points out that the City of London was where the 'developing' economies of the world beyond Europe came for the capital to 'build the infrastructure that would bring their products to market. By 1913 perhaps half the world's total of foreign investment had been raised in London. Whether constructing a railway, sinking a mine, or laying out a plantation, the first step was to write a prospectus for a share issue in London.'

Meanwhile, the economist Ronen Palan, in the process of observing that nearly 40 per cent of the world's financial assets are located in city-state jurisdictions like Gibraltar, the Cayman Islands, Bermuda, the British Virgin Islands, Singapore and Hong Kong associated with British empire, argues that the dominance of the City and finance in our national life goes back to empire. The position of the City, described in the *Investor's Chronicle* recently as 'the UK's economic powerhouse, which contributes roughly a quarter of its GDP', goes back, according to Palan, to an imperial age when it became 'bloated' and 'politically powerful'.

> Indeed, British domestic politics in the twentieth century is often interpreted in terms of the famous City–industry divide. The City of London developed at the heart of the British Empire, somewhat divorced from the UK's mainland economic needs, to finance trading and manufacturing throughout the formal and informal British empire . . . The Bank of England consistently pursued policies that favored the City's position as a world financial center, even when such policies were seen as harmful to the UK's mainland manufacturing needs.

The economic legacy of empire is also tangible in aspects of our national infrastructure. To get a sense of just how significant empire once was to us, you need do no more than walk through the docks of Limehouse, West India, East India and Millwall, which once buzzed with the task of importing tons of goods from the colonies (and elsewhere). You can sense it in the size of Liverpool, which by 1740 was seeing thirty-three slave ships set sail annually,[9] and which grew from an enclave of just a few streets in 1207 to a grand eighteenth-century city controlling over 60 per cent of the entire British slave trade. Liverpool's cotton and linen mills and support industries such as rope-making created mass employment, and by the 1780s Liverpool had become the largest slave-ship building site in Britain.[10] The academic Jon Stobart maintains that by the late eighteenth century Liverpool's elite were so anxious about its reputation for inhumanity that they made efforts to project a more cultivated image, through the foundation of institutions such as the Botanic Garden, the Liverpool Institution and the Lyceum Library. In Bristol, which sent fifty ships per year to Africa between 1728 and 1732, transporting more than 100,000 Africans,[11] the impact of empire can be seen through the legacy of Edward Colston, who, everyone now knows as a result of his depedestalization, made a vast amount of money from the slave trade and donated much of it to good causes in the city. Further north, the eighteenth-century imperial trade in tobacco and sugar was key to industrialization in Scotland. In his book *The Scottish Nation: 1700–2007*, T. M. Devine asserts that during the Victorian and Edwardian age heavy industrial economy in Scotland was geared towards the export market – ships and trains were built and bound for the colonies. In Glasgow, the 'second city of empire', its imperial history and its specific links to the tobacco trade are visible everywhere: from its shipyards to its street names, to the City Chambers, on whose façade there is an illustration of Queen Victoria surrounded by figures representing Great Britain and its colonies.

Then there are our country houses, of course, which are as steeped in the history of the slave trade as they are in the history of the East India Company. The screenwriters for the hit show *Succession* had their fictional media mogul Logan Roy put it crudely in series one when he surveyed a stately home and remarked: 'I mean, look at this fucking place . . . Slaves. Cotton. Sugar. This country's nothing but an off-shore laundry for turning evil into hard currency.' But Stephanie Barczewski provides detailed evidence for the sentiment when she identifies 211 estates acquired by planters between 1700 and 1850. One of the more famous examples is Penrhyn Castle, financed from the profits of slavery by the plantation-owning Pennant family, along with nearby slate quarries and an art collection, the Telford Road (now the A5) and the suspension bridge over the Menai Straits (completed 1828) which opened up the route to Holyhead and Ireland. There is also the grand Harewood House in Yorkshire, home of the Lascelles family, who were already landowners in Yorkshire when the West Indian trade made them yet wealthier in the first half of the eighteenth century. Barczewski points out that some houses went through both nabob and planter ownership, while Tillman Nechtman observes, fascinatingly, that there was a marked difference in the way the newly minted nabobs and the West Indian planters were perceived by the upper echelons of British society. Although both were obviously 'new money', the planters' wealth came from landed estates, a source of income and power that the aristocracy understood and respected, whereas the nabobs' riches were seen as shady and disreputable. Slavery is nowadays regarded as one of the worst features of empire, but in those days what Brits did to India was deemed worse.

The economic legacy of empire is tangible in other ways. There is a case to be made that the East India Company was important in the rise of the office place – some 30,000 people in London were employed in commercial and industrial establishments connected to the Company, generating colossal amounts of documentation, and this incredible bureaucracy was an important stage in the history and development of the office.[12] Geoffrey Jones, in 'Merchants to Multinationals', has pointed out that many British multinational companies have roots in nineteenth-century merchant firms operating in empire, which over time diversified their activities into new regions and industries.[13] For example, Harrisons & Crosfield, based in Liverpool, began as a tea-trading firm in the nineteenth century, but through the establishment of overseas offices in both British and Dutch colonies expanded into wider import and export trade, and eventually diversified into the production of tea, tobacco and rubber through the purchase of plantations – it ultimately became part of Elementis plc, one of the UK's largest speciality chemicals and personal-care businesses, which is listed on the London Stock Exchange. The common Brexiteer accusation, following Brexit, that Britain has become 'far too addicted' to using workers from overseas echoes an economic tradition that goes back centuries, with slave labour, and then indentured labour from Asia, propping up the imperial economy (albeit not in Britain itself).

As a result of the self-examination inspired by the Black Lives Matter campaign, a bunch of companies have come forward to announce that they would make amends for their role in the slave trade. They include the insurance giant Lloyd's of London and the brewer Greene King, the former's connection to slavery being through Simon Fraser, one of its founding subscribers, who owned at least 162 enslaved people and ran the Castle Bruce estate in Dominica, and the latter company being founded by Benjamin Greene, who operated sugar-cane plantations in the West Indies and owned at least 231 slaves.[14] Other institutions which have proffered apologies have included the Bank of England, Lloyds Banking Group, RBS, the law firms Freshfields and Farrer & Co., the University of Glasgow and All Souls College Oxford. And if these institutions are aware of their role in slavery, it is partly because of the excellent work done by the 'Legacies of British Slave-ownership Project' at University College London. The ongoing study, which has produced blogs, symposiums and books, traces where £20 million of slavery compensation money went (as the *FT* has explained, 'if half the money bought corporate debt with proceeds reinvested, it would now be worth £150bn'), and has produced many striking revelations,[15] not least how deeply involved the establishment were. Seventy-five baronets were named in the compensation records, along with fifty MPs in 1831 and forty-two in 1833. Overall, it estimates that between 5 and 10 per cent of the British elites in the 1830s (measured by both social and political criteria) had an interest in slavery, as owners, mortgagees, trustees or executors. Familiar names descended from slave-owning families include the writers George Orwell and Graham Greene, the architect Sir George Gilbert Scott, the two Lord Chancellors Douglas McGarel Hogg and Quintin McGarel Hogg, as well as the descendants of Aretas Akers-Douglas, 1st Viscount Chilston, George Hibbert, whose family seat survives at Munden in Hertfordshire, and Robert Cooper Lee Bevan, who founded what would become Barclays Bank.

British banks financed the slave economy. Half of the sixty banking firms listed in 1835 – later to become part of Lloyds, Barclays and RBS – have been noted in the slave compensation records, and many of the men involved became extremely rich from their ventures. Of the twenty-six directors of the Bank of England in 1801, five were West India merchants. British law firms, such as Freshfields, were also in on the action,[16] while two of the four big international accountancy firms have their roots in families who either owned slaves or had loans secured on them. Edwin Waterhouse, the son of Liverpool cotton broker Alfred Waterhouse, founded Price Holyland Waterhouse (now PricewaterhouseCoopers) in 1865; and William Welch Deloitte was the grandson of a West Indies planter. Infrastructure projects, too, had direct links to slavery. Walton Bridge in Surrey was a legacy of the Jamaican slave owner Samuel Dicker, and Conwy Suspension Bridge in North Wales was part funded by John Gladstone, father of William Gladstone. When the Edinburgh & Northern railway company was launched, over 40 per cent of its initial subscribers were slave owners and their families. And another institution with connections to the slave trade was my newspaper, *The Times*. Three prominent nineteenth-century *Times* men were the sons of slave owners: Thomas Chenery, editor between 1877 and 1884; Sir George Webbe Dasent, assistant editor for twenty-five years from the mid-1840s; and Mowbray Morris, manager of the paper from 1847 to 1873. Also, *The Times'* Paris correspondent during the Crimean War, Georgina Frances de Peyronnet, was the daughter of a West Indies plantation owner, George Whitefield.

The researchers, led by Catherine Hall, Nick Draper and more recently Matthew Smith, tackle some of the common myths about slavery. Did money from it finance our railways? Well,

> by definition, slave compensation was only a small fragment of that total . . . But the evidence suggests, first, that slave-owners were often among the most active of the subscribers, and, second, that in some railway companies, but a distinct minority, slave-owners subscribed a

significant part of the total. For example, the Glasgow, Paisley, Kilmarnock and Ayr Railway Company was one of the focal points of
slave-owning investment. In 1837, some 10 per cent of the total of
£452,900 raised can be attributed to slave-owners.

Did Jews play a disproportionate role in the slave trade – a narrative commonly propounded by anti-Semitic conspiracy theorists?
There is no evidence the community owned a disproportionate number of slaves at emancipation. The Church and certain charitable
bodies were involved, though. Almost 150 Anglican clergymen in
Britain and Ireland appear in the Compensation Commission records,
as well as the Minister and Elders of Kilmarnock, the Commissioners
of Greenwich Hospital and the Society for the Propagation of the
Gospel in Foreign Parts (which branded the letters 'Society' on to the
flesh of their slaves).[17] Even more surprising: *the descendants of slaves*
were compensated for abandoning slave ownership. The slave business in the colonies was not always a case of white against black: some
'free coloureds' had also ventured into slave ownership. A notable
example is Nathaniel Wells, who was born to an enslaved woman and
white father in St Kitts in 1779, was educated in Britain, inherited
much of his father's estate and married Harriet Este, the daughter of
King George II's chaplain. In 1802, he bought the estate of Piercefield
in Monmouthshire, and later became Sheriff and Deputy Lieutenant
of that county. He also owned eighty-six slaves, and in 1837 was paid
£1,400 9s 7d in compensation for their loss.

Which seems like a good place to conclude. Did empire benefit the
colonies? People argue about it fiercely, but according to Bishnupriya
Gupta's Tawney Lecture, levels of per capita income grew very little
across the colonial period in India.[18] Did slavery or money from India
finance the Industrial Revolution or our railways? Opinion is divided.
Did Britain give up on slavery for mainly economic or moral reasons? As summarized earlier, people like Eric Williams and Seymour
Drescher make the case strongly, for both. Was London Mayor Sadiq
Khan right when he declared on the removal of the statue of the
slave trader Robert Milligan from West India Quay that 'it's a sad
truth that much of our city and nation's wealth was derived from the

slave trade'? No, the claim isn't true even of empire as a whole: even during the heyday of imperialism, Britain's links to countries outside the empire were more important in terms of value and scale by a substantial margin than connections with colonies.[19] But his claim in a later online video that 'we owe a significant portion of our wealth to [slavery]' feels truer.

After all, the trade explains the wealth of cities like Bristol and Liverpool, why Manchester did well, producing cloth from cotton grown on plantations worked by slaves, and why people like Richard Pennant MP, who inherited a large estate in Jamaica, had the cash to invest in the aforementioned slate quarries near Bangor and became the first Baron Penrhyn. As Robert Winder puts it: 'the fortunes founded on slavery . . . shaped the structure of British life as decisively and irrevocably as had William the Conqueror's gifts of land to his favoured knights.' Indeed, the riches of empire were so prevalent in Britain that they paid for the purchase or rebuilding of a notable portion of our country houses and established political dynasties. British empire helped both to establish the City of London as a leading world financial centre and to ensure it dominates our national economy, while our slave trade was so deeply entrenched in our economy that even church ministers, abolitionists and people of colour received some of the £20 million (£17 billion) compensation. Compensation that was so large and significant that we, as a nation, finished paying it off only in 2015.[20]

9. The Origins of Our Racism

Jallianwala Bagh was far from being an isolated incident of extreme racialized violence during British empire. Just as harrowing was the British response to the Vellore Mutiny of 1806, when Indian mutineers, enraged by new British regulations regarding headgear, facial hair and caste marks which both Muslims and Hindus considered offensive, seized the Vellore Fort in South India, killing 130 British troops while doing so. Catastrophic slaughter followed once the British had re-established control, one study putting the number killed at around 650 sepoys, at least a hundred being executed in a fives court, where they were crowded in together and fired at with guns at a distance of about thirty yards. Two days after the mutiny, one Captain Marriott reported that 'near seven hundred have been killed inside and outside and the work of death has only stopped this morning. I never in my life experienced such horrid, horrid sentiments and scenes.'[1]

Even worse was the harrowing brutality of what happened after the Indian Uprising of 1857, when Indian troops in Meerut, Delhi, Lucknow and beyond revolted, ostensibly over the introduction of a new Enfield rifle. A rumour had spread that the cartridges for the gun, the ends of which had to be bitten off before loading, were lubricated with a mixture of pigs' and cows' lard – the ingesting of which was considered offensive by Muslims and Hindus. But events quickly escalated beyond the issue, with various parties responding to mounting dissatisfaction about British India and seizing the rebellion as an opportunity to drive the British out. The mutineers tried to restore the emperor in Delhi, shot British officers and were responsible for massacres of Britons including women and children, and the British empire's subsequent rage was often unconstrained.

John Nicholson, who led the retaking of Delhi, suggested that rebels be tortured and/or skinned alive. The former Governor-General, Lord Ellenborough, thought every surviving man in the city, mutineer or not, should be castrated. In Britain, Charles Dickens wrote: 'I wish I were a commander-in-chief in India . . . I should do my utmost to exterminate the Race upon whom the state of the late cruelties rested.' In the end, the Brits settled on, among other things, blowing Indians from guns – the rebel bound to the mouth of the cannon before it was fired – which had the additional result, through the scattering of body parts, of violating various religious and caste sensibilities and denying the families a proper funeral. A relative of the Nawab of Farrukhabad was arrested, tortured, choked with pork and hanged.[2]* One William Hodson burned alive twenty-three sepoys who had fled for their lives into a house in Delhi. Brigadier-General James Neill took a steamship down the Ganges and gunned down bystanders, as well as razing entire villages to the ground. Even civilians who were not involved in the violence were massacred, in some villages all adult men were shot and, as Sir John Kaye, the first prominent British chronicler of the revolt, put it in *History of the Sepoy War*, military officers hanged men 'with as little compunction as though they had been pariah dogs or jackals, or vermin of a baser kind', boasting about the creativity of their murder, hanging men from mango trees and employing elephants as drops. While placing more emphasis on Indian than on British atrocities, he conceded the racist motivation of British violence: 'The very sight of a dark man stimulated our national enthusiasm almost to the point of frenzy. We tolerated those who wore our uniforms and bore our arms, but all else were, in our eyes, the enemies and persecutors of our race.'

A few years later there was the Morant Bay Rebellion of 1865 which began when Jamaicans, led by preacher Paul Bogle, protested about injustice, unemployment, poverty and disease, and the island's Governor, Edward John Eyre, responded as if he was facing another rebellion in the vein of the Indian Uprising. 'Rebels' were tied to

---

* Major Anson, 9th Lancers: 'No wild beast could have attracted more attention. He was forever being surrounded with soldiers, who were stuffing him with pork and covering him with insults. He was well flogged and his person exposed, which he fought against manfully, and then hung, but as usual the rope was too weak and down he fell and broke his nose; before he recovered his senses he was strung up again and made an end of . . . He it was who wouldn't spare our women, and treated them with every possible indignity.'

trees and flogged before being shot, used for rifle target practice (soldiers firing from a distance of 400 yards) and made to hang one another. One woman was flogged and then left overnight with a noose around her neck to encourage her to reveal the whereabouts of Bogle, condemned men were hanged from a ruined courthouse arch, and elsewhere on the island the sadistic Provost Marshal, under the pretext of martial law, flogged black men for misdemeanours as minor as neglecting to remove their hats in his presence or answering back, even killing one man because he ground his teeth. In total, Eyre had 400 Jamaicans murdered, including women and children, and hundreds more flogged.

But worst of all was what happened in Tasmania.³ Following Abel Tasman's 'discovery' of the island in 1642 and Captain Cook's landing in 1777, the British decided to colonize Tasmania with a view to establishing a penal colony. In 1803, when the settlers arrived in force, the island was home to thousands of nomadic Aboriginal Tasmanians (estimates range from 4,000 to 8,000). Ethnically distinct from Aboriginal Australians, and isolated, they lived as hunter-gatherers who wore kangaroo skins and slept in caves.⁴ The island, in those days called Van Diemen's Land, was run by Governor Sir George Arthur. Captain Cook reportedly found the Tasmanians trusting and peaceful, but relations between the indigenous population and Arthur's settlers – a ferocious crowd of mostly bushrangers and sealers – quickly soured. The Europeans tended to find the short, dark Tasmanians repulsive to look at and demonized them as subhuman. Their population already weakened by diseases introduced by the first Europeans on the island, they were terrorized by both convicts and free settlers, who not only attacked them for their land but maimed and killed them for sport and pleasure. Women were raped and forced into harems; men used for target practice and hunted on horseback. There is a report of one European carrying around a pickle tub full of the severed ears of Tasmanians whom he had shot, and there is no record of any European being punished for murdering a Tasmanian, though a settler was reportedly flogged when he forced a woman to wear the freshly severed head of her husband around her neck as he took her off to his shack.

As their numbers dwindled, the Tasmanians responded to the violence, attacking and burning farms, and in 1827 they raided Launceston, the island's second town. Finally, the settlers could claim to be the terrorized party, that the problem with Tasmania was the Tasmanians. The Solicitor-General Sir Alfred Stephen, later Chief Justice of New South Wales, spoke at a public meeting in Hobart in the late 1830s about 'the Aboriginal problem', saying that if the colony could not protect its convict servants from Aboriginal attack 'without extermination, then I say boldly and broadly exterminate!' Martial law was announced against the indigenous population, and a hapless campaign followed, during which trees, kangaroos and black swans were frequently mistaken for the intended targets. Nonetheless, the Tasmanians were crushed. Between 1831 and 1835, Christian missionaries rounded up what was left of the population – around 200 people – and for their own safety took them to Flinders Island, a dozen miles away. There they were given shelter, clothing and food and introduced to the Bible. But for the Tasmanians any initial hope for a better life faded. The island was barren. They died in droves, and by 1847 there were fewer than fifty left. The project was abandoned and the remaining few were shipped back to Tasmania, where they were dumped in an abandoned penal settlement at Oyster Cove. This was essentially a slum where the Tasmanians were left to fend for themselves, occasionally observed by visiting anthropologists. By 1855, only sixteen were still alive. A man defined at the time as the last 'full-blooded' male Tasmanian,* an alcoholic seaman nicknamed King Billy Lanney, became a public spectacle, and was introduced to Prince Alfred when he visited Hobart in 1868. King Billy died a year later, of chronic diarrhoea. His grave was ransacked and his skull snatched, possibly on behalf of the Royal Society of Tasmania, whose members were always keen to secure bones to help them study what they deemed differences between races.

* Belief that Tasmanians were wiped out as a race in 1876 by colonizers endured until the 1970s, at which point, members of the Tasmanian community found a collective voice. Subsequently, there has been a significant rise in people identifying as Aborigine, Aboriginal Australian or Indigenous Australian, and today there are communities that practise traditional cultures.

Reading accounts of what happened I find myself not only feeling sick at the inhumanity of the acts, but also queasy at the way some British historians still write about the events. Jan Morris pens a characteristically elegant account, in peerless prose, but then quotes the ethnologist H. Long Roth describing the genocide as 'one of the greatest losses Anthropology has suffered' – seemingly rather missing the point as to who really suffered as a result of a catastrophe which was used as a case study when, after the Second World War, the lawyer Raphael Lemkin formulated the concept of 'genocide'.[5] She also engages in some wild racial generalizations which are surely based on the contemporaneous accounts of people who have since been proven to be genocidal maniacs ('Physically they seem to have lacked stamina: their senses were uncannily acute, and they were adept at running on all fours, but they were not very strong, nor very fast, nor even particularly agile') and then proceeds to claim that 'the British were not often physically cruel.' She continues: 'They were more generally unsympathetic, or misunderstanding, or contemptuous, while the experience of the Mutiny made them congenitally suspicious. They were also terribly aloof, sometimes deliberately, sometimes through shyness . . .'

Frankly, it feels absurd to use what the celebrated critic Robert Hughes described as 'the only true genocide in English colonial history' as a launchpad to measure the goodness of the British during empire. And the comment briefly makes me wonder whether you need to be a descendant of the colonized or a person of colour to feel the full gut-wrenching horror of it all, which, in turn, brings us to one of the most controversial and contentious of all the modern legacies of British empire in Britain: our racism. It's not a correlation, as I detailed earlier in relation to Wolverhampton's post-war racial politics, that I have a problem with, and neither does the Jamaican-British poet Linton Kwesi Johnson who has said: 'I'll be crucified for saying this but I believe that racism is very much part of the cultural DNA of this country, and probably has been since imperial times.' Meanwhile, the journalist Yasmin Alibhai-Brown remarked in 2000 in relation to the murder of Stephen Lawrence that Britain was not 'catching up with a globalized world' but is 'still locked into an imperial past'. The academic Marcus Collins concluded in a study that 'most whites literally prejudged West Indian men and saw no reason to revise attitudes unaltered in their essentials since colonial days.'[6] And the author Salman Rushdie has commented that 'four centuries of being told that you are superior to the Fuzzy-Wuzzies and the wogs leave their stain. This stain has seeped into every part of the culture, the language and daily life; and nothing much has been done to wash it out.' And so, for many, colonialism and empire are synonymous with racism. Others, however, are wary, questioning (a) whether empire was really racist and/or (b) whether, even if it was racist, it can really explain racism or racist attitudes in Britain today.

Taking the former question first, there are good reasons to be cautious, not least that for a significant period of British empire, 'race' and 'racism' didn't exist in the sense that they do now. As Fredric Weizmann explains, 'the word "race" itself first appeared in European languages between the 13th and 16th centuries. It had multiple meanings, including the modern meanings of a race as a contest of speed, a strong river current, or rapid forward motion. In the 16th and 17th centuries, race began to be used increasingly in the sense of "lineage".' Also, the popular idea that empire was racist in practice and/or in intent is difficult to tally with the consensus that there were in fact no clear motivations behind its establishment (acquired, as Seeley famously claimed, 'in a fit of absence of mind'), with the consensus that slavery began for economic reasons (as the renowned West Indian historian Eric Williams put it: 'A racial twist has . . . been given to what is basically an economic phenomenon. Slavery was not born of racism: rather, racism was the consequence of slavery'), or with the fact that the Enlightenment, the intellectual age of supposed Reason that dominated the world of ideas in Europe between the seventeenth and nineteenth centuries, gave birth to ideas about the 'oneness' of humankind and the potential of all societies to progress (Britain's civilization might be clearly the best, but it was thought that all the others, even the most primitive, such as the Indians who practised sati, or inhabitants of the South Sea Islands who had a predilection for eating one another, could improve if they put their minds to it).

Moreover, when it came to brutal racial violence, it has been argued that the colonized were also capable of racialized horror. The single most commonly cited example is the so-called Black Hole of Calcutta,[7] a notorious incident in June 1756, when, following the capture of the city by the Nawab Siraj al-Dawlah of Bengal, a group of British colonists surrendered and were taken prisoner. A total of 144 men and two women were crammed into the fort's 'black hole', a cell measuring 18 feet by 14 feet 10 inches. It was horrendously hot, and the prisoners fought each other to get near the two small windows, and over the limited supply of water, begging for their lives while the guards laughed at their plight. The story goes that the next morning, only twenty-three of the prisoners were still alive, among a pile of corpses. Also, though there's a strong argument to be made that it was less about race and more about resisting subjugation, both the Vellore Mutiny of 1806 and the Indian Uprising of 1857 featured examples of gruesome violence against the British, with Lord William Bentinck remarking in relation to the former that 'the white community for many nights together went to bed in the uncertainty of rising alive'; a single monument in a church in Delhi conveys the horrors endured by the British in the latter, marking as it does the deaths of Thomas Collins, a deputy collector of the city, his wife, his mother, his brother and a further twenty-three members of their extended family, including three grandchildren.[8] At the Siege of Cawnpore, an episode in the Uprising of 1857, British hostages, largely women and children, were slaughtered and their bodies unceremoniously dumped in a well. As British troops descended on Cawnpore, they were appalled and devastated by the bloodshed of innocents. Military men responded with a ruthless vengeance, and a killing spree quickly followed. 'Remember Cawnpore!' was their battle cry. And, as onerous as it is for me to face, Sikhs participated in the bloody crackdown after 1857 along with the British, the historian Lawrence James reporting that 'Sikh hatred for Muslims mirrored that of British soldiers towards the sepoys. In one incident during the capture of Lucknow in March 1858, a band of Muslim fanatics, wearing green scarves, defended a bungalow to the last man, killing a British officer from a Sikh unit. The Sikhs snatched the survivor and stabbed and burned him to death as British officers and men stood by untouched by his screams for mercy.'[9]

There is another reason people are sometimes openly sceptical of broad claims of empire's racism: when formal notions of racism did emerge, they did not, somewhat bizarrely, always emerge in a black-and-white manner. In the eighteenth century, a theory developed that tribes of light-skinned Indo-European-language speakers, who called themselves Aryans, colonized India around 2000 BC, conquering the dark-skinned barbarians living there and becoming the source of the Indian civilization as we know it today. Some commentators in India – both British and Indians who had an interest in maintaining British rule – used this theory to claim that British imperialism was essentially a reunion of Aryan tribes.[10] A Bengali writer encapsulated the effect of it all in the *Calcutta Indian Mirror* in 1874 when he exclaimed, crudely: 'We were niggers at one time. We now become brethren.' Disturbingly, this Aryan philosophy is still alive in India in the twenty-first century and is one of the reasons why Adolf Hitler's *Mein Kampf* is a distressingly common sight in Indian bookshops – the 37th Indian edition appearing in 2007, the 55th in 2010.[11]

However, none of these reservations amount to much. Sure, some interpretations of Aryanism generously included some Indians like me – but it was still *Aryanism*, excluded most brown people and was essentially the historical equivalent of Tommy Robinson claiming he can't be racist because he has some Sikh supporters. Besides, British adherents to the Aryan theory found ways to modify it in order to justify colonialism – arguing that while these Indians may have been our ancient relatives, they were nonetheless inferior and needed to be governed, their 'inferiority' being explained by various hereditary racial factors or their environment. Yes, the colonized also committed acts of vicious racial violence, but they were, more often than not, responses to dehumanizing colonization, and the facts got routinely exaggerated by the British. In 1959, the author Brijen Gupta suggested, for instance, that the number of prisoners involved in the Black Hole of Calcutta tragedy was actually sixty-four, rather than 146 as claimed, and that twenty-one of those survived,[12] while Lawrence James describes the stories 'of women raped, children tortured and, in one persistent tale, roasted alive and fed to their parents' in the Uprising of 1857 as 'invariably exaggerated'.

It is undeniable that race and racism didn't exist in a formal way during the early phase of British empire in the way they do now, but there was a whole load of dehumanizing behaviour which more or less amounted to racism. As David Roediger puts it in *How Race Survived US History*, 'earlier Europeans did of course note differences between their skin colors and those of non-Europeans.' As Andrew Porter concedes in an essay in *The Cambridge Illustrated History of the British Empire*, 'racialist attitudes, with their elements of hostility, unthinking abuse, and aggression, existed before "races" were scientifically identified or classified.' And as Patrick Wolfe stresses in *Traces of History: Elementary Structures of Race*, even though it was only in the later eighteenth century that 'race' became a distinctive concept, 'this is not to suggest that Europeans failed to recognise and act on observable phenotypic differences until the 1780s. Precursors, "blackmores" and their ilk, are legion. Nor is it to pretend that an overland journey from, say, Botswana to Finland would fail to disclose a significant degree of anatomico-geographical correlation.' George Best, an Elizabethan sea captain, in 1578 described Africans as being 'black and loathsome'. The eighteenth-century Bihari historian Gholam Hossain Khan Tabatabai commented on the cultural disdain the English had for Indians in the 1780s, writing: 'not one of the English Gentlemen shows any inclination or any relish for the company of the Gentlemen of this country . . . Such is the aversion which the English openly show for the company of the natives, and such the disdain which they betray for them, that no love, and no coalition can take root between the conquerors and the conquered.'[13]

Even some leading lights of the Enlightenment were not, in practice, enlightened: David Hume remarked in 1753 that 'I am apt to suspect the negroes to be naturally inferior to whites'; in the eighteenth century, the influential Swedish naturalist Carl Linnaeus made an attempt to designate various ethnicities within the human race, differentiating Europeans from Africans and American Indians and allocating character traits to each group. Europeans were 'acute' and 'inventive' whereas black people were 'negligent, crafty' or even 'governed by caprice'.[14] Then we have slavery, which was economic in original motivation but, over time, began to be justified in deeply racist ways. In the nineteenth century, the American historian George Bancroft claimed that the negro race was treated with disgust as soon as slaves were imported as part of the transatlantic slave network, and in 1959 the historian Carl Degler argued that black people have never been treated equally to whites. Meanwhile, George Fredrickson states in *Racism: A Short History* that 'Between the sixteenth century and the nineteenth, slave traders and those who purchased their merchandise referred frequently, if casually and inconsistently, to the curse [of Ham] as an explanation of why all their slaves happened to be black or African.' The Curse of Ham is a biblical narrative derived from Genesis and interpreted in a deeply racist manner by some Christians, Muslims and Jews as an explanation for black skin, as well as being used as a justification for slavery.*

Furthermore, while slavery illustrates the fact that in the early centuries of British empire the relationship between race and empire was not neat – as Catherine Hall and Sonya Rose have put it, 'The story of how race was naturalised, made part of the ordinary, is both linked to and overflows from that of the Empire' – what Britain was *doing* at the time to most of the black people it interacted with is surely significant. Frankly, when I hear that 'race' wasn't a thing during this period of history, I can't help but remember that by 1670 English merchants had probably overtaken the Portuguese and Dutch as the leading European carriers of slaves from Africa to America. When I

---

* Felicia R. Lee explains in the *New York Times*: 'In the biblical account, Noah and his family are not described in racial terms. But as the story echoed through the centuries and around the world, variously interpreted by Islamic, Christian and Jewish scholars, Ham came to be widely portrayed as black; blackness, servitude and the idea of racial hierarchy became inextricably linked. By the 19th century, many historians agree, the belief that African-Americans were descendants of Ham was a primary justification for slavery among Southern Christians. The debate about just what the story of Ham and Noah means has marched on into the 21st century. Today scholars are increasingly reading documents in the authors' original languages and going further back in time and to more places, as well as calling on disciplines like sociology and classics.'

hear people claim that the colonized were just as racially violent towards their white colonizers, I can't help but recall that between 1670 and 1807, when British participation in slave carrying was outlawed by Parliament, the English continued to dominate the slave-shipping industry. Sure, Aryanism, as practised by some Britons, included some North Indians, but the fact is that in 150 years the British carried as many slaves to the New World as all the other slave-shipping countries combined. And yes, the Enlightenment did sometimes (but not always) encourage the belief that humanity was one, but any intellectual theorizing is surely overshadowed by the fact that between 1660 and 1807 Britain shipped around 3 million Africans to America, the slaves kept shackled to each other or to the deck to prevent mutiny during the Middle Passage, stacked in tiers, with no space to stand or turn, the dysentery, suicides, epidemics and murders killing so many Africans on the way that sharks frequently pursued slave ships on their journey west. Character, as they say of people, is action: what people do tells you who they are. And over this extended period, which some people argue could not be 'racist' because 'race' didn't exist as it does now, Britain was dehumanizing black people on a super-industrial scale.[15]

Besides, and this is the single most important point to be presented to people who quibble that 'race' meant different things to British people in history, or pick out the differences between 'biological racism' and 'cultural differentialism', and between 'racism' and 'racialism' in empire: as British empire grew and peaked in the nineteenth and twentieth centuries, it morphed into nothing less than a wilful, unapologetic exercise in white racial supremacy. When I made my documentary about Jallianwala Bagh, some people were surprised that I was surprised by this. One TV reviewer wrote: 'It feels like a genuine revelation to Sanghera that the British empire is, as he describes it, "an exercise in institutionalised racism". Don't many of us know this?' All I can say is that I probably felt it as a possibility, but, perhaps because we Sikhs have a complex relationship to empire, and maybe because my history education was so poor, I didn't appreciate the depth and detail of it. Certainly, I was unaware that attitudes to race hardened and became formalized during the nineteenth century.

The reasons are difficult to isolate, but one factor was simply the success of the enterprise: when your people run the largest empire in human history, rule over tens of millions in India with a force of a mere few thousand civil servants, it is hard to resist the feeling that you're born to rule. Another factor was that the Enlightenment view that all human beings could be saved came up against bitter experience: emancipation and abolition hadn't resulted in a renaissance in Africa or the Caribbean; experiments with Indian reform had seemingly led only to the bitterness of the Uprising of 1857; everywhere imperialists looked, it seemed that the 'natives' were not taking advantage of generous opportunities for advancement and redemption. Then there was the emergence of race 'science'. In the mid-nineteenth century, some anthropologists and craniometrists measured skulls and argued that blacks were more related to apes than they were to whites. The French anthropologist Gustave le Bon published a diagram showing white Europeans at the top of an evolutionary pyramid. Darwin's *Origin of Species* was published in 1859 and his Theory of Evolution seemed to lend weight to these spurious theories. Darwin himself was generally reluctant to apply his ideas to human societies, but he didn't help the lot of the Tasmanians when he visited in 1836, while he was still formulating his theories, and proclaimed of the island: 'I do not know of a more striking instance of the comparative rate of increase of a civilised over a savage race.'* Such racism turned out to be a rather convenient way of retrospectively justifying what Britain had already done through its empire – as the geneticist Dr Adam Rutherford has put it: 'The emergence of a scientific approach to human taxonomy coincided with the growth of European empires . . . While it is true that some of the pioneers of anthropology had scientific principles at heart, the othering of people in potential or actual colonies has the effect of permitting subjugation.'

---

* Full quote from Darwin's *Beagle* journals: 'All the aborigines have been removed to an island in Bass's Straits, so that Van Diemen's Land enjoys the great advantage of being free from a native population . . . Thirty years is a short period, in which to have banished the last aboriginal from his native island, – and that island nearly as large as Ireland. I do not know a more striking instance of the comparative rate of increase of a civilized over a savage people.'

In short, the British began to see themselves as an imperial race, and, as P. J. Marshall puts it in *The Cambridge Illustrated History of the British Empire*: 'for nearly all imperialists, the British race was an exclusively white one. The non-white peoples of the empire were its subjects. They were citizens of the empire in the sense that they had rights, but they were not regarded as full citizens, capable of controlling their own destinies.' There were countless manifestations of this white supremacy from the nineteenth century, not least what happened in Tasmania. Kipling in 1899 popularized the idea, through a poem, of 'the White Man's Burden' – presenting the notion that whites had a moral duty to rule over non-whites and encourage their cultural, social and economic development. The *Spectator* pronounced in 1865 that 'the negroes are made on purpose to serve the whites, just as the black ants are made on purpose to serve the red.' Warren Hastings disembarked at Calcutta in 1814 and noted in his journal that Hindus possessed 'no higher intellect than a dog, an elephant or a monkey'. Fervid stories of triumph over the fuzzy-wuzzies were fed to schoolchildren, the British nicknamed themselves 'the heaven born', James Mill's *History of British India* in 1817 featured the claim that 'in India there is no moral character', while Walter Bagehot opined that when it came to the British and Indians 'the two are not en rapport together. The higher being is not and cannot be a model for the lower; he could not mould himself on it if he would, and would not if he could.' The year 1810 saw Saartjie Baartman, a woman from 'the interior of South Africa', being toured in London as a kind of racial freakshow, with people paying to see what they regarded as an oversized bottom and sexual organs.[16] As colonization expanded, so did the European fascination with the 'other', people considered ludicrous characters of colour. In the nineteenth century, human zoos – a new trend of exotic exhibition of real people of black or Asian ethnicity – became popular in European cities as part of international trade fairs. African Zulus toured Europe and inhabitants of villages from colonized areas of the world were transported as a form of sinister entertainment and expected to act out rituals, dance and traditional custom, indigenous to their homeland, all for a European audience. Victorian adverts for Pears Soap depicted a white child helping a black child to become more like him, holding up a mirror for his astonishment and edification.[17] In 1889 Cecil Rhodes, who with his British South Africa Company founded the southern African territory of Rhodesia (now Zimbabwe and Zambia), declared that the Anglo-Saxon race was 'the first race in the world'. He added, 'We happen to be the best people in the world, with the highest ideals of decency and justice and liberty and peace, and the more of the world we inhabit, the better it is for humanity.' In his 'Confession of Faith', a document he composed in 1877, setting out his views on imperialism, Rhodes imagined his ideal world: 'Just fancy those parts that are at present inhabited by the most despicable specimen of human being, what an alteration there would be in them if they were brought under Anglo-Saxon influence . . . if there be a God, I think that what he would like me to do is paint as much of the map of Africa British Red as possible.'

Which brings us to the question of whether this historic white supremacy has any relevance to Britain now. It's the single question that provokes more anger, when it comes to empire, than any other, the passions it can evoke becoming apparent recently when Piers Morgan berated the academic Kehinde Andrews on live TV for suggesting that Britain was built on racism. 'Why live in a country you loathe?' he asked. I can see why it provokes such resistance: it challenges the image we have of ourselves as the nation which defeated the racist Nazis and abolished slavery; racism exists everywhere, not just in Britain, and in nations with no history of empire; empire feels like a long time ago and most of us grew up in a post-colonial age; the British had a history of crude xenophobia way before it had an empire, some of the darkest episodes in relation to its intolerance of Jews; and Britain has accepted, if not necessarily wholeheartedly embraced, multiculturalism. Meanwhile, in *Absent-Minded Imperialists*, Bernard Porter, who, if you remember, does not believe empire had much of an influence on British life, argues more specifically that 'it could be argued that other peoples are more arrogant (the French and Americans are the usual candidates),' that 'tabloid and hooligan chauvinism seems to be mainly based on the belief that Britain had won World War II' rather than on empire, and that the idea that 'residual imperialist attitudes undermined British business management in the post-colonial years' is 'essentially unknowable'. He proceeds to state that it is 'arguable in fact that one of the effects on Britain of her very variegated empire was to ensure that British views of other peoples were not as generalized, simplistic, and stereotypical as in countries that only had their ignorant prejudices to guide them. Imperialism could have had a marginally anti-racist effect, therefore.'

As it happens, I find myself agreeing with Porter, despite his ultimate thesis. To say Britain has a dark history of racism which influences contemporary psychology and culture, just as America's traumatic history with slavery is played out in its contemporary politics and culture, does not preclude, for me, the fact that it simultaneously, albeit inadvertently, inspired anti-racism. Imperialists didn't set out to do it, it only came about indirectly, as a response to the racism of empire, but just as it is obscene to omit the fact of the slave trade when debating the racism of empire, it is wrong to omit the fact of abolition, our war against the Nazis, the roundabout success we have made of multiculturalism and so on when discussing empire's racist legacy. Britain not only ended its slave trade, and enforced its abolition around the world, but the campaign pioneered by people like Olaudah Equiano and William Wilberforce had a legacy of its own in providing a model for countless social justice campaigns that followed. The abolitionist movement arguably laid the groundwork for all sorts of progressive shifts in society. Movements like trade unionism and Chartism in the mid-nineteenth century were supported – even led – by members of the immigrant community in Britain we have already come across such as William Cuffay, the son of a liberated slave who became a Chartist speaker at rallies, before he was arrested and eventually deported to . . . Tasmania.

Furthermore, even as empire became fervently jingoistic, there was resistance to colonialism within the enterprise from all sorts of quarters. George Orwell wrote in *The Road to Wigan Pier*: 'All over India, there are Englishmen who secretly loathe the system of which they are part.' Every aforementioned episode of ruthless racial violence was met with both applause and condemnation – for example, when a Royal Commission was set up to investigate Eyre, the controversial

Governor of Jamaica, it split the intelligentsia and country in two: on one side a 'Jamaica Committee', including John Stuart Mill, Charles Darwin, Frederic Harrison, John Bright and Herbert Spencer, attempted to prosecute Eyre privately, while a group of working-class radicals burned an effigy of him in London; on the other an 'Eyre Defence Committee', featuring the likes of Alfred Tennyson, Thomas Carlyle, John Ruskin, Charles Kingsley and Charles Dickens, established a fund to pay the Governor's legal expenses, while supporters within the clergy and House of Lords raised a rumoured £10,000 (£7 million today) on his behalf. The progressive Governor of Hong Kong, John Pope-Hennessy, tried to improve the lot of the poor Chinese and was known to them as 'Number One Good Friend'. Robert Winder, who does such a great job of showing how immigration shaped Britain, rightly points out that while at the turn of the twentieth century Britain 'had sullen manners and crude racial instincts' it was 'still an incomparably open country. There were Jews in Parliament, Germans and Italians in boardrooms, Indian civil servants and doctors, lawyers and even African missionaries. A runaway American slave called William Wells Brown was amazed, in 1852, by the ease with which a man of his colour could move through London: "In an hour's walk through the Strand, Regent Street or Piccadilly," he wrote, "one may meet half a dozen coloured men, who are inmates of the various colleges in the metropolis." '

Not that there is any equivalence between this indirect legacy of anti-racism and the direct legacy of imperial racism. In what precise ways does the racism that has overshadowed, defined and curtailed the lives of millions of Britons in the twentieth and twenty-first centuries have imperial roots? Well, I made an attempt earlier on to explain how these things might have worked with British Sikhs, and many of the points apply more generally, racial violence being the most obvious place to start, given that the 'manhunting' that followed the Uprising of 1857, which saw, in the words of Lawrence James, 'cross-country chases after fugitives' and which 'appealed to the sporting officer', was replicated by 'wog-bashing' and 'Paki-bashing' gangs who saw racial violence as a sport and tormented immigrants from empire in twentieth-century Britain. I challenge anyone to read about how gangs of Teddy Boys 'cruised the streets' in the 1950s with iron bars, table legs and knives, looking for West Indians, Africans or Asians to assault, or Paki-bashing skinhead gangs who murdered taxi drivers, students and restaurant workers in the 1970s and 1980s, and not be taken back to the atmosphere of the 1857 Uprising or the Morant Bay Rebellion. I guess I can't prove it, any more than I can prove that most slave traders were racist, or a woman followed home from work every night by a strange man can prove that he has ill intent. But I bet that the West Indian in Glasgow who in 1975 was murdered by a member of the National Front (who told the police that 'Niggers mean nothing to me, it was like killing a dog') felt, in his final moments, like the mutineers who in the 1850s were flushed out of cornfields as if they were partridges. 'The best sport,' recalled an officer.

Another imperial racist import is fear of miscegenation. Sexual relations were, as empire matured, forbidden: you had to keep distance to maintain authority. And these imperial attitudes were imported into Britain: as Humayun Ansari points out, when during the First World War wounded Indian soldiers were brought to Brighton to convalesce, their contact with white women was severely restricted, for fear that the men might get the wrong idea and that any 'ill-advised' conduct might be damaging to the prestige of European rule in India. No women were allowed to work at the hospital, and any man spotted talking to a woman was severely censured. There were also several incidents in the twentieth century where 'race riots' – more often than not events where white mobs attacked people of colour – were sparked by fear of miscegenation. The catalyst for the Notting Hill race riots of 1958 was an interracial relationship; 1919 saw similar eruptions of violence in working-class areas of Cardiff, South Shields, Liverpool, Glasgow and London, where black men were attacked and white women with black partners vilified. As Philippa Levine puts it: 'The [1919] riots were not focused exclusively on interracial sexual liaisons; broader racism as well as economic antagonism also kindled these hostilities, but sex was always central.'

Then we have the colour bar which ran through both imperial society and post-war Britain like letters through seaside rock. We have heard already about how empire Britons preferred to socialize among themselves (and developed the imperial club as a medium through which to do so), preferred to live with one another (and set up segregated areas in many towns and cities, often referred to as 'cantonments' or 'civil lines', to do so) and kept plum jobs for themselves (Lord Curzon once observed that 'there were no Indian natives in the Government of India because among all the 300 million people of the sub-continent, there was not a single man capable of the job'). India, as a shared physical space between British colonials and 'native' Indian people, had changed drastically from the end of the eighteenth century into the nineteenth. Indian people lived in 'Black Town' or the 'native quarter', described as a 'walled area, enclosing a mass of narrow, winding streets, peopled by a swarming mass of filthy natives, including a generous sprinkling of beggars, lepers, cripples and other grotesques'. The British cantonment regions, however, were completely different. Houses were spacious, Palladian in style, and were often part of a private compound with land, gardens and quarters for servants. The British even lived within their own time zone. When the Indian people would begin the evening feasting and dancing, the British would go to bed. Before the Indians stirred in the early hours, British women were up for their morning ride so that the daytime sun would not affect their complexion. The British were encouraged to be aloof, intimidating, to dress differently from Indian people.[18] This was behaviour that would be more than familiar to thousands of people of my parents' generation who found themselves routinely excluded when they arrived as immigrants to Britain. Asian entrepreneurship is often praised as one of the positive outcomes of multiculturalism, but many immigrants set up their own businesses only because of the racism of the jobs market. Officially, the government condemned prejudice – when, in 1943, the Trinidadian cricketer Learie Constantine was famously turned away, with his family, from the Imperial Hotel in London, the Under-Secretary of State for Dominion Affairs Paul Emrys-Evans stated that 'the government most strongly condemns any form of racial discrimination against Colonial people in this country.' Yet on it went. Immigrants looking for housing were subject to undisguised racism: in 1959 in Leamington, thirty residents protested to the town hall when a Sikh was given a council mortgage; in 1975 in Liverpool, an employment agency admitted that a covert colour bar governed the job market: only one-fifth of black people were successful in finding a job.

This brings us to the most obvious racist import from empire: wild racial stereotypes.[19] Throughout empire, the British found ways not only to distinguish themselves from brown people, but to distinguish types of brown people from one another. I've cited the Tasmanians and the Sikhs as examples already, but there were countless others. The Gurkha, according to a handbook on the subject, was the ideal light infantry soldier due to his 'compact and sturdy build . . . keen sight, acute hearing, and hereditary education as a sports man'. Following the Uprising of 1857, the Bengalis, once considered the stalwarts of the colonial army, fell from grace, being described as 'feeble even to effeminacy', men for whom 'Courage, independence, veracity are qualities to which his constitution and his situation are equally unfavourable.' At the same time, those from southern India were declared to 'fall short, as a race, in possessing the courage and military instincts', and the Punjab was anointed 'the home of the most martial races of India'. A series of official Recruiting Handbooks for the Indian Army included photos of the types of men deemed suitable to recruit, with physical requirements described in detail. One prominent anthropologist, Herbert Hope Risley, working at the turn of the century, even believed that caste could be discerned from the nose, the finest noses naturally belonging to the upper castes.

Needless to say, there was no consistency in this absurd generalizing. As Tayyab Mahmud explains, when 1.5 million Indians went overseas as indentured labour between 1834 and 1920, filling the gaps created by the abolition of slavery in the European colonies in the early nineteenth century, they endured being stereotyped in often entirely contradictory ways. Initially, it was standard to portray Africans as lazy and untrustworthy, while Indian workers were deemed industrious, reliable and obedient. However, once Indians were ensconced on the plantations and having to contend with brutal hardships and humiliations, they fell from favour. In truth, the planters suddenly claimed, the Indians were weak, dishonest and filthy. Now,

Chinese workers looked a far better bet: 'fully alive to the necessity of authority for their regulation and control . . . generally tractable and manageable, not averse to foreigners'. The modern legacies of this nonsense are legion. As outlined earlier in relation to Sikhs, many of the ethnic groups labelled 'a martial race' by the Victorians still cling to the idea across the world and, amazingly, a significant proportion of the army of the Republic of India is still recruited along the spurious ethnic lines defined by the British back then, while Sanjoy Chakravorty has argued that caste-based reservations in independent India were created by Britons who took a complex system of faiths and social identities and simplified them crudely, creating new categories and hierarchies, stuffing the mismatched together and toughening flexible boundaries.[20] In 1958, the Colonial Office, in an inversion of how indentured labourers were viewed, was making a distinction between the two types of migration: West Indians being viewed favourably, seen as hard-working and talented, while Indians and Pakistanis were deemed the opposite – 'lazy, feckless, and difficult to place in employment'.[21] More recently, a study in 2017 by NatCen and the Runnymede Trust found that racial stereotypes are still widely prevalent; for example, 44 per cent of those surveyed thought that 'some races are born harder working than others.' And I have felt the effect of these stereotypes myself when one of the first job offers I ever received was from an editor who stated baldly: 'I like Indians, they work hard.' The concerning implication being, of course, that he believed that other ethnicities were wired to be less diligent.

This is not to say that every claim that has been made about this legacy of divide and rule quite works. When Neha Shah, an activist and researcher at the University of Oxford, suggested that the presence in the Tory Cabinet of a bunch of British Asians with family roots in Uganda, Kenya and Tanzania could be explained by the fact that in the early twentieth century thousands of Indians (mostly Goans, Gujaratis and Punjabis) were imported into East Africa as 'subcolonial agents of civilisation . . . required to work in colonial administration and serve in the colonial police and army, to keep the "native peoples" in order', it felt uncomfortable. To imply that any individual has a certain political view because of their ethnicity feels like a generalization too far. But imperial conceptions of racial groups explain so much about the different ways different ethnic groups are treated in Britain, with notions of good and bad immigrants. And as for the ultimate argument that always crops up in relation to this theme, that the racism of empire can't have influenced modern Britain because it was such a long time ago, well, none of this feels particularly ancient. The British empire, with all its racial extremism, was still a thing when much of this racism was emerging in Britain in its crudest forms. Around the time that one new arrival from Jamaica was being threatened with a knife during his first weekend in London in 1954 ('You blacks, you niggers, why don't you go back to the jungle?'), Barbara Castle was on a fact-finding mission to Kenya, financed by the *Daily Mirror*, and discovering stories of torture and murder in British colonial jails, such as the deaths of eight Mau Mau prisoners in the Hola internment camp. In 1959 Castle received a letter which described the brutal beating of a detainee who had previously collapsed carrying buckets of earth: the beating was so severe that he was killed.[22] A 1911 textbook entitled *A School History of England*, written by Rudyard Kipling and C. R. L. Fletcher 'for all boys and girls who are interested in the story of Great Britain and her empire', included racist 'facts' such as how West Indians were 'lazy, vicious and incapable of any serious improvement or of work except under compulsion',[23] remained in print until 1930 and was reissued under a different title in 1983, a time when those of us who were still growing up would hear such attitudes expressed all the time. And in a personal essay for the *New Statesman* Richard Evans, Regius Professor Emeritus of History at Cambridge University, described the multiple ways in which the racism of empire influenced his 1950s childhood.*

* 'I learned to read from a primer called *Little Black Sambo* about a Tamil boy and his parents, Black Mumbo and Black Jumbo. The coronation of Queen Elizabeth, which I remember watching with our neighbours on a tiny television set in 1953, was the occasion for a magnificent display of the empire's power and extent, with special attention paid to colonial figures such as the revered Sir Robert Menzies, prime minister of Australia, or the much-loved (and much-patronised) Queen Salote of Tonga. The *Eagle* boys' magazine, edited by the Reverend Marcus Morris in a vain attempt to provide a respectable alternative to the *Beano* and *Tiger*,

Just as the experience of the Indian Uprising created the need for notices in Indian hotels that read 'Gentlemen are requested not to strike the servants,' and just as such attitudes led in 1903 to the cricketer and writer Cecil Headlam advising that 'You must be very careful how you hit a man in India . . . it is best to carry a cane and administer rebuke upon the calves and shins, which are tender and not usually mortal,'[24] it seems clear to me that our experience of empire has influenced, if not created, the distinct brand of racism practised in Britain. It doesn't explain it all, but you can hear the echoes of imperialism in the almost daily headlines highlighting racial injustice and inequality – from the fact that, according to a report from Green Park, an executive search and diversity consultancy, less than 5 per cent of the most senior jobs are held by people from ethnic minorities, with ethnic minorities being virtually absent in the leadership of key areas such as healthcare, education and criminal justice, to the fact that a third of the companies in the Financial Times Stock Exchange (FTSE) 100 Index still lack any ethnic minority representation on their boards, even though ethnic entrepreneurs have proved themselves a million times over. The same echoes can be heard in the almost total absence of black academics in the most senior leadership roles, in the claim from a recent report that trainee doctors from black and ethnic minority backgrounds are less likely to be approved for jobs than their white counterparts, in the conclusions of recent official reports that the Metropolitan Police and the Home Office are 'institutionally racist',

---

serialised comic strips about great imperial lives, including those of Cecil Rhodes and David Livingstone, who, I learned, were hugely appreciated by the Africans for trying to civilise them. When my mother's home-made marmalade ran out, usually in August, we bought Robinson's Golden Shred, which came with a free miniature "golliwog" figure. In the late 1950s, after we got a TV set, we watched *The Black and White Minstrel Show* every week, in which George Mitchell's white singers blacked up and accompanied their performances with stereotypical "black" gestures, body movements and Al Jolson accents – or at least, some kind of approximation to them (the show was enormously popular, winning audiences of more than 20 million at its height). Over dinner, I listened to my parents arguing with one of their schoolteacher friends over whether black people were further down the scale of evolution than whites, located somewhere in the vicinity of the apes, as their friend maintained, or perhaps a bit higher up.'

in the assertion of a review that the Home Office displayed 'profound institutional failure' and 'ignorance and thoughtlessness' on the issue of race during the *Windrush* scandal and in the fact that, as Theresa May said on entering Downing Street, black people are 'treated more harshly by the criminal justice system'. Of course we like to remember the abolition of the slave trade and the defeat of the Nazis, and sometimes even the success of multiculturalism and our history of anti-racism and the social justice campaigns it inspired, but we also dominated the slave trade for a significant period, ran one of the biggest white supremacist enterprises in the history of humanity and dabbled in genocide, and the stain of it has seeped into many aspects of our contemporary culture, from the jobs market to the sinister re-emergence of violent white supremacy.

At this point I am reminded of the fact that, in 1876, a few years after the tragic death of King Billy Lanney, it was thought there was only one 'full-blooded' Tasmanian Aborigine left – a woman named Truganini. Her life, which had spanned the colonization, had been harrowing beyond imagination: her mother shot by a soldier, her sister kidnapped, her stepmother abducted, her fiancé drowned in her presence by Europeans who also raped her. Beset by STIs, she became a prostitute for Europeans. In her later years she had partnered up with King Billy Lanney, dubbed the last-surviving full-blooded male in his lifetime, and had been horrified by what happened to his body after his death. When, aged sixty-four, she died, her last words were: 'Don't let them cut me, but bury me behind the mountains.' She did not get her wish. Although initially buried in a prison grave, after two years she was dug up, her body boiled of its flesh and her skeleton strung together for exhibition in the Tasmanian Museum, where she remained on display until 1947.[25]

10. Empire State of Mind

One of my last outings before the coronavirus lockdown was a re-union at my old school, Wolverhampton Grammar. For the first time since I left, twenty-five years ago, initially for a bleak summer job in a hospital laundry, and then university, I caught up with the people I spent most of my teenage years with, and it was unnerving. Accepting that the most handsome boy in the year was somehow even better-looking at forty-three than he was at eighteen as I increasingly resembled Salman Rushdie was not great for self-esteem. There was the discovery that every other classmate seemed to have gone into medicine and, to be honest, it was hard not to feel frivolous in comparison. But most disorientating of all was the poshness.

WGS had been an independent grammar school for a couple of years by the time I attended, and while it was certainly more pretentious than the comp my siblings attended, many of us were on fully or partially Assisted Places, and it was hardly Harrow. Nevertheless, here we were having a three-course dinner in our old assembly hall before a stained-glass window celebrating more than 500 years of history, singing the school song (in Latin), toasting the Queen and breaking into a spontaneous rendition of 'Jerusalem'. Had I wilfully forgotten that I had attended the Black Country's answer to Charterhouse? I guess it explained quite a lot, not least why I had made it on Fleet Street while friends at my state primary at least as clever as me were doing minimum-wage jobs in town.

Moreover, was there a distinct imperial tone to proceedings? By this stage I had spent more than a year immersed in British empire and was wary of the possibility of seeing legacies where there are none, becoming like social networker @cholenacree who tweeted: 'Do I believe everything happens for a reason? Yes. And the reason is colonialism.' But the after-dinner speaker, a former pupil and diplomat, repeated a joke about the honours he had received which I'd first read in Niall Ferguson's book on empire (CMG = Call Me God, KCMG = Kindly Call Me God, GCMG = God Calls Me God)* and which the historian had cited as an illustration of how empire's administrative hierarchy became increasingly elaborate in the nineteenth century, with 'no fewer than seventy-seven separate ranks' in 1881. Standing in the oldest part of the school I was reminded that our assemblies regularly involved the recital of the 'Founder's Prayer' which urged us to 'answer the good intent of our founder and become profitable members of Church and Commonwealth'. And singing an abbreviated version of the school song, 'Carmen Wulfrunense', I remembered it featured a verse which positively gloried in colonialism: 'Occidens et oriens / Nostram vim sensere / Caelum terras maria / Nostri domuere' ('The West and the East / Have felt our force / The skies, the lands, the seas / Our brothers have subdued'). I don't really see WGS as a public school, given that it was a state grammar until a few years before I joined, and my fees were paid for in entirety by the government, but, strictly speaking, it was, and maybe I had been influenced in ways I had never fully appreciated by the culture of imperialism that has infiltrated and sustained Britain's public-school system.

For the fact is that the success of Britain's public schools is another legacy of British empire – many of them thriving during the Victorian age, and in some cases being established, because they served as preparation, even training, for a role in empire.[1] Schools such as Uppingham saw a third of their leavers depart England for opportunities overseas. While Eton produced those destined for the highest echelon, such as viceroys and field marshals, newer institutions such

* The Most Distinguished Order of St Michael and St George is a British honour founded in 1818 by the Prince Regent (later King George IV) to commemorate the British protectorate over the Ionian Islands and Malta. Originally membership was restricted to inhabitants of the Ionian Islands (Greece) and Malta, but after 1879 any British citizen could receive it. Traditionally, the honour is given mainly to diplomats, foreign-service workers and people who have done important work within the Commonwealth. William IV established three classes of the order: Knight Grand Cross or Dame Grand Cross (GCMG); Knight Commander or Dame Commander (KCMG or DCMG); and Companion (CMG). See https://www.royal.uk/order-st-michael-and-st-george.

as Clifton more usually trained the men who took up lowlier but still prestigious positions in the military and imperial service, and below this a clutch of minor public schools catered to a mass of mixed-ability middle-class boys, helping to sustain all levels of recruitment. 'The lodges of public-school freemasonry spread throughout the empire and became part of its power structure,' James Epstein has observed. 'The public schools formed part of a network of associations sustaining a gentlemanly ethos of privilege manifest in the practice of elite domestic and imperial rule.'

Victorian public schools did not work exclusively to produce staff for empire, but their focus on the values of fair play, resilience and duty made them perfect for the task, and of these nothing was more important than fair play, the nineteenth-century notion of, wherever possible, according indigenous rulers and local tradition due respect and observance. It was notoriously articulated by the Victorian author Sir Henry Newbolt, whom we met earlier as the presenter of a BBC Empire Day special and as a friend of Sir Francis Young-husband of the Tibet expedition, but who is most famous for his 1897 poem about a schoolboy cricketer who, as an adult, travels to Africa to battle for empire. The hero's memory of his school sports master spurs him on to triumph in battle, and the poem's famous line 'Play up! Play up! And play the game!' encapsulates the popular view that the war spirit was seeded on the sports field. And it says something that when, in order to keep Tsarist Russia from getting near India, Britain fought a series of arduous Afghan wars, the battles were dubbed the 'Great Game', with Lord Curzon, later Viceroy of India, remarking that 'Turkestan, Afghanistan, Transcaspia, Persia' were to him 'pieces on a chessboard upon which is being played out a game for the domination of the world'.★

★ Though chess, football and rugby, which rapidly became popular across empire's white dominions, weren't the ultimate imperial games. That accolade went to cricket – a sport that is used as a proxy not only for good British behaviour (hence the phrase 'it's just not cricket'), but for empire too. The historian Prashant Kidambi points out that, in the late nineteenth century, cricket became the imperial sport, crucial to the British sense of identity, purpose and morality. Chester Macnaghten, one of the headmasters of the aforementioned public schools that

The most notorious remark on this theme came, of course, in the form of the Duke of Wellington's apocryphal line about how 'the battle of Waterloo was won on the playing fields of Eton', and in the case of Eton you can get a sense of how imperialism might have been indoctrinated in the nineteenth century through a story that Lord Meath, the founder of Empire Day, tells in his autobiography. Apparently when he and his classmates once dared to brush snow off their knees on a bitterly cold day, a master launched into a diatribe complaining that such actions were spineless and unimperial. 'You young worms!' he exclaimed. 'Do you call yourselves British boys? . . . Shame on you! Your fathers are the rulers of England, and your forefathers have made England what she is now. Do you imagine that if they had minded a little snow that Canada would ever have been added to the empire, or if they had minded heat we should ever possess India or tropical Africa? Never let me see you shrink from either heat or cold. You will have to maintain the empire which they made.' Meanwhile, the lingering imperial tone of the twentieth-century Etonian education was conveyed in a recent essay in the *London Review of Books* by the literary critic James Wood in which he recalled how first-year Etonians of his generation were, for history, given a copy of *Heaven's Command*, the first volume of Jan Morris' trilogy

---

opened up in India to educate the aristocracy, made it a habit to read out to students a passage from *Tom Brown's Schooldays* where Tom, captain of the cricket XI, triumphed in a match. Macnaghten was known to pronounce afterwards: 'In hours so spent you will learn lessons such as no school instruction can give – the lessons of self-reliance, calmness and courage . . .' Meanwhile Scouts-founder Robert Baden-Powell, who excelled at sport at Charterhouse before heading into an army career in India, Afghanistan and Africa, compared the famous siege of Mafeking to a cricket match when he was a colonel in command of a regiment during the Second Boer War. He wrote: 'Just now we are having our innings and have so far scored 200 days, not out, against the bowling of Cronje, Snijman, Botha . . . and we are having a very enjoyable game . . .' Such sentiments were routine. At the Battle of Ladysmith, fought in November 1899 also during the Second Boer War, officers were funnelling the wounded into makeshift hospitals during a brief armistice. 'We are only sportsmen,' one injured officer is reported to have remarked.

about the rise and fall of the British empire, along with bits from the other two books.

> The trilogy is a lush, romantic account of the enormous, bloody, dust-filled adventure of empire. Morris – who as James Morris had fought in the 9th Queen's Royal Lancers during the Second World War – describes military expeditions, noble defeats and brutal victories with the same rousing relish. It was a good book to give to dreaming 13-year-old boys. But now I wonder at the school's reflexive turn towards Britain's imperial past, and its choice of this glitteringly nostalgic text. Morris doesn't exactly hide the racism and genocidal violence of the imperial enterprise, but they're somehow swept up in the sheer mad gusto of the narrative.

Wood analyses the impact the 'propaganda' had on him and may have had on contemporaries who went into politics, pointing out that Jacob Rees-Mogg 'triples down on sickly imperial nostalgia in his recent book [on the Victorians], telling us in his acknowledgments, amid nods towards patient wife and beneficent nanny, that "it was *Heaven's Command* by Jan Morris that sparked my interest in history"' and that Boris Johnson's book about Winston Churchill 'effectively ends where Morris ends her history', in January 1965, when Churchill, 'the great lion of empire', is being laid to rest at a funeral where, in the words of Morris, 'a hundred nations were represented . . . and twenty of them had once been ruled from this very capital'. And if I accept Wood's argument that such imperial nostalgia influenced these individuals and, in turn, the country they ended up running, I cannot escape the question of how the imperialism of my education may have affected me – both private and state, given that, according to John MacKenzie, 'public schools were taken as the model for the rest of the educational system' and 'in state schools, the symbols and rituals of imperial life were no less apparent.' I don't recall empire being taught to me, explicitly. Besides, we were a relatively sceptical generation: while other year groups, going back to the 1950s, lead the singing at the school reunion, several of my former classmates at our table can't quite bring themselves to join in. Also, our Latin, only compulsory for a year or two, was never good enough to comprehend the lyrics of the school song, and talk of 'Commonwealth' in the school prayer is not quite the same thing as empire: depending on when it was written, the meaning could actually have been 'nation' or 'society'. But I do think my education at WGS and beyond, a classic British education in many ways, was shaped by colonial attitudes in its assumptions and omissions. And to understand how such assumptions and omissions might shape minds, you need to consult Edward Said's *Orientalism*.

In 1978, when James Wood and his contemporaries might have been reading Jan Morris, the youth of Britain were confronting the demise of the Sex Pistols and *Dallas* was beginning, Said, the late Professor of Literature at Columbia University who is often cited as a founder of post-colonial studies as an academic field, was examining the reductive assumptions the West makes about the civilizations and people of Asia, North Africa and the Middle East. Characterizing these patronizing representations of the East as 'Orientalism', he argued that Western thinkers had dismissed the artistic and intellectual life of the globe beyond their own as fruitless, tyrannical, exotic, unrewarding and unthinking. He added elsewhere that the purpose of such cultural disparagement was to marginalize empire's subjects – 'regulating and confining the non-European to a secondary racial, cultural, ontological status'. And this, I realize, is the gaze through which my education encouraged me to view the non-Western world – even my own heritage. I may not, like some immigrants to Wolverhampton, have grown up believing that white people were superior – attitudes which led one woman migrating to the Black Country from Barbados to express shock at the sight of white folks sweeping the street ('we always put the white folks up on a pedestal, we were taught to believe they were better than us').[2] I may have had a different, authentic, Punjabi view of India presented to me by my Indian family. And no one who taught me ever disparaged non-Western culture outright in the way that Hugh Trevor-Roper, Regius Professor of History at Oxford, did in a lecture on BBC radio in 1963 when he declared: 'Perhaps, in the future, there will be some African history to teach . . . at present

there is none: there is only the history of the Europeans in Africa.'*
But my quintessentially British, private-school Oxbridge education
taught me to value Western history, Western literary forms
(such as the novel and the memoir) and Western geopolitical forms
(the nation state) above their non-Western counterparts, and encouraged me to view my own Indian heritage through patronizing
Western eyes.

It would be an understatement to say I am persuaded by Said's
argument that the cultural self-confidence of the colonized was
destroyed through the relentless running down of their indigenous
beliefs and way of life and the promotion of colonial knowledge. It
hits me in the gut. It makes me appreciate that my 'excellent education' was no such thing really: through its assumptions and relentless
omissions, it was narrow and encouraged me to belittle most non-
Western thought, history and literary forms as irrational and illogical,
including the heritage that my parents attempted to inculcate in me
through bedtime stories, Bollywood movies and weekend Punjabi
language lessons. I may never have described myself as colonized, but
reading Said makes me realize that my view of South Asia has been
heavily influenced by books written by Britons, or by South Asians
writing for Britons, and that, psychologically, I may well have been
colonized. Furthermore, that education can be a tool of colonialism
is reflected in the fact that imperialists routinely used it as a weapon.

When establishing the British Raj and conquering royal Indian
kingdoms, the British attempted to remould the Indian aristocracy in
order to create a natural ally from within India. Young princes or
maharajahs were educated in the 'British manner', in the hope that
with a traditionally British public-school education young boys
would inherit the same British imperial values. The colonizers
imagined reshaping the Indian aristocracy through a system of

---

* He continued: 'The rest is darkness, like the history of pre-European, pre-
Columbian America. And darkness is not a subject for history ... History, I
believe, is essentially a form of movement, and purposive movement too. It is not
a mere phantasmagoria of changing shapes and costumes, of battles and conquests ... the unrewarding gyrations of barbarous tribes in picturesque but
irrelevant corners of the globe.'

subsidized Indian public schools. Lord Curzon hoped that through this type of education the Indian ruling classes would eventually become 'colleagues' of the British: educating people out of their traditional cultural values was a way of ensuring his idealized homogeneity. Meanwhile, Thomas Babington Macaulay, who played a key role in the introduction of English and Western concepts to Indian education, argued in 1835 that 'it is impossible for us, with our limited means, to attempt to educate the body of the people. We must at present do our best to form a class who may be interpreters between us and the millions whom we govern, – a class of persons Indian in blood and colour, but English in tastes, in opinions, in morals and in intellect.'[3]

The ultimate defeat of the Sikh kingdom was achieved not on the battlefield after the Anglo-Sikh Wars but through the British tutoring of Duleep Singh, the last Maharajah of the Sikh empire.[4] Singh attained his position at the age of just five, with his mother, Maharani Jind Kaur, as regent. When the English declared war on the Sikhs in 1845, Singh was painfully separated from his mother and placed under the care of the British Resident, Henry Lawrence, as a nominal ruler. Lawrence wished to educate the young Maharajah in the ways of the English and orchestrated trips to the races so that he could mix with young Europeans. However, after Lawrence left India on sick leave, Duleep Singh ended up in the care of Dr John Login, a medic in the Bengal Army originally from Orkney, and under his tutelage Singh was brought up in the manner of a British boy, under the original orders of Henry Lawrence who wished him 'not left to grow idle and debauched in India, with nothing to do'. In 1853, Singh converted to Christianity and a year later went to live in exile in England. His change in religion greatly impressed Queen Victoria, who praised him for embracing 'our faith' and insisted that 'being a Christian, the first of his high rank who has embraced our faith, must incline everyone favourably towards him'. Duleep Singh's formative years were spent being Anglicized in every possible respect, stripping him of the cultural heritage he was born into. He was given books to read, such as *The Boy's Own Book*, a text frequently read by British public schoolboys, and the British even tried to find common ancestral ground with the Maharajah with one

Colonel Sleeman, best remembered for his supposed oppression of criminal gangs in India known as 'Thughee', remarking in a letter that the young man was descended from 'Jutes', as were people in Kent, going on to suggest that he might therefore find cousins in England and thus providing an illustration of how absurd Aryan theories about race sometimes worked in practice.*

Over time, Singh educated himself, became reconnected to his heritage, rebelled and embraced Sikhism again, but it was too late by then to lay claim to the Sikh empire. And his journey is one that many colonial subjects seemed to travel in the colonial age. My obsession, Dean Mahomed, went from being Indian to a version of a British gent, to then embracing and even marketing his Indian heritage. Jawaharlal Nehru, the Indian independence activist and first Prime Minister of India, was educated at Harrow and Trinity College Cambridge and once remarked, 'In my likes and dislikes I was perhaps more an Englishman than an Indian . . . I returned to India as prejudiced in favour of England and the English as it is possible to be.' But he rebelled against this Anglicization. Even during his time

---

* Sleeman's letter, which a Sikh historian friend struggled to make sense of given that Duleep was unlikely to have been from a family of the Punjabi 'Jatt' caste, goes: 'I have been reading up the book I spoke to the Maharajah about ("Pictorial History of England"), since he left. You must get it for him, and let him see for himself that he is of the same race as the men of Kent. They were from Jutland, and came into England with the Saxons from Friesland and Angles from Holstein, who dispossessed the old Britons in the fifth century. They were the Juts or old Getae of the Greeks and Romans, who came from the countries about Kashgar. Some came down and settled on the banks of the Indus, whence they spread to the Jumba and Chunbal; whilst others went and settled in western Europe (Sweden and Denmark): from them Jutland received its name. Tell His Highness that their chiefs, Hengist and Horsa, were Juts, like himself; their family came from Kashgar and the Caspian, and settled in Jutland, while his part of the family settled on the Indus, spreading to the Punjab. The Juts took possession of Kent, and some of the first kings were Juts, like the Maharajah's ancestors, and both might, with equal justice, boast descent from Odin, the god of war; they also took possession of the Isle of Wight and the Isle of Thanet. All the old Kentish families are descendants of Juts, and of the same race as Duleep Singh. You can show him some of the beauties of Kent, as you go up the Thames, and he will have an opportunity of seeing it if he visits Lord Hardinge.'

at Cambridge, he expressed an interest in radical social reform, shar-
ing socialist ideas and empathizing with the Sinn Fein movement in
Ireland that pushed back on the English right to rule.[5] By 1922, the
British Viceroy, Lord Reading, described him as 'fanatical in his hostility towards government', and in 1929 Nehru gave an anti-imperial
speech at the Lahore Congress, massively unsettling British officials
in India. Then there was Surendranath Banerjea, who like Nehru
became a member of the Indian National Congress, standing up
against British imperialism. Banerjea had trained in England to be a
member of the Indian Civil Service but lost faith in the system after
he experienced institutionalized racism while studying in London.[6]

I can't help but feel that I'm on a similar journey, that in embarking
on this project I'm making an effort to decolonize myself, and the
question of how imperialism shapes the psychology of the colonized,
and the children of the colonized, raises another question: how might
the experience of British empire have shaped the psychology of the
colonizers? It's a slightly more esoteric theme but one that has been
tackled by a number of analysts. In *The Intimate Enemy*, Ashis Nandy,
a fellow at the Centre for the Study of Developing Societies in Delhi,
argues that colonialism damaged both colonized and colonizing societies, cites a famous psychiatric case study of a police officer in Algeria
who carried his torture of freedom fighters back home with him,
becoming violent to his family, and applies it to colonialism at large,
quoting the *Mahabharata*, one of the two major Sanskrit epics of
ancient India: 'Do not do unto others what you would that they do
not do unto you, lest you do unto yourself what you do unto others.'
In *After Empire*, Paul Gilroy reflects upon the harrowing effect that
colonial violence may have had on the colonized, pointing out that
while 'the practice of blasting prisoners to death by tying their bodies
over the mouths of cannon' was meant to terrorize and subjugate Indians, it also had a dehumanizing effect on the British: 'The vastly
more interesting issue of what this grisly spectacle might have meant
and done to its British organizers, spectators, and enthusiasts gets
smuggled out of sight,' as does the experience of 'onlookers who
were covered by blood and fragments of flesh . . . to say nothing
of the plight of an unfortunate bystander who was hit by one of the

vanished prisoners' flying heads that, singed but intact, fell back to earth from a height of several hundred feet.' Most famously there is George Orwell, who for the sake of balance I should point out was also an Etonian, and whose time as an imperial officer inspired a great deal of anti-colonial writing, not least his essay entitled 'Shooting an Elephant', broadcast on BBC radio in 1948. In it he describes the experience of an Englishman, perhaps Orwell himself, working as a police officer in Burma when he is called upon to shoot an out-of-control elephant. He does so against his instincts, his torment increased by the elephant's bungled death. The message of the story is that colonialism can not only dehumanize colonizers, but render them absurd. 'I perceived in this moment that when the white man turns tyrant it is his own freedom that he destroys. He becomes a sort of hollow, posing dummy, the conventionalized figure of a sahib. For it is the condition of his rule that he shall spend his life in trying to impress the "natives", and so in every crisis he has got to do what the "natives" expect of him.' The narrator adds that he felt pressured to act because 'The crowd would laugh at me. And my whole life, every white man's life in the East, was one long struggle not to be laughed at.'

The essay could be read as a response to Kipling's poem 'The White Man's Burden', which some fifty years earlier had proposed that settler colonialism was nothing less than a moral obligation. And, in turn, the likes of Said, Gilroy and Orwell raise the question of how imperialism may have shaped British psychology more generally. It's an issue that most imperial historians end up addressing at some point or other. We have Jan Morris, for instance, acknowledging how, during the period known as the New Imperialism in the late nineteenth century, when empire became popular, 'a vigorous kind of brainwashing was in full swing' conducted by national newspapers, the government and pressure groups, and observing that the British continued to 'believe in the power of their prestige' even when empire had expired and become a 'deception'. We have John Darwin observing in *Unfinished Empire* that 'an imperial mentality was still deeply entrenched at all levels of British society' even after India had been granted independence; right into the 1950s, the British were portrayed with an imperial bent in novels and publications, especially those aimed at the young, such as the reissued adventure novels of the popular Victorian writer G. A. Henty and the *Eagle* comic. Linda Colley meanwhile theorizes in *Captives: Britain, Empire and the World, 1600–1850* about how Britain's modest size and its aggressive colonization are connected, suggesting that 'domestic smallness and a lack of self-sufficiency made for continuous British extroversion, not to say global house-breaking, violence and theft.'

I inevitably end up psychoanalysing my home nation as I demarcate imperial patterns in our contemporary culture and anthropology. The anxiety about money imported by East India Company nabobs which inspired the writer and politician Horace Walpole to complain that England was now 'a sink of Indian wealth', for instance, echoes so much modern anxiety about the influence in Britain of foreign cash, Russian, Indian, Chinese and otherwise. When Niall Ferguson talks about how 'time and again, in the inter-war period' there was a pattern consisting of 'a minor outbreak of dissent, a sharp military response, followed by a collapse of British self-confidence, hand-wringing, second thoughts', I am reminded of the hesitant progress of so many British projects from the third runway at Heathrow to HS2, of US Secretary of State Dean Acheson's famous remark in 1962 that 'Great Britain has lost an empire and has not yet found a role' and of Norman Davies' conclusion in *The Isles* that 'the United Kingdom was established to serve the interests of empire, and the loss of empire has destroyed its raison d'être.' It seems we are incapable of doing anything as a nation nowadays without succumbing to self-doubt and endless hand-wringing. Also, our contemporary neurosis about being unable to afford our global ambitions is nothing new: in the 1860s Prime Minister Gladstone was so concerned about the heavy expense of empire that his government mooted the idea of separation from the colonies – or, at least, a 'friendly relaxation' of the relationship – while in the 1890s General Sir Henry Brackenbury, the Director of Military Intelligence, complained in an all too familiar way that Britain was 'attempting to maintain the largest empire the world has ever seen with armaments and reserves that would be insufficient for a third-class Military Power'.

Some imperial psychological legacies are more profound than

others, however, and one of the bigger ones is surely our national distrust of cleverness. It's a contradiction that while Britain is renowned abroad for the excellence of its private education system, with public schools like Dulwich College now operating branches as far afield as China, our society is resolutely anti-intellectual. Sure, the rise of the mediocre privileged man is an international phenomenon, inspiring the psychologist Tomas Chamorro-Premuzic to pen a book entitled *Why Do So Many Incompetent Men Become Leaders?*, but we Britons are world experts at resisting smartness. The pressure to disguise intelligence starts early: talking about exam rituals the anthropologist Kate Fox observes that 'modesty is important: even if you are feeling reasonably calm and confident, it is not done to say so – you must pretend to be full of anxiety and self-doubt, convinced that you are going to fail'; 'if you have clearly swotted like mad, you can admit this only in a self-deprecatory context'; 'those who do well must always appear surprised by their success.' Zinnia Wormwood remarks in the film adaptation of Roald Dahl's *Matilda* that 'a girl does not get anywhere by acting intelligent.' Elsewhere, the phrase 'too clever by half' is in common currency; Michael Gove famously stated when campaigning for Brexit that 'people in this country have had enough of experts'; during the coronavirus crisis a BBC *Newsnight* correspondent reported a 'senior Tory' calling opposition leader Keir Starmer a 'smartypants', as if, as Twitter wag @TobyonTV put it, 'having someone smart in a position of responsibility is less preferable to someone who has been notoriously pantless'; Boris Johnson once dismissed his predecessor David Cameron in a leaked Cabinet memo with the insult 'girly swot'; and while he himself managed a 2:1 at Oxford, Johnson became famous as a result of a series of media appearances where he wilfully played the role of a bumbling upper-class twit.

Matthew Parris recently observed that 'Regrettably, [Boris] Johnson has an Etonian distrust of intellect among colleagues,' but might it be more accurate to say that Johnson displays an imperial distrust of cleverness, instilled in him at Eton? For there is no doubt that a phobia of cleverness was institutionalized during empire. When reflecting on the role of public schools in empire, Jeremy Paxman observes that they 'were trying to turn out steady, reliable chaps whose minds would be free of the danger of seditious thoughts – or, indeed, too much thought of any kind'. It was a philosophy reflected in the headline of a leading article in Marlborough College's magazine *The Marlburian* in 1888, which declared 'Knowledge puffeth up', and in remarks made in 1895 by the headmaster of Harrow School, who advanced the popular view that public schools had an obligation to produce men who would go on to run the empire, and that imperial strength was derived from the games pitch: 'England owes her empire far more to her sports than to her studies.' They thus echo Thomas Carlyle's depiction of the English as 'the stupidest in speech, and the wisest in action', and novelist Charles Kingsley, who had Sir Francis Drake say in his 1855 novel *Westward Ho!* that 'book-learning is not business; book-learning didn't get me round the world; book-learning didn't make Captain Hawkins, nor his father neither, the best shipbuilders from Hull to Cadiz; and book-learning, I very much fear, won't plant Newfoundland.' Meanwhile, the Sudanese Political Service preferred their recruits to be reliable rather than bright: one candidate was famously rejected because he left his copy of *The Times* lying about, with the crossword completed.[7]

After the First World War, the man in charge of recruitment at the Colonial Office was Major Ralph Dolignon Furse, a decorated war hero, a keen rugby and cricket player and, crucially, holder of a poor third-class degree from Oxford. Furse's selection process was designed to eliminate anyone too smart: dependability was the thing most desired. The last thing anyone wanted was for men in the field to analyse what they were doing. Andrew Thompson reports on how Furse's emphasis on practical experience over intellect was reflected in the fact that after 1900 one in twenty recruits to the administrative arm of the Colonial Service had a business background, as did around 20 per cent of the technical and professional employees signing up. Observing the British in India, Adolf Hitler expressed his admiration for the public-school system that produced such 'men of inflexible will and ruthless energy who regard intellectual problems as a waste of time but know human nature and how to dominate other men in the most unscrupulous fashion'.[8]

It didn't always work out, of course, which leads us to another significant psychological legacy of imperialism: heroic failure. As well as being responsible for an authoritative study of the influence of British empire upon our country houses, Stephanie Barczewski is the author of *Heroic Failure and the British*, a fascinating study of how 'glorious disaster and valiant defeat' have become essential aspects of the British national character over the past two centuries. She points out, among other things, how the British have a curious predilection for celebrating heroic failure in our monuments – take, for instance, Waterloo Place, off Pall Mall, where you'll find statues of Captain Robert Falcon Scott, who lost the race to reach the South Pole and then expired on his way home in 1912, and Sir John Franklin, who died in a doomed attempt to reach the North-west Passage in 1848, a mission which also cost the lives of 129 men. She quotes the comedian John Cleese on how the failure of people like Scott gets to the heart of what being English is truly about (as he puts it, it's 'not just that the highest form of English heroism is stoicism in the face of failure, but that in Scott's case a whiff of success might have tarnished the gallantry') and George Orwell, who once observed that while Ypres, Gallipoli, Mons and Passchendaele are household names, the British triumphs of the Great War were not so readily recalled. And it is notable that, alongside the monuments to Scott and Franklin, Waterloo Place also hosts several to that catastrophe, the Crimean War.

Barczewski concludes that the British belief that true heroism requires disaster is so entrenched in our psyche that we sometimes even reimagine parts of our history as disasters when they were not, such as the retreat at Dunkirk, and it's easy to think of other examples of heroic failure being fetishized. In football, we talk about the Hand of God incident involving Diego Maradona as much as our 1966 World Cup victory; Paul Gascoigne's tears during the 1990 World Cup semi-final are more famous than many glorious goals; and our most popular football song, 'Three Lions', features a chorus that celebrates 'thirty years of hurt'. In athletics the image of the Brownlee brothers – triathletes Alistair and Jonny – losing the World Triathlon Series in Mexico because Alistair shunned the chance to win the race to help his younger sibling, became as famous as any victory that year, while Fintan O'Toole has argued that Brexit has been a 'perfect vehicle for this zombie cult'. Barczewski is in no doubt about where this 'conscious sense of celebration of the striving for an object that was not attained' all comes from: empire. She illustrates her argument with the case of the Battle of Isandlwana in 1879, the first major conflict in the Anglo-Zulu War. General Lord Chelmsford, Commander in Chief of the British Army, considered his force to have superior military might, in both numbers and artillery. Confident that the Zulus would avoid pitched battle, he was strategically complacent, allowing a surprise attack from a massive Zulu force of 20,000 men. With no ability to consolidate, the British were defeated with a vast loss of life: 922 British soldiers were killed, as well as 840 African auxiliaries. The final death count reached 75 per cent of the original force. In order to draw some positives from the appalling loss of life, the British focused heavily on the last men standing who were surrounded but fought to the death – even when their ammunition failed them, they pulled out their knives. Poems were written about their bravery, and in 1884 the Irish artist R. T. Moynan painted a depiction of the last survivor in a Christ-like stance.

Then we have the example of General Gordon, the former Governor-General of the Sudan, who was present at the burning of the Imperial Summer Palace in China, and died in Khartoum in 1885 after being sent back to the country to deal with a Mahdi revolt. A hero to the British people – after he had commanded the army that put down the Taiping Rebellion during the Second Opium War – Gordon was ordered to evacuate the city of Khartoum immediately, before it was overrun by the Mahdist army. Instead, he resolved to stay, possibly in an attempt to rescue every civilian, but with the expectation that the British would send reinforcements. The relief came two days too late and by then Gordon was already dead. The British retreated from the Sudan and the whole exercise proved to be a massive failure. However, Gordon's memory received national recognition in a day of mourning and two services, held at Westminster Abbey and St Paul's Cathedral. Gordon's death captivated the nation: he was eulogized in portraiture, in poetry – his epitaph composed by Tennyson – and in popular notions of chivalry and Arthurian legend, in comparisons to the mythical Sir Lancelot. Apparently, the British government hadn't wanted to send Gordon there in the first place, but if Gladstone did so it was because the popular press, such as the *Pall Mall Gazette*, campaigned for him to embark on the mission, leading to crowds gathering to chant 'Gordon must go!'[9] – which brings us to the imperial psychological legacy that is jingoism.

Aggressive expressions of extreme patriotism have been a fact of life in the British media my entire lifetime, whether it was the *Sun* publishing headlines including 'STICK IT UP YOUR JUNTA!' 'INVASION!' 'IN WE GO!' and 'GOTCHA' during the Falklands War, or Piers Morgan's *Mirror* carrying coverage about a 1996 football tournament under a headline proclaiming 'THE MIRROR INVADES BERLIN'. 'There is a strange smell in Berlin,' claimed the piece. 'And it's not just their funny sausages. It's the smell of fear.' But such jingoism has accelerated in recent years with then Education Secretary Michael Gove penning an essay for the *Daily Mail* in 2014 in which he announced that the centenary of the First World War should be about 'battling left-wing myths that belittle Britain' and denounced historians who 'denigrate patriotism'. Not long afterwards Brexit was giving newspapers an excuse to run coverage variously campaigning for the return of blue British passports and dragging Big Ben out of hibernation to celebrate our withdrawal from the EU. At one point amid a row with Spain and the EU over the status of Gibraltar, readers of the *Daily Telegraph* were informed that although the once mighty Royal Navy was weaker than it used to be, it could still 'cripple' Spain if required. Such behaviour goes back directly to the age of New Imperialism of the late nineteenth century, when two Conservative popular newspapers were founded and embraced empire with enthusiasm. Colonialism was central to the *Daily Express* and the *Daily Mail*, the former declaring that its policy was 'patriotism' and its party 'the British empire', the latter defining itself as 'independent and Imperial' in its politics, and both of them investing considerable sums in detailed reporting of the Boer War. Kennedy Jones, the business partner of the *Daily Mail* owner, once remarked that imperialism 'was the policy on which we worked for the whole of my journalistic career – One Flag, One Empire, One Home. We are a single family . . . I have always found the British public deeply interested in Imperial affairs. There is a personal bond, a domestic tie.'[10]

Frankly, the tone of the *Daily Mail*'s coverage of empire during the jingoistic age of New Imperialism was not much different to its tone now in relation to Brexit, with the newspaper claiming that the festivities to mark Queen Victoria's sixty years on the throne, which under the influence of Colonial Secretary Joseph Chamberlain doubled as a 'Festival of the British Empire', testified to the 'Greatness of the British Race'.[11] The newspaper's star reporter waxed lyrical not only upon the fact that 'we possess all these remote outlandish places' but also that 'these people are working, not simply under us, but with us – that we send out a boy here and a boy there, and a boy takes hold of the savages of the part he comes to, and teaches them to march and shoot as he tells them, to obey him and to believe in him and to die for him and the Queen.' In 1929 the *Daily Express* organized a huge rally for Empire Day featuring parades, bands, choirs and addresses from the likes of Stanley Baldwin and the Bishop of Kensington. And, again in the age of New Imperialism, jingoism spread beyond the press to novelists (the popular writer G. A. Henty producing a stream of books with titles like *By Sheer Pluck*, *The Young Colonists* and *A Roving Commission, or, Through the Black Insurrection at Hayti*), advertisers (Colman's Flour were fond of the imperial leitmotif) and poets (the Poet Laureate Lord Tennyson was parodied in a journal called *Truth* in a poem entitled 'The Laureate Rampant or, Patriotism gone mad'). As with Brexit, it was not always clear whether these people and publications were whipping up jingoism or just reflecting its existence in the general population, but they all held the view that being British was the best thing that could happen to anyone, which brings us to another psychological legacy of empire: our national sense of exceptionalism.

We have already explored how British politics is shaped and defined by a profound sense of being special, but the idea that we are different to everyone else extends deeper into our culture and psychology. There is a popular view that Shakespeare is the best writer any country has ever had, that we have the best pop music and the most beautiful countryside and that we alone defeated evil in the twentieth century. When in the week of the seventy-fifth anniversary of VE Day *The Times* commissioned YouGov polls in four Western countries to explore perspectives on the Second World War, it found that while those in Germany, France and the US believed that America's efforts had contributed most to achieving victory in Europe, the British saw themselves as key. We Britons see the Second World War as a time when we 'stood alone' against Hitler. And Boris Johnson took up the theme in *that* imperialism-flecked conference speech of 2016, gloating about how we have a 'language that was invented and perfected in this country and now has more speakers than any other language on earth', how 'British soft power' is spearheaded by the global popularity of Jeremy Clarkson, J. K. Rowling and the BBC, how our athletes, coming from 'a country that can boast only 1 per cent of the world's population . . . came second in the Olympic and Paralympic games', and declaring that 'we have in the Foreign Office the finest diplomatic service in the world – covering far more countries than the French with only 70 per cent of the budget,' that 'we have the world's most superb intelligence services.' He added: 'Churchill was right when he said that the empires of the future will be empires of the mind.'

I wouldn't judge any Briton if they are moved by the gist of this – I am proud of some of these things too. The endless claims by our political leaders that we are 'world-beating' are occasionally right. I could even add some items to the list, such as the success of the Premier League around the world, our dominance of Formula 1 racing, the brilliance of our fashion designers, our facility for developing world-dominating TV formats, our theatre. And you can't blame anyone for being moved by the basic facts of the imperial project. After all, the British empire, on which the sun famously never set, was not only the biggest thing that ever happened to us, but one of the biggest things that ever happened to the world. At its height it covered a quarter of the world's land surface and governed nearly a quarter of the world's population – some 412 million people, according to the OECD. It embraced large swathes of Asia, Africa, North America and Australia, while forging close trade links with other regions, especially in South America. And it was all done with so few people. In 1899, the Colonial

Service had just 1,500 officials.[12] As Robert Tombs explains in 2014's *The English and their History*, there were fewer British soldiers in the whole of Northern India in 1857 than there were in Northern Ireland in the 1980s; in 1903 the Colonial Office comprised 113 clerks who oversaw an empire of over 100 separate political units and 600 Indian princely states, half the number of people in the modern Ministry of Defence's press office. The Indian Civil Service in the late nineteenth century numbered no more than 2,000 – smaller than Ofsted, today's school inspection service. The problems begin when you begin to miss it, when you fail to remember what actually happened – when these empires of the mind become a toxic cocktail of nostalgia and amnesia.

11. Selective Amnesia

Empire nostalgia is a veritable industry, literally in some instances. The tour operator Millis Potter, for example, offers 'Tea & Tiffin Colonial India Tours' which will, according to the marketing, let you 'delve into India's colonial past' and 'visit hill-stations, imperial cities and tea estates'. A firm called Mahlatini sells 'colonial-style safaris' which 'offer a taste of a bygone era where decadence, exploration and adventure were the spirit of the day' (with no mention of the violent racial suppression of the era) and allow you to stay at the Victoria Falls Hotel in Zimbabwe, which apparently has a 'colonial era . . . ambience' reminiscent of a time when, they say, Cecil Rhodes dreamed of building a railway from the 'Cape to Cairo' (no mention of Rhodes' other stated dream, 'the furtherance of the British empire and the bringing of the whole uncivilized world under British rule, for the recovery of the United States, and for making the Anglo-Saxon race but one empire'). Meanwhile, the Oxford Union flogged a cocktail called the Colonial Comeback during a debate about slavery reparations in 2015, Gourmet Burger Kitchen launched a burger called the Old Colonial in 2016, a London rum bar decided to call itself The Plantation in the same year and, incredibly, in 2020, the East India Company exists as a retail outlet.

You may have assumed that the East India Company was not a viable brand, considering it stopped existing in a meaningful sense in 1858 following decades of corruption, rebellion and misrule, yet today you can spot its name on shops from Central London to Qatar. Poetically, given that the Company's competitive advantages over colonial American tea importers led to the Boston Tea Party, tea is their main offering, including one called Royal Flush, from a bush planted by the Duke of Edinburgh in Ceylon in 1954 and served at the Queen's Diamond Jubilee in 2012, alongside other British essentials such as marmalade, digestive biscuits, cordial and nuts enrobed in chocolate. It is hard to conjure up a more ill-judged commercial venture. And it makes no odds that among the commemorative coins on sale there are a couple featuring Gandhi, or that the man heading the business, one Sanjiv Mehta, is Indian-born. In interviews, he has described the Company as 'the Google of its time' (I don't believe that Google has an army) and asserted that the East India Company 'brought the world together' (missing out the fact that it did so through force). He has also stated that 'the fact that an Indian now owns the East India Company means that the negative has become a positive,' but, you know, it really hasn't.

But I can imagine how a businessman might have thought it was a good idea to resurrect the brand. Presumably his people did some market research, and presumably this research brought up a notorious YouGov poll from 2014 in which 59 per cent of respondents deemed the British empire to be 'something to be proud of', only 19 per cent claimed to be 'ashamed' of its misdeeds, and more than a third claimed 'they would like it if Britain still had an empire.' Two years later, in January 2016, a YouGov poll found that 44 per cent of Britons thought their country's 'history of colonialism' was something to be proud of, and 43 per cent deemed the British empire to be a 'good thing'. More recently, in March 2020, a global YouGov poll found that 30 per cent of Britons believe former colonies were better off as part of the British empire.

So the number of people who feel nostalgic about empire might be falling but around a third of people in the UK still believe Britain's colonies were better off for being part of an empire, a higher proportion, according to the *Guardian* report of the poll results, 'than in any of the other major colonial powers'. And who can be surprised given the number of high-profile names who have emerged in recent years to celebrate empire. In bestselling books and popular TV shows, Niall Ferguson has argued that British empire shaped the modern world, spread democracy and was significantly more benign than other empires. Jeremy Black has offered a defence of empire, noting in a book 'the prominence of imperial rule in history and in the world today, and the selective way in which certain countries are castigated'; Andrew Roberts has argued that 'empire allowed two centuries of respite from the bloodshed that had been there before and which was likely to come again'; Michael Palin has claimed that the British empire is not as 'wicked' as it is often portrayed and we should stop apologizing for our past; while Nigel Biggar, Regius Professor of Moral and Pastoral Theology at Oxford University, has repeatedly complained that academics are too frightened to stand up for the British empire because it is not 'fashionable' and they fear they would get 'mobbed'.

The revivers of the East India Company may also have been encouraged by the popularity of the imperial aesthetic in Britain – an aesthetic that another tour operator, Ampersand, offering a 'GRAND COLONIAL TOUR OF ASIA: INDIA, SRI LANKA, BURMA, VIETNAM & SINGAPORE', highlights in its marketing when it trills about the appeal of 'polished teak floors, whirring ceiling fans, palm trees swaying in the breeze, clipped green lawns and crisp white linen-clad butlers serving you the perfect G&T'. It goes on to suggest that anyone starting the tour in London should dine at Gymkhana, before spending the night at Blakes Hotel. As it observes, the 'boutique hotel in South Kensington . . . has been decorated with echoes of empire', while Gymkhana has been inspired, according to the restaurant's own website, 'by the elite clubs of India where members of high society socialise, eat, drink, and play sport'. It's a vibe that has been fetishized by TV and film for as long as I can remember, through productions such as *Heat and Dust* in 1983, *The Jewel in the Crown* on ITV in 1984, David Lean's adaptation of E. M. Forster's *A Passage to India* in the same year, *The Best Exotic Marigold Hotel* in 2011, *Indian Summers* in 2015 and *Victoria & Abdul* and *Viceroy's House* in 2017.[1]

The single most tangible expression of nostalgia comes in the routine accusation that any commentary on the darker aspects of British empire is 'anti-British'. There was an illustration recently when Children's BBC posted a clip on Twitter of a song recorded for its *Horrible Histories* programme which had Queen Victoria discovering in musical form the foreign roots of so many typically British things. She was finding out, for instance, that British tea is actually from India ('Yes, for your cuppa thousands died and many wars were fought'), that sugar is from the Caribbean ('For sugar in your cup of tea, slavery's been supported'), that her British cotton vest is made from cotton from America, and picked by slaves again ('your empire's built on fighting wars, that's how your income's swollen'), and, in conclusion, that 'your British things are from abroad and most are frankly stolen'. It didn't strike me as particularly controversial, especially in the context of a show that employs comedy to educate, but the online reaction was intense. The journalist Iain Martin tweeted: 'Is the BBC on a mission to get itself closed down?' The broadcaster and publisher Andrew Neil tweeted: 'This is anti-British drivel of a high order. Was any of the licence fee used to produce something purely designed to demean us?' Admittedly, the outrage may have been amplified by the fact that the video was introduced by the comedian Nish Kumar, who linked the video's theme to Brexit, but such a response is routine in a country where, in the words of Jon Wilson, Professor of Modern History at King's College London: 'the broader public debate about empire is extremely thin and gets used as a proxy for nationalism.' When the Labour MP Lisa Nandy said she wanted to remove the word 'Empire' from the OBE (Officer of the Most Excellent Order of the British Empire) she was accused by Toby Young of being anti-British. When activists pulled down a statue of a seventeenth-century slave trader in Bristol, Melanie Phillips claimed that the very fabric of British identity was under assault: 'the freedom and values we hold dear are in peril.' When it was suggested there would be no singing along to the jingoistic 'Rule Britannia' at the 2020 BBC Proms, Nigel Farage tweeted: 'The woke agenda is to make us ashamed of who we are.' On a local level, in my home region, whenever it is pointed out that the linked chains featured on a new flag for the Black Country were produced in the region not only for industry but for the slave trade,[2] there are fevered accusations of disloyalty.

In short, there is a popular view that if you don't celebrate the empire you're 'anti-British'. And along with the demand that I be more 'grateful' for what Britain has given me (which I get whenever I comment critically on any aspect of British life), the suggestion that I am insulting Britain has been a common reaction to any comments I have made in public about the dark chapters of British empire, a reflex which is in itself, as we established a few chapters ago, a symptom of imperialism.* It's incredible that it even needs to be said, but to interrogate the dark episodes of British empire is not to criticize Britain, any more than discussing kamikaze pilots of the Second World War is anti-Japanese or talking about America's Civil War is anti-American. For this kind of nostalgia to blossom as it does, though, something else needs to thrive: selective amnesia. As Robert Saunders has put it: 'It is probably only possible to be nostalgic for empire if you forget most of its history.'

We have already touched upon some illustrations of such amnesia: as a nation we routinely forget the imperial precedents for modern wars; as a society, we forget not only that black and Asian people were invited to work here, but that many came as citizens; we forget more generally that Britain was built on immigration, Robert Winder observing that 'Britain has an amnesiac streak . . . when it comes to acknowledging the immigrant blood in her veins'; the imperial nature of the wealth that built and sustained many stately homes was deliberately concealed by owners and has been wilfully forgotten since. And it is easy to think of further examples of selective amnesia. Activists have been keen to point out during the national debate about statues that while Winston Churchill is remembered as a great war leader, his colonial attitudes, which arguably led to up to 4 million Indians dying

---

* For what it's worth, I am actually grateful for a great deal. And because the accusation will inevitably be levelled at me, I might as well spell out what I am grateful for: for having had a free education at one of the best grammar schools in the country; for having attended (for free) one of the best colleges at one of the most successful universities in the world; for an NHS that cares for the people I love the most; for a welfare state that saved my family from the most crushing consequences of poverty; for the chance to live in the greatest city on earth and work on two of the greatest newspapers in the world; for British pop music; for the glorious British countryside; for Pizza Express. But I resent being instructed to demonstrate my gratitude whenever I analyse any aspect of British life, when my white colleagues don't get the same treatment. Yes, I have had a better life than I would probably have had in India, but *I was born here*, not India, I am British, I am as entitled to comment on my home nation as the next man and the endless insistence that I display my gratitude is rooted in racism. Racism which is, in itself, rooted in the fact that the children of imperial immigrants born here are not always seen as fully British.

in the Great Bengal Famine of 1943–4, are erased. In the summer of 2020 more than 175 historians called on the Home Office to remove the history element of the UK citizenship test because of its 'misleading and false' representation of slavery and empire, including the way 'the abolition of slavery is treated as a British achievement, in which enslaved people themselves played no part', its silence 'about colonial protests, uprisings and independence movements', the highly contentious claim that slavery was illegal within Britain itself and the erroneous assertion that 'there was, for the most part, an orderly transition from empire to Commonwealth, with countries being granted their independence'. It has been argued that the imperial project has been ignored by literature, with Jonah Raskin claiming in 1971 that 'No Victorian wrote a good novel about the colonial world,' and our most famous painters preferring other subjects such as landscapes. Turner might have a watercolour of *The Fortress of Seringapatam* in his name, but he had never visited India himself: he relied on sketches by an amateur draughtsman.

The most significant manifestation of imperial amnesia is surely the way we forget the contribution empire made in both world wars. In 1914, it was not only Britain which took on the Germans and their allies, but the entire British empire: over 3,000,000 men from across the empire and Commonwealth supported the British Army; one academic has estimated that the war might have been 10 per cent more expensive without the colonies' support and British wartime deaths 30 per cent higher without imperial soldiers.[3] In the Second World War, the number of imperial soldiers was just as significant, including 1,440,500 troops from India, 629,000 from Canada, 413,000 from Australia, 136,000 from South Africa, 128,500 from New Zealand and more than 134,000 from other colonies.[4] Lizzie Collingham highlights how British empire sustained Britain in terms of 'supplies of men, arms and ammunition, raw materials and, above all, food' throughout the Second World War. There have been a few times when the imperial contribution has been recognized: during the First World War, British propaganda praised the assistance and co-operation of its Dominions and dependencies, asserting that the empire would emerge from the war as an even stronger entity. In

1921, the Chattri Memorial was constructed on the South Downs on the site where First World War Hindu and Sikh soldiers had been cremated after being hospitalized in Brighton's Royal Pavilion, Dome and Corn Exchange; in 2001 a commemorative gate appeared on London's Hyde Park Corner in honour of the overseas soldiers who fought for Britain in both wars. But in reality the aftermath of the First World War saw empire troops packed off back home with unseemly haste, and the huge celebratory Peace March that took place in London in July 1919 did not include any of these non-British troops.[5] In 1995 Norman Tebbit referred to the 'overwhelmingly English-speaking armies, from the United States of America, the empire and the Kingdom itself, which liberated Western Europe from the Nazi darkness'. In 1998 the late comedian Bernard Manning went on *The Mrs Merton Show* and declared 'there were no Pakis at Dunkirk' (he was not wrong in the literal sense: they were Indians at the time) and in 2020 the actor Laurence Fox became a media sensation after complaining about the inclusion of a British Sikh soldier in the First World War movie *1917*.

Indeed, the most serious and painful omission of my education was that during the years of being taught about world wars and sitting through endless remembrance services, no one cared to tell us, a racially diverse student body, that our people were there too. It is a form of amnesia in itself that our national story is built almost entirely around what this country did in two world wars, when, as Gideon Rachman has observed in the *Financial Times*, 'for a Martian historian, the most interesting thing about modern British history would surely be that the country built a massive global empire.' What a difference it would make if, within this story we endlessly tell ourselves, we acknowledged the truth of empire's role. Which brings us to the imperial amnesia of our education system. It's a challenging area to navigate because we all had an education, and the question of how much we were taught about empire quickly becomes one of competing biographies. Furthermore, it is difficult to discern exactly what, if anything, is taught to many children about empire today because academies, a fast-growing education sector, are not required to follow the national curriculum.

But the *Guardian* gathered GCSE exam data in 2020 and found that only up to 11 per cent of GCSE students are studying modules that refer to black people's contribution to Britain and less than one in ten are studying a module which concentrates on empire. No modules in the GCSE syllabus for the most popular exam board, Edexcel, mention black people in Britain. The Runnymede Trust has told us that of the students who choose to do history for GCSE only about 4 per cent of pupils are taking the 'Migration to Britain' option, which focuses on empire. Meanwhile, a campaign group pushing for the mandatory teaching of empire in schools called The Impact of Omission has been conducting an ongoing online survey and as of autumn 2020 has found that while 86 per cent of people were taught about the Tudors at school, and 72 per cent were taught about the Battle of Hastings and 73 per cent learned about the Great Fire of London, just 37 per cent were taught about transatlantic slavery, just 10 per cent were taught about the role of slavery in the British Industrial Revolution and just 8 per cent learned about the British colonization of Africa. As the economic anthropologist Jason Hickel put it in a tweet: 'If British people understood colonial history half as well as they understand the details of Henry VIII's wives, Britain would be a different country.' Furthermore, only 13 per cent of historians in UK universities specialize in the histories of Asia, Africa, Latin America or the Middle East, while the Royal Historical Society recently concluded in a report based on a year of research and a survey of over 700 university-based historians that 'the narrow scope of the school and university History curriculum is an obstacle to racial and ethnic diversity in History as a discipline.' It continued: 'if History wishes to improve its recruitment of BME students and to present a broad and inclusive range of perspectives on the past, the privileging of an "island story" of Britain (in both school-teaching and university-teaching) will need to be addressed.'

People who have attested to the poor teaching of empire include the historian Bernard Porter who has written that he did 'not remember the empire ever being discussed or even mentioned at home as a child', and at school he 'studied no imperial history whatsoever'. He first came to the subject at postgraduate level. The commentator Ian

Jack has written that when he 'did history at school, in the late 1950s and early 60s, we chose not to see [empire] at all', his history education sticking to 'the safe grooves offered by the causes of the Franco-Prussian war. Looking back, it seems an extraordinary omission.' The novelist Charlotte Mendelson tweeted recently that she did history at Oxford and supposedly had 'one of the best educations Britain can offer' from the ages of four to twenty-one, but she had been 'taught nothing about slavery or colonialism. Nothing. Ever.' Meanwhile, the former Prime Minister Tony Blair admitted in his autobiography that when Britain handed Hong Kong back to China in 1997, and the Chinese said it was an opportunity finally to put the past behind them, he 'had, at the time, only a fairly dim and sketchy understanding of what that past was'. A Gallup poll conducted in 1997 found that nearly two-thirds of people did not know which country Robert Clive was from, more than three-quarters had never heard of Cecil Rhodes, nearly four out of five could not identify a famous poem by Rudyard Kipling, nearly half thought Australia was still a colony and more than half did not know that the United States of America had once belonged to Britain. And the fact that the outrage and counter-outrage over the toppling of statues led to a group of men standing guard over a statue of the novelist George Eliot in Nuneaton (a writer known, by the way, for opposing slavery and anti-Semitism), surely speaks volumes.

There is perhaps an even starker illustration of imperial amnesia, and how it mingles with nostalgia to produce dysfunctional attitudes to empire, in Britain's obsession with India's railways. It feels impossible in the third decade of the third millennium to turn on the TV on any evening and not happen across a show like *Indian Hill Railways*, *Great Indian Railway Journeys*, *India's Frontier Railways* or *Extreme Railway Journeys* in which an invariably white presenter travels on trains in India and informs us how they were a gift British empire bestowed upon India. And after 'be more grateful' and 'where is your patriotism?', 'what about the railways?' has been another common response to any public remarks I've ever made about empire. In fact, it is so standard a response to any analysis of British empire that the historian Katherine Schofield has started employing the hashtags

#OccasionalMassacre #ButTheRailways to highlight examples of 'tiresome tub-thumping jingoism' on Twitter, and around a quarter of the letters I got about Jallianwala Bagh mentioned them. 'I was saddened that you too, a respected journalist and writer, seem to have fallen into the trap of generalising that all the British in India during the time of the empire were racists,' went one. 'You also asked what the British did for India. How long have you got? Do construction and other infrastructure projects count; railways and rolling stock, metalled and all-weather roads, bridges, reservoirs, canals and irrigation systems . . . A television programme on all these construction projects in India would redress the balance.'

Redress the balance? There are so many series about the Indian railways that it's actually more difficult to think of presenters who have *not* presented such shows than of presenters who have. And the myth they propound about Britain's generosity is expertly disassembled by Christian Wolmar in *Railways & the Raj*, where he approaches the subject not as an imperial historian but as a specialist on transport, with a bunch of authoritative books about railways under his belt. He acknowledges that the British may have been partly motivated by a 'civilizing mission' in India, quoting an official as saying 'if we are not in India to civilize and raise India, we had better leave it as soon as we can,' yet he is categorical that they did not build the railways there as an act of charity. Accessing India's rural states meant that goods manufactured in Britain could reach a huge market. As well as commercial interests, railway construction in India was also intended to aid the empire's military: troop trains would allow faster mobilization, and so enable the British to reduce their reliance on expensive military garrisons. As a result, some stations, such as the one at Lahore, were fortified and 'looked more like a medieval castle than a welcoming entrance to a key transport network'. During the First World War, a vast number of carriages were removed and taken to France, with some lines stripped bare – never mind the local population that relied on the train service.

Furthermore, the financing of railway construction was intended to benefit the British rather than the Indians. In 1849, the British government announced that it would guarantee private companies a 5 per cent return in the scheme; the shortfall would be the responsibility of the Indian government (in other words, the Indian taxpayer). Many British investors seized the opportunity, and the system inevitably bred inefficiency, because getting a guaranteed steady return meant that the investors were not incentivized to ensure competence. There was much corner-cutting in the construction process; moreover, the assumption that British materials were innately superior meant that Britain did not allow the development of a local industry to supply the rolling stock and locomotives for the railways, preferring to import what was needed from home. In 1869, there were a thousand steam locomotives running in India; not a single one had been built there. Industries that supported the railways, such as steelworks and coal-mining, were also dominated by British-based companies. During construction, the British railway companies made no effort to ensure the health and safety of their local employees, who were also exposed to diseases such as cholera: as a result many were killed, not least the estimated 25,000 who lost their lives during an eight-year construction of just two railway sections crossing the Thal and Bhor Ghats, making it possibly 'the deadliest railway project ever undertaken in the world'. A significant minority of the Indian workforce – and presumably of this body count – were children. Even for the best-paid local workers, wages were desperately low, and frequently suffered deductions without cause or were completely withheld. And there was no chance of promotion: the British believed that Indians were inherently incompetent, and so they were not allowed near most managerial, supervisory and technical positions. Simply put, the system of employment on the railways was overtly racist.

The first-class service on Indian trains was described by the author Mark Twain as the best of any luxury trains in the world – 'no car in any country is quite its equal for comfort (and privacy)' – but the third-class carriages, used by the vast majority of Indians, were a different story. Not only were they wildly overcrowded, because railway operators oversold tickets, but there were no toilet facilities, and for the first two decades of railway service the doors of carriages were even locked during stops. In the event of death or injury during the journey, 'native' passengers were not eligible for the same

compensation as the British received. The system also fostered existing class and religious divisions, such as on the East Indian Railway,
where Hindus and Muslims had separate waiting rooms. And perhaps
the worst outrage of all, although the railways were hailed by the
British authorities as a means of alleviating famine, in reality the
officials used funds which had been ring-fenced for famine relief for
private sector railway expansion. So well-upholstered British politicians and civil servants benefited from the taxes of poverty-stricken
peasants, which should have been used to prevent widespread starvation. Finally there is the false implication in many British TV shows
on Indian railways that the British bequeathed the legacy of a railway
system that remains intact and in use today. True, the British left
behind a basic framework for further expansion, but the transformation
of the railways into a nationwide system came as a result of the efforts
and innovations of an independent India, which also vastly improved
welfare standards for those working for it and travelling on it.

I was so struck by Wolmar's book that, in addition to the challenge
of turning this project into a TV series in the middle of a global pandemic, I pitched the idea of a documentary about the true story of the
Indian railways to a producer. His reply? 'Viewers don't like to have
their prejudices challenged.' The remark depressed me, but I also
appreciated his frankness, for it is a fact that terrestrial television's
increasingly elderly viewers watch railway programmes to be com-
forted, and probably wouldn't be interested to learn that their favourite
shows are based on a myth. Unfortunately, this is also seemingly what
we, as a nation, want from our history. As the former British Museum
Director Neil MacGregor once put it: 'What is very remarkable about
German history as a whole is that the Germans use their history to
think about the future, where the British tend to use their history
to comfort themselves.' But why are we like this? Why do we struggle to
look our history in the eye? When other countries with difficult histories, such as Germany, do not? Having spent nearly two years
thinking about it, a number of explanations have transpired, not least
the fact that we have not, as a nation, been invaded or occupied in
modern times. As a result we have never been forced to interrogate
our behaviour, in the way that the Germans, the Japanese and the

French were forced to do after the Second World War. As the character Whisky Sisodia remarks in Salman Rushdie's *Satanic Verses*, 'The trouble with the Engenglish is that their hiss hiss history happened overseas, so they dodo don't know what it means.'

Furthermore, we have a long tradition of playing down imperialism in this country. As William Dalrymple points out, while the East India Company 'had always found it useful to behave with great ostentation in India' it 'had correspondingly found it advantageous to downplay its immense wealth at the London end of its operations'. In 1621, twenty years after it had been established, the Company had only six permanent members of staff, and operated out of the home of its Governor, Sir Thomas Smythe. Only when it had been in business for almost half a century did it finally move to a dedicated building in Leadenhall Street. This new HQ was modest, but a clue to its character lay in its first-storey façade, which featured a frieze of galleons cutting through the sea. As several academics point out in essays in *The East India Company at Home, 1757–1857*, while a couple of nabobs celebrated their subcontinental links, company employees were generally careful to conceal how exactly they came into their wealth. The British profited from slavery for many decades, brutalized and exploited millions, paid compensation of £20 million to former slave owners while offering the slaves nothing – but the moment Britain abolished it, abolition became the main narrative. After losing the First Opium War against Britain, China was forced to open itself to free trade in hard drugs, an episode which set in motion what the Chinese refer to as the 'Century of Humiliation',* but the *Illustrated London News* took a different tack, portraying the conflict as a righteous crusade against an Eastern dictatorship in the name of free trade, while the Treaty of Nanking, which ended the war, didn't even mention opium.[6] And the narrative that empire was

---

* Writing in 1895, the Chinese scholar Yan Fu described these events thus: 'A group of island barbarians wearing wild clothes, with a birdlike language and animal-like faces, sailed to our shores from thousands of miles away and knocked on our gates, requesting access. When they failed to attain their aims, they breached our coastal defenses, imprisoned the officials of our land, and even burned the palaces of our emperor.'

a noble enterprise dedicated to improving the lives of its subjects even survived the Boer Wars when Lord Kitchener's 'scorched-earth policy' resulted in as many as 30,000 homes being destroyed and around 48,000 people dying in British concentration camps in South Africa.[7]

Also, evidence of imperialism was sometimes deliberately destroyed or obscured. In 1961, the Secretary of State for the Colonies, Iain Macleod, ordered that post-independence governments be denied access to any material that 'might embarrass' Her Majesty's government or members of the police, military forces or public servants, or that might compromise intelligence sources, or that might 'be used unethically by ministers in the successor government'. Meanwhile, an official review concluded in 2012 that thousands of documents detailing deplorable acts committed during the dying days of the British empire had been destroyed, while others were kept sealed, in breach of legal obligations to pass them into the public domain. Among these illegally hidden papers, secreted for half a century in a Foreign Office archive, out of view of historians, journalists and other interested parties, were records proving that ministers in London were aware of the horrors inflicted on Mau Mau insurgents in Kenya, including the murder of a man who was said to have been 'roasted alive'; intelligence reports on the 'elimination' of those opposed to the colonial regime in 1950s Malaya; and details of how the UK forcibly displaced islanders from Diego Garcia in the Indian Ocean around 1970.[8]

Fourth, historians have observed how constituent parts of the United Kingdom have struggled to accept their role in imperialism and slavery for their own particular local reasons. 'The speed with which Scots have forgotten about the British empire and the prominent part they played in it is itself pathological,' Neal Ascherson has observed in an essay.[9] 'Rising national consciousness has much to do with this amnesia. Scotland, to generalize, prefers to regard itself as a virtuous little country which has tried to do good things in the world but has often been misled by its big neighbour: as Jackie Kay put it, sardonically: "a hard-done-to wee nation, yet bonny and blithe".' Meanwhile Andrew Thompson has asked out loud why there has 'been so little writing on Welsh involvement in empire', and concluded that it is because 'For far too long [historians have] conveniently buried aspects of both Welsh and imperial history. Dominated by the ideologies of socialism and nationalism, post-war Welsh politics proved reluctant to integrate colonial activity into Welsh history – similar silences have also been observed in the history of Glasgow.'

A fifth reason we struggle, as a country, to accept what happened with British empire is that the public have arguably never been particularly aware of empire in Britain. The extent of what the public ever understood about Britain's imperial projects is the subject of intense academic debate, but during the First World War H. G. Wells famously observed that 'nineteen people out of twenty, the lower class and the middle class, knew no more of the empire than they did of the Argentine Republic or the Italian Renaissance.' In 1860 John Bright observed that 'the English people . . . are very slow and very careless about everything that does not immediately affect them. They cannot be excited to any effort of India except under the pressure of some great calamity, and when that calamity is removed they fall back into their usual state of apathy.' Meanwhile, people like Lord Meath and the Royal Colonial Institute fretted so much about the lack of public appreciation of empire that they tried to do something about it, the former setting up Empire Day and the latter running essay competitions on imperial topics for schoolchildren and university students. Nevertheless, a survey in 1948 found that three-quarters of people were unaware of the distinction between a colony and a dominion, that nearly half could not name a single colony and that 3 per cent believed the United States was still part of empire. One person cited 'Lincolnshire' as a colony.[10]

Sixth, there is the realization I was hit with when I started this project: that empire is a really difficult thing to comprehend. As Samir Puri puts it, 'it is . . . far easier to comprehend the six-year event of the war [of 1939–45], with its clear beginning and end, than it is to take in the empire which was a five-centuries-long state of being and of mind . . . empire defies straightforward characterization, and lasted for too long, spread over too large an expanse, for it to be easily encapsulated in a simple formula.' He adds that empire

cannot be dismissed or celebrated as entirely exploitative or benevolent, nor did it end at one clear point, instead being undone over
various episodes, 'gradually depositing its various legacies into the
British psyche. So there was no single moment of public reckoning
when the empire collapsed.' I would add that the Second World War
story, in which we defeated the evil, racist Nazis, is easier to digest
morally too.

Which brings us to another possibility that presents itself: that the
history is just too painful to digest. I've had personal experience of
how such amnesia can work with individuals, having written a memoir confronting the darkest episodes in my family history. I spent
years reconstructing the story, going over it again and again in
incredible detail, but as soon as I finished I began forgetting it: in the
years that have followed publication, I've done such a good job that I
sometimes meet strangers who seemingly know more about my family life than I do. I've since realized that families have secrets for a
reason: it is hard to function if you walk around with full knowledge
of every terrible thing that has ever happened. It is important to forget for your own mental health, and that the same might be true for
nations was alluded to as a possibility by Ernest Renan when he
observed that 'the essence of a nation is that all of its individuals have
many things in common, and also that everyone has forgotten many
things.' And there is an illustration of how such amnesia might work
in practice in the single best book I've ever read on slavery – *The
Trader, The Owner, The Slave* by James Walvin.

Coming in at just over 250 pages of generously spaced text, it is
certainly not the longest book on the subject. Nor is it the most
famous. But in efficiently telling the stories of three men – John
Newton, the captain of a slave ship, who later became a preacher,
Thomas Thistlewood, a slave owner who made a small fortune from
a plantation in Jamaica, and the black slave Olaudah Equiano, who
secured his freedom, wrote an autobiography and became a leading
black figure in the campaign against the slave trade – Walvin not
only humanizes a trade that can feel complex, but deftly reveals how
slavery, like so many aspects of empire, has been erased from the
British consciousness and conscience. As the historian David Olusoga

has observed, 'Few acts of collective forgetting have been as thorough and as successful as the erasing of slavery from Britain's "island story",' and the complex ways this amnesia may have worked is revealed through these characters.

Olaudah Equiano, for instance, provides an illustration of how the slaves themselves have been forgotten. The man led a truly extraordinary life: a child slave, he was sold several times, including to a Royal Navy officer, before purchasing his freedom in 1766 and becoming a prominent abolitionist. His autobiography, *The Interesting Narrative of the Life of Olaudah Equiano*, in which he wrote about the horrors of slavery, was reprinted nine times in his lifetime and helped the cause to gain traction, leading to the British Slave Trade Act of 1807, which abolished the trade. The book was remarkable not just for exposing the horrors of the slave trade, but also for what it revealed about Equiano – how, for instance, when he first saw a sailor reading, he assumed the man was talking to the text ('I have often taken up a book, and have talked to it, and then put my ears to it, when alone, in hopes it would answer me; and I have been very much concerned when I found it remained silent'). Equiano was also a pioneer, like Dean Mahomed, in his private life, marrying Susannah Cullen, from Cambridgeshire, who had subscribed to his book and probably met him during one of his book tours, and having two children with her.

But after his death, like Mahomed and so many early British multicultural figures, he was forgotten. Within a few years he and his autobiography had been erased from public memory, abolition seemingly removing his importance and relevance. It took more than 150 years for his reputation to be resurrected, and the way abolition made so many forget about the fact that Britain had ever engaged in the global slave trade crops up repeatedly as a pattern. As Margot Finn and Kate Smith point out: 'Moral revulsion for Britain's central role in slavery and the slave trade encouraged propertied and powerful families to remove both material and text-based evidence of Caribbean colonialism from the historical record.' And as Alice Procter observes in *The Whole Picture*, no paintings of black abolitionists such as Olaudah Equiano, Ottobah Cugoano and 'the other members of the London-based Sons of Africa group, formerly enslaved Black men who were campaigning to end slavery well before Wilberforce got involved', have ever been identified. In the UK, there are many more monuments to notable men and women who owned slaves, and to William Wilberforce, the white man most strongly associated with abolition, than to the actual victims and survivors of enslavement. The human victims of this crime against humanity have been forgotten.

The next figure in Walvin's book is John Newton, the author of hymns including 'Amazing Grace' and 'Glorious Things of Thee Are Spoken', who provides an illustration of how the British have always struggled to face up fully to the brutality of what they did. His story appears at first to be one of reconciliation: of a man facing up to his mistakes and thenceforth living a life of repentance. After several years at the heart of the slave trade, captaining slave ships, Newton found God, renounced his past and became a vocal supporter of abolitionism. His testimony in pamphlets like *Thoughts upon the African Slave Trade*, in which he claimed that his personal story 'will always be a subject of humiliating reflection to me, that I was once an active instrument in a business at which my heart now shudders', was a powerful weapon in the battle for abolition. But when *The Times* remarked in his obituary on his 'unblemished life', they were off the mark. A superficial survey of his life tempts you to imagine that his religious awakening made him see the evil in the buying and selling of human souls, but the fact is that it was *after* his supposed epiphany that Newton became the first mate and then the captain of a number of slave ships, and it wasn't until much later that he began to question the morality of his trade. Moreover, when he wrote and talked about his experience, he didn't face up to what he had done with full frankness. For instance, in *Thoughts upon the African Slave Trade* he wrote that 'I have seen them [slaves] agonizing for hours, I believe for days together, under the torture of the thumbscrews; a dreadful engine, which if the screw be turned by an unrelenting hand, can give intolerable anguish.' But he hadn't just witnessed it, he had ordered it, and on several occasions. When he claimed later that he 'felt the disagreeableness of the business very strongly', that 'the officer of gaoler, and the restraints under which I was forced to keep my prisoners, were not suitable to my feelings', he failed to mention his considerable wages and bonuses. When he joined the campaign for abolition, he wrote that the slave trade was an 'unhappy and disgraceful branch of commerce', which formed a 'stain of our national character', but he had not complained about it in all the years he had participated or in the decades that had passed since giving it up.

Such distancing seems to be common among Britons involved in the slave trade. Edward Said noted it in his reading of Jane Austen's *Mansfield Park* (1814), in which we're told that Sir Thomas Bertram, the owner of Mansfield Park, got rich from business interests in the West Indies, but when, at one point, a character mentions she had brought up the subject of slavery with Bertram, she reports, 'there was such a dead silence!'* Such repression has been observed in real life too, former slave owners who received colossal amounts of compensation gloating about Britain's moral superiority and castigating other slave-owning nations, and the nation identifying itself as the country that enforced abolition. It is a narrative which is maintained today, with Michael Gove able to talk in an important speech about how we led the world in abolition, without mentioning that we also led the slave trade for decades beforehand.

The most disturbing form of erasure, however, is presented in Walvin's third case study: Thomas Thistlewood, a slave owner in Jamaica. What he demonstrates is not amnesia in a precise sense but the denial, or cognitive dissonance, which surely leads to amnesia. The man was nothing less than a sadist. When he bought his slaves, they were branded with 'TT' on their shoulder, renamed and their characteristics listed, and he kept detailed notes in his diary on what he did to them. This tells us that he once broke an English oak stick when beating a slave. He had a runaway slave savagely whipped, and then had the wounds marinated in salt, pepper and lime juice. When one slave was discovered eating sugar cane because food was scarce, Thistlewood 'had him well flogged and pickled, then made Hector [another slave] shit in his mouth'. When a third slave ran away, he 'gave him a moderate whipping, pickled him well, made Hector shit in his mouth,

---

* 'Did you not hear me ask about the slave trade last night?'

'I did – and I was in hopes the question would be followed up by others. It would have pleased your uncle to be inquired of farther.'

'And I longed to do it – but there was such a dead silence!'

immediately put in a gag whilst his mouth is full and made him wear it 4 or 5 hours'. The next week he did the same twice to a female slave and also whipped Hector for losing his hoe and made New Negro Joe piss in his eyes and mouth. He also 'gagged' a slave, 'locked his hands together, rubbed him with molasses and exposed him naked to the flies all day and to the mosquitoes all night'.

Throughout his time in Jamaica Thistlewood was also a serial rapist of female slaves, taking whoever he wanted whenever he wanted, not caring who saw him. He lived in Jamaica for thirty-seven years and by his own account had sex on 3,852 occasions, infecting many of his slaves with venereal disease. In a typical year he had fourteen different sexual partners and had sex 108 times. Handing out a whipping never prevented him from returning to the same woman for sex: having chastised them physically, he punished them sexually. Occasionally slaves told him to his face that they despaired of life, and he noted their misery: we hear in his diary, for example, that Moll drowned herself in 1756, that Mocho Jimmy tried to hang himself in 1780, that Phoebe was flogged 'for wishing she was dead already', while his house servant, Jimmy, remarked that 'if this is living, he did not care whether he lived or died'. But the thing is, at the same time Thistlewood saw himself as refined. He read widely, considered himself a man of the eighteenth-century Enlightenment, kept himself informed of the latest intellectual trends, was a book lover, amateur scientist and botanist, gaped in wonder at the appearance of Halley's Comet in 1759 and was seemingly always eager to improve himself. Despite living on the edge of British empire in the furthest corner of Jamaica, he and his fellow bookworms indulged in the sophisticated pleasure of reading and book ownership. For more than thirty years he kept a regular account of the weather in all its tropical variety. Between 1765 and 1768 he imported 139 varieties of flora from England. Also, a black slave, Phibbah, became his common-law wife. When Thistlewood left for another plantation, she gave him a gold ring and also visited him in his new post. Their relationship lasted thirty years, she had a son (Mulatto John) and when Thistlewood died in 1785 his will requested her manumission.

It would be hyperbolic to say this man is typical of imperial Britons in any way. But his cognitive dissonance, his ability to compartmentalize, his refusal to accept the brutal reality of what he was doing even as he cultivated a sophisticated demeanour, echo a psychological pattern that is common in British approaches to slavery. You see it in the way *The Oxford Dictionary of National Biography* swerves away from the phrase 'slave owner' in favour of euphemistic expressions like 'plantation owner' and 'West Indies merchant', while slavery is described as possessing 'considerable property in Jamaica'. It is evident when you read historians describe slave owners as 'adventurers' and the slavery system as 'plantation agriculture', and use euphemistic terms such as 'appropriation' and 'importation' when they're talking about theft, kidnapping and forced enslavement. And you see examples of such cognitive dissonance in British attitudes to empire in general. Such as when Jan Morris tells a story about 'the young Mahdist commander Emir Mahmoud, captured by Kitchener at Berber in 1897': 'Chains were riveted around his ankles, an iron halter was put around his neck, his hands were bound behind him, and he was paraded in ignominy through town' behind Kitchener, sometimes being dragged, sometimes running, being whipped when he fell. Morris then claims in the next paragraph that while 'Every empire rests on force . . . the British were not habitually cruel.' Such as when Prime Minister David Cameron declared while visiting the Indian city of Amritsar, scene of the 1919 infamous massacre, 'I think there's an enormous amount to be proud of in what the British empire did and was responsible for.' And such as when Liam Fox claimed that 'The United Kingdom is one of the few countries in the European Union that does not need to bury its twentieth-century history.'

We are not alone in this refusal to face up to difficult facts. The aforementioned 2020 YouGov survey of international attitudes to colonialism found that the Dutch are actually even more proud of their former empire than us, with half of Dutch people saying their old empire – which counted South Africa and Indonesia among its territories – is something to be proud of rather than ashamed of. And a few years ago I took a 500-mile round trip across the Deep South, where there were once nearly 50,000 slave plantations, powered by a slave labour force which hit 4 million at its height. Touring some former plantations – or 'great historic houses', as they call themselves – I discovered that they don't do a brilliant job of relaying their history. At the Greek Revival Anchuca Mansion in Vicksburg, Mississippi, none of the visitor bumph I read, nor the video played for me, mentioned the word 'slave'. The Monmouth Plantation in Natchez, Mississippi, briefly acknowledged the existence of slaves in its official material, but the tour guide shied away from the subject, talking, for instance, about how all the bricks for the house were made on site, neglecting to mention that they were made by slaves on site, and referred to the giftshop as originally being the 'servants' quarters', when it was actually used to house slaves. Meanwhile, at the Oak Alley Plantation Mansion in Vacherie, Louisiana, I struck up conversation with a white Southerner who remarked, casually: 'People emphasize the negative side of slavery too much.' But slavery is at least present as a fact in US popular culture: the trip was commissioned as a result of the success of *12 Years a Slave*, and I went to the Oak Alley Plantation because it was one of the locations used in the film. In Britain, in contrast, we act like we were never involved in slavery, let alone acknowledge that there were actual black slaves in Britain.

The impulses behind such amnesia are easy to understand. There have been many stages in educating myself about British empire when I have wanted to look away. When reading about Thistlewood, or about Captain Cornelius Hodges, a man who worked for the Royal African Company in the Gambia area and who, when his African wife had given birth to a black baby, accused her of committing an infidelity and crushed the infant in a mortar and fed it to dogs,[11] I have longed to do something else instead. I love my country and want to believe the best things about it. If I found nostalgic BBC2 programmes about the Indian railways soothing, I would have happily watched them instead. But the problem is, if you don't face up to these uncomfortable facts, you'll never be able to navigate a path forwards. Freudian psychoanalysts believe that if you deny or repress a traumatic experience, you risk acting out versions of the original trauma in ways that can be self-defeating. If we don't confront the reality of what happened in British empire, we will never be able to work out who we are or who we want to be.

12.   Working Off the Past

It has been surreal and exciting to see my concerns, towards the end of my journey into imperial history, inspire national news stories and debate. As the Black Lives Matter movement has encouraged a re-evaluation of imperial monuments, mainstream programmes like the *BBC News at Ten* have run items on how British empire explains racism not only in Britain but in the USA too, there have been debates across the British media about the economic legacies of empire, and major institutions like the National Trust and the Bank of England have started to assess their colonial heritage out loud.

The only thing I can compare it to, emotionally, is being a fan of an obscure R&B artist from Barnet, who became momentarily famous when Robbie Williams covered one of his songs, and I started hearing his music being whistled by builders on my street. I didn't, in truth, think these themes would *ever* become a mainstream concern, yet alone so suddenly and quickly. But if I do not consider our monuments worthy, in themselves, of lengthy discussion as an imperial legacy, it's because they're *just monuments*. The debates they have inspired have been thrilling, but I doubt most people were aware of the statues which are now deemed so contentious, and it doesn't feel particularly controversial that some are being taken down.

Those upset by the removal of statues routinely claim that such gestures 'erase' history. But monuments are not in themselves history. As Simon Schama has put it: 'It is more usually statues, lording it over civic space, which shut off debate through their invitation to reverence.' Nazi history was not deleted when streets were given back their old names after the defeat of Hitler in Germany, and Iraqi history was not altered by statues of Saddam Hussein being toppled after his defeat in the Iraq War of 2003. And, frankly, some of the most controversial commemorations were provocative when they were put up. The statue of Colston in Bristol was put up nearly two centuries after his death by businessman James Arrowsmith, whose efforts to raise £1,000 (£448,000 in today's prices) failed even after the statue was unveiled in 1895.[1] And when it was proposed that a tribute to Robert Clive be put up in Whitehall, the Viceroy of India, Lord Minto, struggling to deal with unrest caused by a predecessor's partition of Bengal, called it 'needlessly provocative'.[2]

Moreover, I hope this book has demonstrated how the British empire is absolutely embedded within us and how there are many more serious and troubling imperial legacies. More important than statues is that the museums which are so part of our national life refuse to engage honestly and sincerely with the question of how they obtained their imperial artefacts. The way we fail to acknowledge we are a multicultural society because we had a multicultural empire makes our national conversations about race tragic and absurd. The manner in which our imperial history inspires a sense of exceptionalism results in dysfunctional politics and disastrous decision-making. Our collective amnesia about the fact that we were, as a nation, wilfully white supremacist and occasionally genocidal, and our failure to understand how this informs modern-day racism, are catastrophic. I can see why it could be offensive for a black person to walk past a statue of a slave trader in their own city, and I personally find it degrading, as a British Indian, that, when I go to see anyone in government, I often have to encounter a statue of Robert Clive, who was widely loathed during his lifetime, who according to Samuel Johnson 'had acquired his fortune by such crimes that his consciousness of them impelled him to cut his own throat', and who when he committed suicide in 1774 was secretly buried in an unmarked grave. But these other legacies are more serious: at worst, they curtail and destroy lives.

It is puerile to reduce imperial history to a matter of 'good' and 'bad': trying to weigh up the positive and negative in this way is like defending the morality of kicking a random old man in the shins one afternoon because you helped an old lady across the road in the morning. The 'balance sheet' approach to British empire is ludicrous: I don't 'love' or 'hate' empire any more than I did when I started. But when you're considering the contemporary legacies of this complicated history, they can be weighed up. And while I'm glad empire gave us our multiculturalism, our internationalism, a certain tradition of anti-racism, and laid the foundations of the welfare state, and while I delight in the fact that our language, art and cuisine reflect our complex history, our imperial legacies and the ways we fail to see them are a burden. At a time of division and anxiety, when we are living through some of the greatest upheavals in modern history, we can progress only if we confront them.

I began by suggesting, half seriously, how a new Empire Day might be part of the solution, but it wouldn't. Like Black History Month, it would perpetuate the idea that imperial history is separate from regular history, when it *is* regular history. There is evidence that Empire Day didn't even work for the imperialists who conceived it: lots of children just saw it as a half-day holiday, barely registering the lessons it was meant to implant. Let's face it, only the balanced and compulsory study of British empire in British schools would solve our many dysfunctions when it comes to imperialism, and increasing numbers of serious people are advocating it. Race-equality think tank the Runnymede Trust has called for lessons on migration, belonging and empire to be made mandatory in every secondary school in England. A campaign calling itself 'Fill in the Blanks', led by sixth-form students from South London, all of whom have family from former British colonies, seeks 'to mandate the teaching of colonial history'. The historian William Dalrymple has described as a 'real problem' the fact that 'in Britain, study of the empire is still largely absent from the history curriculum . . . Now, more than ever, we badly need to understand what is common knowledge elsewhere: that for much of history we were an aggressively racist and expansionist force responsible for violence, injustice and war crimes on every continent.'

Notably absent from this campaign are most of the aforementioned historians and public figures who argue that British empire was glorious. Which makes you wonder: if it was so glorious, why not back initiatives calling for the balanced teaching of it to become compulsory? There is also a vocal group of anti-'woke' protestors who complain whenever organizations like the National Trust make efforts to educate the public about the imperial history of their assets: threatening to cancel their membership of an organization that highlights history for the crime of highlighting actual history. These tensions focus attention on a serious stumbling block in the way of achieving the goal: in more than a hundred years, we have not, as a country, ever reached a consensus as to what should be taught. I promise this is the last time I draw a parallel with the past, but arguments about how and what we should teach British children about imperialism go back to the age of empire, when everyone from Lord Meath to the Navy League, the League of Empire and the Royal Colonial Institute campaigned to encourage the teaching and celebration of empire. As Andrew Thompson explains, they faced opposition in the early twentieth century from local education authorities which 'did not wish to see their classrooms converted into pulpits', from the National Union of Teachers which 'jealously guarded the autonomy of the individual teacher' and from individual teachers, some of them Communists and socialists, who refused to participate in Empire Day activities and, in isolated cases, proffered alternative views of colonialism.

Such tensions have only deepened and re-emerged in the modern age, with every sign of progress seemingly being matched with a regressive move. As I write, Tim Reeve, the Deputy Director of the V&A, has indicated in remarks to the Cheltenham Literature Festival that his museum has started talks with the Ethiopian embassy over returning looted treasures in its collections.[3] But at the same time, Oliver Dowden, the Culture Secretary, has recently warned museums and galleries, in a leaked letter, to cease removing controversial artefacts or risk losing funding. Prime Minister Johnson has just marked the start of Black History Month with a social media message celebrating notable black Britons and remarking that 'all too often we often forget that Black history and British history are one and the same.' But at the same time he has criticized Black Lives Matter protestors (making the same argument), and insisted he is a 'huge admirer' of an aide who has previously questioned the existence of institutional racism and hit out at a 'culture of grievance' among anti-racism campaigners.[4] And it's not surprising that, in the face of this, some are defeatist.

There have been times during the past two years of personal investigation when I have felt bleak about the lack of consensus – not least when the government rejected calls to add more black, Asian and ethnic minority history to the English national curriculum. Sometimes it feels as if our national divisions over empire are deepening, not healing. Ultimately, however, I am optimistic that things can improve, not least because the experience of other countries dealing with difficult histories shows that narratives can change. On a visit to Algiers in early 2017, President Macron gave a speech in which he said that his country's colonialism was 'a crime against humanity, a real barbarity. It is a past that we must confront squarely and [we must] apologize to those we have harmed.' His statement conflicted with the 2005 law that compelled places of education to teach the 'positive' aspects of French imperialism, and he has since followed through with a number of specific policies on subjects such as the repatriation of colonial artefacts in French museums. New Zealand recently announced changes to its education curriculum which will see a wider range of experiences incorporated into history teaching (everything from the arrival of Māori in Aotearoa and first encounters and early colonial history of Aotearoa New Zealand to New Zealand's role in the Pacific) and more of the country's history becoming mandatory in schools.

There has also been movement in America, which we like to see as more screwed up than us, but which has started taking the idea of reparations for slavery seriously. A report for the Roosevelt Institute think tank, written by Duke University professor William Darity and A. Kirsten Mullen, suggested that a figure between $10 trillion and $12 trillion could 'serve as the baseline for black reparations in the 21st century' payable by the United States – a sum that may be a fraction of the $777 trillion that we earlier heard the African World Reparations and Repatriation Truth Commission has suggested the West pays as compensation for lives lost during the African slave trade, and equivalent to half the annual GDP of the US according to the *FT*. While such a payout seems unlikely, high-level Democrats like Elizabeth Warren, Kamala Harris and Joe Biden have called for a national dialogue, with Biden declaring he would support financial reparations to African Americans and Native Americans if studies showed them to be feasible, and California recently became the first American state to pass legislation to begin the process of paying reparations.[5] Reflecting on the change of tone in the conversation, Sue Neiman, an American philosopher, cultural commentator and essayist, has expressed her surprise that what had once been 'a minority position' should play a role in a presidential race and that the *New York Times* should print an argument for reparations.

> Polls show that the majority of white Americans still oppose them, as the majority of Germans opposed reparations for the Holocaust in the early years after the war. Yet the fact that what was so recently the province of a few intellectuals is now part of a national conversation is as good a sign of progress as any I know . . . Americans could start by simply asking Congress to pass H.R.40, a resolution made and denied every year since 1987, which would create a commission to study appropriate remedies for slavery. It cannot be too much to expect the U.S. Congress to do in the twenty-first century what the German parliament did in 1952.

Neiman makes the comparison between the USA and Germany in *Learning from the Germans*, a fascinating study of how the two countries have dealt with their respective racist legacies, which reflects her own experience of growing up in the American South during the civil rights era and spending her adult life around Berlin as a Jewish woman. The book explains how the Germans have a word – *Vergangenheitsaufarbeitung*, which translates as 'working off the past' – to describe how they have come to terms with Nazism and the Holocaust in a deep and systematic way. The nation's acts of remembrance and remorse have included: Willy Brandt, as Chancellor of Germany, sinking to his knees at the Warsaw Ghetto in 1970 to apologize to Polish Jews for the Holocaust; an art scene (including TV and cinema) which regularly confronts Nazi crimes; 'public rites of repentance' around events such as Kristallnacht and the liberation of Auschwitz; the establishment of the Holocaust Memorial in the very centre of Berlin; the erection of hundreds of monuments to the victims of the Nazi tyranny; the banning of the swastika and the taking down or recontextualization of Nazi monuments; the incorporation of the history of Nazi policing into the training of police cadets, including a mandatory visit to a former concentration camp; and the installation of *Stolpersteine* – 'stumble stones' – raised commemorative brass plates on pavements in more than 1,200 locations inscribed with the names of Nazi victims.

It is rarely useful to make a direct comparison between Nazi Germany and British empire – we should perhaps instead talk about imperial episodes such as the Herero and Nama genocide, arguably the first genocide of the twentieth century, waged by the German empire against the Ovaherero, the Nama and the San in what was then German South West Africa. And these international examples of debate, some of them still propounding balance-sheet views of history, are not suggested as templates for Britain. They're just illustrations of how national conversations can at least change. We clearly have no such progress afoot, nothing resembling *Vergangenheitsaufarbeitung* exists in Britain in relation to empire and there is no sign of a sensible government emerging that would introduce the formal and balanced teaching of empire in our schools: in recent years both the Labour and Conservative parties have behaved like culture warriors when it comes to imperialism.

Having said that, however, our politicians do not necessarily define our national culture, and there are signs of progress. For example, the fact that education policy is devolved and academies and private schools don't have to follow the national curriculum has given certain educators the freedom to innovate. Professors Claire Alexander and Joya Chatterji embarked, for instance, on a project called 'Bangla Stories', in which they attempted to teach British history through the stories of Bengali Muslims caught up in the 1947 Partition, the Bangladesh War of Liberation and migration to Britain, with their website offering lesson plans for teenaged students.[6] Desmond Deehan, head teacher of Townley Grammar School, a large girls' school in outer London, has devised curriculums where history students are taught about immigration to Britain, about kings and queens around the world, rather than just their own, and about the Black Lives Matter movement and LGBT history; in French lessons, children ask directions not only to the bakery, but to the synagogue, mosque and temple.[7] Meanwhile, the Welsh government is conducting a review into the way black and minority ethnic history is taught in schools ahead of the introduction of a new curriculum in 2022.

In higher education, there are a bunch of educational establishments following in the footsteps of UCL and highlighting the role that slavery has played in our national story: the University of Glasgow announced in 2018 that it was setting up a 'centre for the study of slavery' with a memorial to the enslaved; the University of Bristol appointed a professor of slavery in 2019 to help to consider whether benefactors who profited from it should still be celebrated on campus; and Cambridge University announced in the same year that it was commissioning its historians to investigate whether the university had previously profited from the slave trade. Institutions like the Migration Museum in Lewisham and the International Slavery Museum in Liverpool are doing important work in their spheres, and William Dalrymple's suggestion that Britain set up a 'museum of colonialism' is inspired,[8] though it would of course be better if national institutions integrated these themes into what they already do, the risk with specialized institutions being that such history gets ghettoized. Activists like Alice Procter have done such a fine job of highlighting alternative narratives about museum artefacts that places like the British Museum have been forced to change.

Other activists behind the Rhodes Must Fall Campaign have done productive work putting on imperial tours of places like Oxford, which have received positive reviews from unlikely places. Museum Detox, a network of BAME heritage professionals, has been highlighting how better racial representation in the sector – which currently stands at around 7 per cent, when Census data puts the overall BAME population of England and Wales at 14 per cent – could make museums and galleries better at what they do. And, actually, there have been some positive steps in politics too. Sure, there is no consensus emerging on education, and British politicians generally resist public apologies for imperial events such as Jallianwala Bagh and slavery, with former Prime Minister David Cameron, whose distant cousin received compensation for slaves he had owned, refusing to apologize during an official visit to Jamaica, saying rather, 'I do hope that, as friends who have gone through so much together since those darkest times, we can move on from this painful legacy and continue to build for the future.' But Britain has already apologized for some imperial events and even paid reparations of sorts: as we have seen, in 1997, Tony Blair formally apologized for the Irish Potato Famine; in 2007 he said sorry for Britain's role in the transatlantic slave trade after meeting Ghana President

John Agyekum Kufuor; and in 2013 we paid £20 million to 5,000 elderly Kenyans who were tortured during the Mau Mau rebellion.

There are hundreds of other campaigns around, and if I have, as a result of going from no knowledge to a little knowledge over the course of about two years, earned the right to proffer a single piece of advice to campaigners, it would be to be positive. Campaigning for things to be torn down or renamed has resulted in some change: many Britons have learned more about imperialism during the subsequent debates than they did during years of schooling. But tearing things down also provokes vigorous opposition, exciting adversaries who feel obliged to launch counter-campaigns, and more would be achieved by campaigns to *create* and *build*. I'm thinking here about how, at my old Cambridge college, Christ's College, a JCR BME officer headed a three-year campaign for more representations of BME alumni in the college. As a result, a portrait of Szeming Sze, co-founder of the World Health Organization, is now displayed, near one of the imperial figure Jan Smuts. I'm thinking about London Mayor Sadiq Khan's decision to put *up* memorials to Stephen Lawrence, the *Windrush* generation and Sikh soldiers. I'm thinking about how Gandhi's statue in Parliament Square, and the possibility he might be commemorated on a British coin, though perhaps inappropriate given that he opposed rampant consumerism ('The world has enough for everyone's needs, but not everyone's greed'), shows we do have it within us to face up to difficult events in our imperial history. I'm thinking of Manchester Museums, which recently returned forty-three sacred and ceremonial objects to Indigenous Australians. I'm thinking of the Pitt Rivers Museum, which exhibits the University of Oxford's anthropological collections, which has recently advertised a vacancy for 'postdoctoral researcher: The Restitution of Knowledge', to 'intervene in current dialogues about restitution by generating knowledge about the ongoing histories of colonial loot', which has removed shrunken heads from display and has been returning human remains, and which has a director who has remarked that 'we can't undo history but we can be a part of the process of healing.' I'm thinking about the website for the National Museum of Australia, which proffers a message, when you log on, that 'acknowledges First Australians and recognises their continuous connection to country, community and culture'. And I'm thinking about how urgent and essential efforts to decolonize curriculums might have a better chance of succeeding if they changed their language, if campaigners talked about *widening* curriculums rather than *decolonizing* them: for that is what decolonizing involves. It is entirely possible to teach the canon and also give students a sense of what sits outside it, to teach the extraordinary and prizewinning works of Naipaul, Ishiguro and Zadie Smith, for example, alongside those of Dickens and Joyce, with a letter from one Brian Luker to the Cambridge University alumni magazine putting it well recently, when he admitted that reports about 'decolonization' had initially infuriated him but he came to realize that 'the widening and deepening of the curriculum and the understanding and possible adoption of alternative viewpoints are wholly admirable . . . And wholly within the academic tradition.'

Some of the best responses to our history in recent years have been in creative fields. I'm thinking here of 'Fons Americanus', the 40-feet-tall working fountain inspired by the Victoria Memorial in front of Buckingham Palace which was exhibited in the Tate Modern recently and, instead of celebrating empire like the original, explored the transatlantic slave trade. I'm thinking of the anti-slavery installation that appeared around Bristol's Colston statue in 2018, which featured dozens of figurines packed tightly as if they were aboard an eighteenth-century slave boat[9] – a chilling visual reminder of how Colston made his wealth. I'm thinking of *We Bury Our Own*, a series of photographic self-portraits from contemporary Aboriginal artist Christian Thompson for the Pitt Rivers Museum in which one of the first two Aboriginal students to study at the University of Oxford sported the university's formal dress and obscured his face, as a way of responding to the museum's historical collection of photographs of Indigenous Australians.[10] And I'm thinking of the time students at the University of Manchester painted over a mural of Rudyard Kipling's 'If . . .' with a mural of Maya Angelou's 'Still I Rise', on the grounds of Kipling's racism and imperialism.[11] Much of the press reaction was hostile, but the students actually created a quietly profound piece of work. Rather than erase 'If . . .' entirely, they left its verses visible beneath those of Angelou. Like all good art, it was less a statement than an invitation to ask questions. A request to tease out the threads of how the present is connected to the past.

Bibliography

Abgarian, Almara, 'Almost half of British people don't try the local food when on holiday', 29/05/2019, https://metro.co.uk/2019/05/29/almost-half-british-people-dont-try-local-food-holiday-9723200/

Accominotti, Olivier, Flandreau, Marc, and Rezzik, Riad, 'The spread of empire: Clio and the measurement of colonial borrowing costs', *Economic History Review* 2011, 64:2, 385–407, https://onlinelibrary.wiley.com/doi/abs/10.1111/j.1468-0289.2010.00536.x

Addley, Esther, 'A one-way passage from India: Hackney Museum explores fate of colonial ayahs', *Guardian*, 1/03/2020, https://www.theguardian.com/culture/2020/mar/01/one-way-passage-from-india-hackney-museum-colonial-ayahs-london

Aderinto, Saheed, 'Empire Day in Africa: Patriotic Colonial Childhood, Imperial Spectacle and Nationalism in Nigeria, 1905–60', *Journal of Imperial and Commonwealth History* 2018, 46:4, 731–57, https://www.tandfonline.com/doi/abs/10.1080/03086534.2018.1452538

Ahmed, Zubair, 'Hitler memorabilia "attracts young Indians"', *BBC News*, 15/06/2010, http://news.bbc.co.uk/1/hi/world/south_asia/8660064.stm

Ahujja, Sahil, 'St. James' Church and Fakhr-ul-Masjid, Delhi', *Pixelated Memories*, 12/01/2016, http://pixels-memories.blogspot.com/2016/01/st-james-church-and-fakhr-ul-masjid.html

Akala, *Natives, Race and Class in the Ruins of Empire*, Two Roads, 2018

Aldrich, Robert, *Cultural Encounters and Homoeroticism in Sri Lanka: Sex and Serendipity*, Routledge, 2014

Alexander, Michael, and Anand, Sushila, *Queen Victoria's Maharaj: Duleep Singh, 1838–93*, Weidenfeld & Nicolson, 2001

Alibai-Brown, Yasmin, *Who Do We Think We Are?*, Allen Lane, 2000

Allen, Charles, *Duel in the Snows: The True Story of the Younghusband Mission to Lhasa*, John Murray, 2004

Allen, Charles, *Plain Tales from the Raj: Images of British India in the Twentieth Century*, BBC Books, 1975

Allen, Robert, *Global Economic History: A Very Short Introduction*, Oxford University Press, 2011

Amos, Owen, 'Is it true only 10% of Americans have passports?', *BBC News*, 9/01/2018, https://www.bbc.co.uk/news/world-us-canada-42586638

Anderson, Benedict, *Imagined Communities: Reflections on the Origin and Spread of Nationalism*, Verso, 1983

Anderson, David, 'Master and servant in colonial Kenya, 1895–1939', *Journal of African History* 2000, 41:3, 459–85, https://www.cambridge.org/core/journals/journal-of-african-history/article/master-and-servant-in-colonial-kenya-18951939/F5117806551B8E9EBEB4F60D7430AA89

Andrews, Kehinde, 'Colonial nostalgia is back in fashion, blinding us to the horrors of empire', *Guardian*, 24/08/2016, https://www.theguardian.com/commentisfree/2016/aug/24/colonial-nostalgia-horrors-of-empire-britain-olympic

Anonymous, 'The seductive dangers of the Hong Kong high life', *The Times*, 5/11/2014, https://www.thetimes.co.uk/article/the-seductive-dangers-of-the-hong-kong-high-life-5dgfp7rsqfd

Ansari, Humayun, *The Infidel Within: Muslims in Britain since 1800*, C. Hurst, 2004

Ansari, Sarah, 'Cornelia Sorabji: India's Pioneer Woman Lawyer: A Biography, by Suparna Gooptu', *English Historical Review* 2012, 127:527, 1013–15, https://academic.oup.com/ehr/article-abstract/127/527/1013/368836

Anthony, Scott, 'Why do educators struggle with the legacy of empire?', *Times Higher Education*, 19/04/2018, https://www.timeshighereducation.com/cn/comment/27701

Appadurai, Arjun, *Modernity at Large: Cultural Dimensions of Globalization*, University of Minnesota Press, 1996

Ardern, Jacinda, and Hipkins, Chris, 'NZ history to be taught in all schools', *Beehive – New Zealand Government*, https://www.beehive.govt.nz/release/nz-history-be-taught-all-schools

Aretxaga, Begoña, *Shattering Silence: Women, Nationalism and Political Subjectivity in Northern Ireland*, Princeton University Press, 1997

Ascherson, Neal, 'Scotland, Brexit and the Persistence of Empire', in Stuart Ward and Astrid Rasch (eds.), *Embers of Empire in Brexit Britain*, Bloomsbury Academic, 2019, pp. 71–8

'Asians face mass expulsion to Britain as Africanisation starts', *Nation*, 4/08/2013, https://www.nation.co.ke/lifestyle/dn2/Asians-face-mass-expulsion-to-Britain/957860-1936760-139mqyz/index.html

Atwal, Priya, *Royals and Rebels: The Rise and Fall of the Sikh Empire*, C. Hurst, 2020

Austen, Jane, *Mansfield Park*, Wordsworth Editions, 1992

Austin, Beth, '1619: Virginia's First Africans', *Hampton History Museum*, 2018, https://hampton.gov/DocumentCenter/View/24075/1619-Virginias-First-Africans?bidId=

Awan, Shazia, 'The British Museum gleams with stolen riches from its colonial past – but Asian names are too "confusing" for inclusion', *Independent*, 14/09/2017, https://www.independent.co.uk/voices/british-museum-tweet twitter-row-asian-names-confusing-curator-colonialism-a7946431.html

Azoulay, Ariella Aïsha, *Potential History: Unlearning Imperialism*, Verso, 2019

Bagehot, Walter, *Physics and Politics, or, Thoughts on the Application of the Principles of 'Natural Selection' and 'Inheritance' to Political Society*, D. Appleton, 1875, https://www.gutenberg.org/files/4350/4350-h/4350-h.htm

Bailey, Ronald W., 'Review: J. E. Inikori's Africans and the Industrial Revolution in England: A Study in International Trade and Economic Development', *International Journal of African Historical Studies* 2002, 35:2, 485–7, https://experts.illinois.edu/en/publications/review-je-inikoris-iafricans-and-the-industrial-revolution-in-eng

Bailkin, Jordanna, *The Afterlife of Empire*, University of California Press, 2012

Balakrishnan, Angela, 'Are the British really the worst-dressed tourists?', *Guardian*, 24/05/2007, https://www.theguardian.com/travel/blog/2007/may/24/arethebritishreallythewor

Ballantyne, Tony, *Orientalism and Race: Aryanism in the British Empire*, Palgrave Macmillan, 2002

Bancroft, George, *History of the United States, from the Discovery of the American Continent*, 10 vols., Little, Brown, 1844–75, https://catalog.hathitrust.org/Record/000333733

Banerjea, Surendranath, *A Nation in Making: Being the Reminiscences of Fifty Years of Public Life*, Oxford University Press, 1925

Bank, Andrew, 'Of "Native Skulls" and Noble Caucasians: Phrenology in Colonial South Africa', *Journal of Southern African Studies* 1996, 22:3, 387–403, https://www.jstor.org/stable/i324968

Barczewski, Stephanie, *Country Houses and the British Empire, 1700–1930: Studies in Imperialism*, Manchester University Press, 2014

Barczewski, Stephanie, *Heroic Failure and the British*, Yale University Press, 2016

Barrie, Joshua, 'How taxpayers were still paying for British slave trade nearly 200 years later', *Mirror*, 13/02/2018, https://www.mirror.co.uk/news/uk-news/taxpayers-still-paying-british-slave-12019829

Barringer, Tim, and Flynn, Tom, *Colonialism and the Object: Empire, Material Culture and the Museum*, Routledge, 1998

Bartlett, Nicola, 'Boris Johnson defends appointing aide who attacked "grievance culture" to race review role', *Mirror*, 17/06/2020, https://www.mirror.co.uk/news/politics/boris-johnson-defends-appointing-aide-22206451

Barton, Gregory, *Informal Empire and the Rise of One World Culture*, Palgrave Macmillan, 2014

Barua, Pradeep, 'Inventing Race: The British and India's Martial Races', *Historian* 1995, 58:1, 107–16, https://www.jstor.org/stable/24449614

Bates, Crispin, *Subalterns and Raj: South Asia since 1600*, Routledge, 2013

Baxter, Peter, *Gandhi, Smuts and Race in the British Empire of Passive and Violent Resistance*, Pen & Sword History, 2017

Bayly, C. A., *Imperial Meridian: The British Empire and the World, 1780–1830*, Routledge, 1989

Beaven, Brad, and Griffiths, John, 'The City and Imperial Propaganda: A Comparative Study of Empire Day in England, Australia, and New Zealand c. 1903–1914', *Journal of Urban History* 2016, 42:2, 377–95, https://journals.sagepub.com/doi/abs/10.1177/0096144214566965

Beetham, David, *Transport and Turbans: A Comparative Study in Local Politics*, Oxford University Press, 1970

Bellot, Leland Joseph, 'Canada versus Guadeloupe in Britain's Old Colonial Empire: A Study of George Louis Beer's Interpretation of the Peace of Paris of 1763', MA thesis, The Rice Institute, May 1960, https://scholarship.rice.edu/bitstream/handle/1911/89064/RICE0099.pdf?sequence=1

Bennett, Rosemary, ' "Racist" Gandhi must fall, say Manchester University students', *The Times*, 17/10/2019, https://www.thetimes.co.uk/article/racist-gandhi-must-fall-say-manchester-university-students-gx205l6cs

Bennett, Tony, *The Birth of the Museum: History, Theory, Politics*, Routledge, 1995

Bennett, Tony, 'The Exhibitionary Complex', *New Formations* 1988, 4, 73–102, http://banmarchive.org.uk/collections/newformations/04_73.pdf

Bennold, Katrin, and Eddy, Melissa, 'In Germany, Confronting Shameful Legacy is Essential Part of Police Training', *New York Times*, 23/06/2020, https://www.nytimes.com/2020/06/23/world/europe/germany-police.html

Benson, Arthur Christopher, and Esher, Viscount, *The Letters of Queen Victoria: A Selection from Her Majesty's Correspondence between the Years 1837 and 1861*, vol. III: *1854–1861*, John Murray, 1908, https://www.gutenberg.org/files/28649/28649-h/28649-h.htm

Bhambra, Gurminder K., 'The imperial nostalgia of a "Small Island" ', *UKandEU*, 4/06/2018, https://ukandeu.ac.uk/the-imperial-nostalgia-of-a-small-island/

Bhambra, Gurminder K., Gebrial, Dalia, and Niancolu, Kerem, *Decolonising the University*, Pluto Press, 2018

Bickert, Sven, *Empire of Cotton: A New History of Global Capitalism*, Penguin, 2015

Biggar, Nigel, 'Don't feel guilty about our colonial history', *The Times*, 30/11/2017, https://www.thetimes.co.uk/article/don-t-feel-guilty-about-our-colonial-history-ghvstdhmj

Biggar, Nigel, 'Rhodes, Race, and the Abuse of History', *Standpoint*, 03/2016, http://www.standpointmag.co.uk/features-march-2016-nigel-biggarrhodes-race-history-rhodes-must-fall

'Biggest Global Sports – A statistics-based analysis of the biggest global sports', *Biggest Global Sports*, 2014, http://www.biggestglobalsports.com/top-sporting-nations/4587465102

Biswas, Soutik, 'Was Mahatma Gandhi a racist?', *BBC News*, https://www.bbc.co.uk/news/world-asia-india-34265882

Black, Jeremy, *The British Empire: A History and a Debate*, Routledge, 2015

Blainey, Geoffrey, 'Lost Causes of the Jameson Raid', *Economic History Review* 1965, 18:2, 350–66, https://www.jstor.org/stable/2592099?seq=1

Boast, Robyn, 'Neocolonial Collaboration: Museum as Contact Zone Revisited', *Museum Anthropology* 2011, 34:1, 56–70, https://anthrosource.onlinelibrary.wiley.com/doi/abs/10.1111/j.1548-1379.2010.01107.x

Boddy, Janice, *Civilizing Women: British Crusades in Colonial Sudan*, Princeton University Press, 2007

Boehme, Kate, and Lester, Alan, 'Time to throw out the balance sheet', University of Sussex, 26/01/2016, https://blogs.sussex.ac.uk/snapshotsofempire/2016/01/26/time-to-throw-out-the-balance-sheet/

Bogart, Dan, and Chaudhary, Latika, 'Extractive institutions? Investor returns to Indian railway companies in the age of high imperialism', *Journal of Institutional Economics* 2019, 15:5, 751–75, https://econpapers.repec.org/article/cupjinsec/v_3a15_3ay_3a2019_3ai_3a05_3ap_3a751-774_5f00.htm

Booth, Martin, 'Anti-Slavery Day Marked by New Artwork in Front of Edward Colston Statue', *B24/7*, 18/10/2018, https://www.bristol247.com/news-and-features/news/anti-slavery-day-marked-by-new-artwork-in-front-of-edward-colston-statue/

'Boris Johnson's conference speech: Full text', *Spectator*, 2/10/2016, https://www.spectator.co.uk/article/full-text-boris-johnson-s-conference-speech

Bowen, H. V., *The Business of Empire: The East India Company and Imperial Britain, 1756–1833*, Cambridge University Press, 2006

Bowlby, Chris, 'The Palace of Shame that Makes China Angry', *BBC News*, 2/02/2015, https://www.bbc.co.uk/news/magazine-30810596

Boxall, Megan, 'Lessons from history: "Prohibition makes anything precious"', *Investors' Chronicle*, 14/08/2020

Bradbury, Rosie, 'Fact check: Jan Smuts portrait and bust were not "toppled" by Cambridge students', *Varsity*, 6/08/2018, https://www.varsity.co.uk/news/15971

Bradshaw, Tim, Neville, Sarah, and Warrell, Helen, 'NHS tracing app in question as experts assess Google–Apple model', *Financial Times*, 6/05/2020, https://www.ft.com/content/d44beb06-5e3e-434f-a3a0-f806ce06576c

Breckenridge, Carol A., 'The Aesthetics and Politics of Colonial Collecting: India at World Fairs', *Comparative Studies in Society and History* 1989, 31:2, 195–216, https://www.cambridge.org/core/journals/comparative-studies-in-society-and-history/article/aesthetics-and-politics-of-colonial-collecting-india-at-world-fairs/173A0D542B56EE2124E1CC9E7F798E1B

Bremner, Alex, ' "Some Imperial Institute": Architecture, Symbolism, and the Ideal of Empire in Late Victorian Britain, 1887–93', *Journal of the Society of Architectural Historians* 2003, 62:1, 50–73, https://www.jstor.org/stable/3655083?seq=1

Brendon, Piers, *The British Empire: How It Was Built and How It Fell*, All You Need to Know series, Connell Publishing, 2018

Brendon, Piers, *The Decline and Fall of the British Empire, 1781–1997*, Vintage, 2008

Brendon, Vyvyen, *Children of the Raj*, Orion, 2005

'Brexit: Gove defends £705m plan for border posts and staff', *BBC News*, 12/07/2020, https://www.bbc.co.uk/news/uk-politics-53375713

'Brexit: UK must not be EU "colony" after Brexit', *BBC News*, 16/12/2017, https://www.bbc.co.uk/news/uk-politics-42375059

'Bristol University appoints History of Slavery professor', *BBC News*, 30/10/2019, https://www.bbc.co.uk/news/uk-england-bristol-50180417

'The British Empire at its Territorial Peak Covered Nearly the Same Area as the Moon', *Brilliant Maps*, 1/01/2019, https://brilliantmaps.com/british-empire-moon/

British Pathé, 'Think and Eat Imperially', 1927, https://www.youtube.com/watch?v=eg7FUp1AXqY

'British worst at learning languages', British Council, 2019, https://esol.britishcouncil.org/content/learners/skills/reading/british-worst-learning-languages

Broadberry, Stephen, *British Economic Growth, 1270–1870*, Cambridge University Press, 2015

Brooks, George E., *Eurafricans in Western Africa: Commerce, Social Status, Gender, and Religious Observance from the Sixteenth to Eighteenth Century*, James Currey, 2003

Brown, Andy, *Political Languages of Race and the Politics of Exclusion*, Ashgate, 1999

Brown, Judith M., *Nehru*, Routledge, 2014

Brown, Judith M., and Louis, Roger Wm., *The Oxford History of the British Empire*, vol. IV: *The Twentieth Century*, Oxford University Press, 1999

Budgen, Nicholas, 'Compulsory Punjabi', *Spectator*, 24/01/1987, http://archive.spectator.co.uk/article/24th-january-1987/13/compulsory-punjabi

Buettner, Elizabeth, *Empire Families: Britons and Late Imperial India*, Oxford University Press, 2004

Buettner, Elizabeth, 'How Unique is Britain's Empire Complex?', in Stuart Ward and Astrid Rasch (eds.), *Embers of Empire in Brexit Britain*, Bloomsbury Academic, 2019, pp. 37–48

Burbank, Jane, and Cooper, Frederick, *Empires in World History: Power and the Politics of Difference*, Princeton University Press, 2010

Burrow, Merrick, 'The Imperial Souvenir: Things and Masculinity in H. Rider Haggard's *King Solomon's Mines* and *Allan Quartermain*', *Journal of Victorian Culture* 2013, 18:1, 72–92, https://academic.oup.com/jvc/article-abstract/18/1/72/4102745

Burton, Antoinette, *After the Imperial Turn: Thinking with and through the Nation*, Duke University Press, 2003

Burton, Antoinette, 'Raj nostalgia: reconsidering the stories through which we view empire', *History Extra*, 11/05/2018, https://www.history-extra.com/period/victorian/raj-nostalgia-reconsidering-the-stories-through-which-we-view-empire/

Burton, Antoinette, and Kennedy, Dane, *How Empire Shaped Us*, Bloomsbury Academic, 2016

Butler, Jeffrey, 'Cecil Rhodes', *International Journal of African Historical Studies* 1977, 10:2, 259–81, https://www.jstor.org/stable/i210958

Byron, Arthur, *London Statues*, Constable, 1981

Cain, P. J., and Hopkins, A. G., *British Imperialism: 1688–2015*, Routledge, 2016

Cameron, A. D., 'The Vellore Mutiny', PhD thesis, University of Edinburgh, 1984, https://era.ed.ac.uk/handle/1842/6856

Campbell, Lucy, 'V&A in talks over returning looted Ethiopian treasures in "decolonisation" purge', *Guardian*, 7/10/2020, https://www.theguardian.com/artanddesign/2020/oct/07/va-in-talks-over-returning-looted-ethiopian-treasures-in-decolonisation-purge

Canny, Nicholas, *The Origins of Empire*, Oxford University Press, 2001

Carrington, Michael, 'Officers, Gentlemen and Thieves: The Looting of Monasteries during the 1903/4 Younghusband Mission to Tibet', *Modern Asian Studies* 2003, 37:1, 81–109, https://www.jstor.org/stable/3876552?seq=1

Carroll, Khadija von Zinnenburg, *Art in the Time of Colony*, Routledge, 2016

Carroll, Ruaidhrí, 'Liberty London Was Built From Two Warships', *Culture Trip*, 11/9/2018, https://theculturetrip.com/europe/united-kingdom/england/london/articles/liberty-london-was-built-from-two-warships/ and https://www.libertylondon.com/uk/information/our-heritage.html

Cavendish, Richard, 'The Black Hole of Calcutta', *History Today* 2006, 56:6, https://www.historytoday.com/archive/black-hole-calcutta

Centre for Critical Heritage Studies, University of Gothenburg, *Critical Heritage Studies*, 8/11/2020, http://criticalheritagestudies.gu.se

Centre for Critical Studies in Museums, Galleries and Heritage, University of Leeds, 2020, http://ccsmgh.leeds.ac.uk

Chakrabarty, Dipesh, *Provincializing Europe*, Princeton University Press, 2000

Chakravorty, Sanjoy, *The Truth about Us: The Politics of Information from Manu to Modi*, Hachette India, 2019

Chakravorty, Sanjoy, 'Viewpoint: How the British reshaped India's caste system', *BBC News*, 18/06/2019, https://www.bbc.co.uk/news/world-asia-india-48619734

Chamorro-Premuzic, Tomas, *Why Do So Many Incompetent Men Become Leaders?*, Harvard Business Review Press, 2019

Chantiluke, Roseanne, Kwoba, Brian, and Nkopo, Athinangamso, *Rhodes Must Fall: The Struggle to Decolonise the Racist Heart of Empire*, Zed Books, 2018

'The Chattri memorial', Brighton & Hove City Council, 2020, https://www.brighton-hove.gov.uk/content/leisure-and-libraries/parks-and-green-spaces/chattri-memorial

Chaudhary, Latika, 'Taxation and educational development: evidence from British India', *Explorations in Economic History* 2010, 47:3, 279–93, https://www.sciencedirect.com/science/article/abs/pii/S0014498310000148

Cheang, Sarah, 'Women, Pets and Imperialism: The British Pekinese Dog and Nostalgia for Old China', *Journal of British Studies* 2006, 45:2, 359–87, https://www.researchgate.net/publication/249106714_Women_Pets_and_Imperialism_The_British_Pekingese_Dog_and_Nostalgia_for_Old_China

Clarkson, Jeremy, 'Stand still, wimp – only failures run off to be expats', *Sunday Times*, 29/3/2009

Coates, Sam, 'Ministers aim to build "empire 2.0" with African Commonwealth', *The Times*, 9/03/2017, https://www.thetimes.co.uk/article/ministers-aim-to-build-empire-2-0-with-african-commonwealth-after-brexit-v9bs6f6z9

Cobain, Ian, Bowcott, Owen, and Norton-Taylor, Richard, 'Britain destroyed records of colonial crimes', *Guardian*, 18/04/2012, https://www.theguardian.com/uk/2012/apr/18/britain-destroyed-records-colonial-crimes

Cohn, Bernard, 'Representing Authority in Victorian India', in Eric Hobsbawm and Terence Ranger (eds.), *The Invention of Tradition*, Cambridge University Press, 2012, pp. 165–201

Colley, Linda, *Britons: Forging the Nation, 1707–1837*, Yale University Press, 2005

Colley, Linda, *Captives: Britain, Empire and the World, 1600–1850*, Pimlico, 2003

Collingham, Lizzie, *The Hungry Empire: How Britain's Quest for Food Shaped the Modern World*, Vintage, 2018

Collins, Marcus, 'Pride and Prejudice: West Indian Men in Mid-Twentieth-Century Britain', *Journal of British Studies* 2001, 40:3, 391–418, https://www.jstor.org/stable/3070729?seq=1

'Coming home to roost: the pleasures and perils of returning to schools in the UK', *Good Schools Guide*, 2020, https://www.goodschoolsguide.co.uk/international/uk/returning-to-schools-in-the-uk

'The Commonwealth and the First World War', National Army Museum, https://www.nam.ac.uk/explore/commonwealth-and-first-world-war

'Consuming South Asian Textiles', Victoria and Albert Museum, http://www.vam.ac.uk/content/articles/c/consuming-south-asian-textiles/

Coombes, Annie, *Reinventing Africa: Museums, Material Culture and Popular Imagination in Late Victorian and Edwardian England*, Yale University Press, 1994

Craggs, Ruth, and Wintle, Claire, *Cultures of Decolonisation: Transnational Productions and Practices, 1945–70*, Manchester University Press, 2016

Crais, Clifton, Scully, Pamela, and Baartman, Sara, *The Hottentot Venus: A Ghost Story and a Biography*, Princeton University Press, 2009

Croft, Jane, 'UK to pay nearly £20m compensation to Mau Mau torture victims', *Financial Times*, 6/06/2013, https://www.ft.com/content/f0aec002-cea9-11e2-ae25-00144feab7de

Cuno, James, *Whose Culture? The Promise of Museums and the Debate Over Antiquities*, Princeton University Press, 2009

Curzon, George, *The Place of India in the Empire: Being an Address Delivered before the Philosophical Institute of Edinburgh*, Adamant Media Corporation, 2003

'Dadabhai Naoroji: The UK's first Indian MP', *The History Press*, 2020, https://www.thehistorypress.co.uk/articles/dadabhai-naoroji-the-uk-s-first-indian-mp/

Dalrymple, William, *The Anarchy: The Relentless Rise of the East India Company*, Bloomsbury, 2019

Dalrymple, William, *The Last Mughal: The Fall of a Dynasty, Delhi, 1857*, Bloomsbury, 2009

Dalrymple, William, 'Robert Clive was a vicious asset-stripper. His statue has no place on Whitehall', *Guardian*, 11/07/2020, https://www.theguardian.com/commentisfree/2020/jun/11/robert-clive-statue-whitehall-british-imperial

Dalrymple, William, *White Mughals: Love and Betrayal in Eighteenth-Century India*, HarperCollins, 2003

Dalziel, Nigel, *The Penguin Historical Atlas of the British Empire*, Penguin, 2006

Darwin, Charles, *Voyage of the Beagle: Charles Darwin's Journal of Researches*, ed. Janet Browne and Michael Neve, Penguin, 1989

Darwin, John, *After Tamerlane: The Rise and Fall of Global Empires, 1400–2000*, Penguin, 2007

Darwin, John, *Unfinished Empire: The Global Expansion of Britain*, Penguin, 2011

Dasgupta, M., *Calcutta Cookbook: A Treasury of Recipes from Pavement to Palace*, Penguin, 2000

David, Saul, *The Indian Mutiny: 1857*, Penguin, 2003

David, Saul, *Victoria's Wars: The Rise of Empire*, Penguin, 2007

Davies, Norman, *The Isles: A History*, Palgrave Macmillan, 2000

Davin, Anna, 'Imperialism and Motherhood', *History Workshop Journal* 1978, 5:1, 9–66, https://academic.oup.com/hwj/article-abstract/5/1/9/576550?redirectedFrom=PDF

Davis, John A., *Naples and Napoleon: Southern Italy and the European Revolutions, 1780–1860*, Oxford University Press, 2009

Davis, Lance E., and Huttenback, Robert A., *Mammon and the Pursuit of Empire: The Political Economy of British Imperialism, 1860–1912*, Cambridge University Press, 1987

Davis, Wade, *Into the Silence: The Great War, Mallory and the Conquest of Everest*, Vintage, 2012

de Freitas, Will, 'Concentration camps in the South African War? Here are the real facts', *The Conversation*, 18/02/2019, https://theconversation.com/concentration-camps-in-the-south-african-war-here-are-the-real-facts-112006#:~:text=More%20than%20a%20century%20after,are%20back%20in%20the%20headlines

Degler, Carl N., *Out of our Past: The Forces that Shaped Modern America*, Harper Perennial, 1983

de Groot, Joanna, 'Metropolitan Desires and Colonial Connections: Reflections on Consumption and Empire', in Catherine Hall and Sonya O. Rose (eds.), *At Home with the Empire: Metropolitan Culture and the Imperial World*, Cambridge University Press, 2009, pp. 166–90

Deo, Ritwik, 'The British abroad: expats, not immigrants', *Guardian*, 9/07/2012, https://www.theguardian.com/commentisfree/2012/jul/09/british-abroad-expats-immigrants-indians

Desai, Kishwar, *Jallianwala Bagh, 1919: The Real Story*, Context, 2018

Devine, T. M., *The Scottish Nation: 1700–2007*, Penguin, 2006

Dirks, Nicholas B., *The Scandal of Empire: India and the Creation of Imperial Britain*, Harvard University Press, 2008

Dixon, Carol Ann, 'Decolonising the Museum: Cité Nationale de l'Histoire de l'Immigration', *Race & Class* 2012, 53:4, 78–86, https://journals.sage-pub.com/doi/10.1177/0306396811433115

Donald, James, and Rattansi, Ali, *'Race', Culture and Difference*, Sage Publications, 1994

Donaldson, Dave, 'Railroads of the raj: estimating the impact of transportation infrastructure', *American Economic Review* 2018, 108:4–5, 899–934, https://www.aeaweb.org/articles?id=10.1257/aer.20101199

Donington, Katie, 'Relics of Empire? Colonialism and the Culture Wars', in Stuart Ward and Astrid Rasch (eds.), *Embers of Empire in Brexit Britain*, Bloomsbury Academic, 2019, pp. 121–32

Donnelly, Jim, 'The Irish Famine', *BBC History*, 17/02/2011, http://www.bbc.co.uk/history/british/victorians/famine_01.shtml

Dorling, Danny, and Tomlinson, Sally, 'Brexit: how the end of Britain's empire led to rising inequality that helped leave to victory', *The Conversation*, 22/05/2019, https://theconversation.com/brexit-how-the-end-of-britains-empire-led-to-rising-inequality-that-helped-leave-to-victory-116466

Draper, Alfred, *The Amritsar Massacre: Twilight of the Raj*, Echoes of War series, Buchan & Enright Publishers, 1985

Draper, Nicholas, 'Possessing People: Absentee Slave-Owners within British Society' and 'Helping to Make Britain Great: The Commercial Legacies of Slave-Ownership in Britain', in Catherine Hall, Nicholas Draper, Keith McClelland, Katie Donington and Rachel Land, *Legacies of British Slave-Ownership: Colonial Slavery and the Formation of Victorian Britain*, Cambridge University Press, 2014, pp. 34–77, 78–126

Draper, Nicholas, *The Price of Emancipation: Slave-Ownership, Compensation and British Society at the End of Slavery*, Cambridge University Press, 2010

Drayton, Richard, 'The wealth of the west was built on Africa's exploitation', *Guardian*, 20/08/2005, https://www.theguardian.com/politics/2005/aug/20/past.hearafrica05

Drayton, Richard, 'Where Does the World Historian Write From? Objectivity, Moral Conscience and the Past and Present of Imperialism', *Journal of Contemporary History* 2011, 46:3, 671–85, https://journals.sagepub.com/doi/abs/10.1177/0022009411403519

Drescher, Seymour, *Econocide: British Slavery in the Era of Abolition*, University of North Carolina Press, 2010

Duncan, Carol, *Civilizing Rituals: Inside Public Art Museums*, Routledge, 1995

Duncan, Conrad, 'Brexiteer complains he has to wait in queue at EU airport: "This isn't the Brexit I voted for"', *Independent*, 14/02/2020, https://www.independent.co.uk/news/uk/home-news/brexit-eu-airport-queue-immigration-brexiteer-amsterdam-airport-schiphol-a9335281.html

Duncanson, Ian, 'Nostalgia and Empire', *Griffith Law Review* 2012, 21:1, 23–35, https://www.tandfonline.com/doi/abs/10.1080/10383441.2012.10854731

Dupraz, Yannick, and Ruada, Valerie, 'There is no "case for colonialism": insights from the colonial economic history', LSE Blog, 17/10/2017, https://blogs.lse.ac.uk/africaatlse/2017/10/17/there-is-no-case-for-colonialism-insights-from-the-colonial-economic-history/

Eder, Jacob S., Gassert, Phillip, and Steinweis, Alan E., *Holocaust Memory in a Globalising World*, Wallstein Verlag, 2017

The Editors of Encyclopaedia Britannica, 'Indian Mutiny', *Encyclopaedia Britannia*, 20/09/2006, https://www.britannica.com/event/Indian-Mutiny

'The Elgin Marbles are going nowhere', *Mail*, 27/09/2020, https://www.dailymail.co.uk/news/article-8777415/Oliver-Dowden-issues-statue-warning-museums-galleries.html

Elsner, John, and Cardinal, Roger, *The Cultures of Collecting*, Melbourne University Press, 1994

Eltis, David, and Engerman, Stanley L., 'The Importance of Slavery and the Slave Trade to Industrialising Britain', *Journal of Economic History* 2000, 60:1, 123–44, https://www.jstor.org/stable/2566799?seq=1

Ember, Melvin, Ember, Carol R., and Skoggard, Ian (eds.), *Encyclopaedia of Diasporas: Immigrant and Refugee Cultures around the World*, 2 vols., Springer, 2005

'Empire Day', *The Times Archive*, 27/04/1909, p. 8, https://www.thetimes. co.uk/archive/article/1909-04-27/8/4.html

'Empire Day', *The Times Archive*, 3/05/1910, p. 4, https://www.thetimes. co.uk/archive/article/1910-05-03/4/4.html

'Empire Day', *The Times Archive*, 24/05/1909, p. 13, https://www.thetimes. co.uk/archive/page/1909-05-24/13.html

'Empire Day', *The Times Archive*, 24/05/1909, p. 15, https://www.thetimes. co.uk/archive/article/1909-05-24/15/12.html

Engels, Ryland, 'Jan Smuts and Walt Whitman: strange bedfellows', *Journal of South African and American Studies* 2016, 17:3, 339–56, https://www. tandfonline.com/doi/abs/10.1080/17533171.2015.1125605

English, Jim, 'Empire Day in Britain, 1904–1958', *Historical Journal* 2006, 49:1, 247–76, https://www.jstor.org/stable/4091747?seq=1

'English turn to booze on holiday', *BBC News*, 27/08/2009, http://news. bbc.co.uk/1/hi/health/8225029.stm

Epstein, James, 'Taking Class Notes on Empire', in Catherine Hall and Sonya O. Rose (eds.), *At Home with the Empire: Metropolitan Culture and the Imperial World*, Cambridge University Press, 2009, pp. 251–74

Erikson, Emily, and Bearman, Peter, 'Malfeasance and the Foundations for Global Trade: The Structure of English Trade in the East Indies, 1601–1833', *American Journal of Sociology* 2006, 112:1, 195–230, https:// www.jstor.org/stable/10.1086/502694

Evans, Chris, *Slave Wales: The Welsh and Atlantic Slavery, 1660–1850*, University of Wales Press, 2010

Evans, James, *Emigrants: Why the English Sailed to the New World*, Weidenfeld & Nicolson, 2017

Evans, Richard J., 'The History Wars', *New Statesman*, 17/06/2020, https:// www.newstatesman.com/international/2020/06/history-wars

Evans, Richard J., *The Third Reich in History and Memory*, Oxford University Press, 2015

'Expatriates Worldwide', *Just Landed*, 2020, https://www.justlanded.com/
english/Common/Footer/Expatriates/How-many-expats-are-there

'Exploring alternative ways of shaping future legacies and assembling
common worlds across different fields of conservation practice', *Heritage
Futures*, 2020, https://heritage-futures.org/

Farmer, Ben, 'British Army examines plans to create a Sikh regiment', *Telegraph*, 23/02/2015, https://www.telegraph.co.uk/news/uknews/defence/
11430070/British-Army-examines-plans-to-create-a-Sikh-regiment.html

Fenske, James, ' "Rubber will not keep in this country": Failed development in Benin, 1897–1921', *Explorations in Economic History* 2013, 50:2,
316–33, https://ideas.repec.org/a/eee/exehis/v50y2013i2p316-333.html

Ferguson, Niall, *Empire: How Britain Made the Modern World*, Penguin, 2003

Ferguson, Niall, 'Home truths about famine, war and genocide', *Independent*, 14/06/2006, https://www.independent.co.uk/voices/commentators/
niallferguson-home-truths-about-famine-war-and-genocide-482314.html

Ferguson, Niall, 'Why We Ruled the World', *The Times*, 6/01/2003, https://
www.thetimes.co.uk/article/why-we-ruled-the-world-3h385rbmllw

Fieldhouse, David, 'For Richer, for Poorer?', in P. J. Marshall (ed.), *British
Empire*, Cambridge University Press, 1996, pp. 108–46

Figes, Alice, 'English "exceptionalism" despite Italy's warning', *Open Democracy*, 19/05/2020, https://www.opendemocracy.net/en/can-europe-make-
it/english-exceptionalism-despite-italys-warning/

Finch, Alan, 'The provision of school meals since 1906: progress or a recipe
for disaster?', *History and Policy*, 14/01/2019, http://www.historyand
policy.org/policy-papers/papers/the-provision-of-school-meals-since-1906-
progress-or-a-recipe-for-disaster

Finkelstein, Daniel, 'Winston Churchill was a racist but still a great man',
The Times, 12/02/2019, https://www.thetimes.co.uk/article/churchill-
was-a-racist-but-still-a-great-man-vnhkhfnpm

Finn, Margot C., 'Material Turns in British History: I. Loot', *Transactions of
the Royal Historical Society* 2008, 28:5, 5–32, https://www.researchgate.net/
publication/328701347_Material_Turns_in_British_History_I_Loot

Finn, Margot, and Smith, Kate (eds.), *The East India Company at Home, 1757–
1857*, UCL Press, 2018

Fisher, Lucy, 'We led the war effort, say British – others disagree', *The
Times*, 8/05/2020, https://www.thetimes.co.uk/edition/news/who-won-

the-war-nations-divided-over-which-allied-power-played-the-biggest-
role-8wpcrowwr

Fisher, Michael, *Counterflows to Colonialism: Indian Travellers and Settlers in Britain, 1600–1857*, Permanent Black, 2004

Fisher, Michael H., *The First Indian Author in English*, Oxford University Press, 1996

Fisher, Michael H., *The Travels of Dean Mahomet: An Eighteenth-Century Journey through India*, University of California Press, 1997

Fleming, Peter, *Invasion 1940*, Common Reader, 2000

Flint, John, *Cecil Rhodes*, Little, Brown, 1974

Flood, Alison, 'UK needs a museum of colonialism, says historian William Dalrymple', *Guardian*, 16/09/2020, https://www.theguardian.com/books/2020/sep/16/uk-needs-a-museum-of-colonialism-says-historian-william-dalrymple

Floud, Roderick, *The Economic History of the English Garden*, Allen Lane, 2019

Foley, Nimah, and Rhodes, Chris, 'Tourism: Statistics and Policy', House of Commons Library, Briefing Paper 06022, 24/09/2019, http://research-briefings.files.parliament.uk/documents/SN06022/SN06022.pdf

Ford, Ford Madox, *The Spirit of the People: An Analysis of the English Mind*, Palala Press, 2015

Ford, Richard, 'Whites dominate most powerful jobs', *The Times*, 28/07/2020, https://www.thetimes.co.uk/article/whites-dominate-most-powerful-jobs-ptwdbowll

Forsyth, Mark, *A Short History of Drunkenness*, Penguin, 2017

Foucault, Michel, *The Archaeology of Knowledge*, trans. A. M. Sheridan Smith, Routledge, 2002

Fox, Kate, *Watching the English: The Hidden Rules of English Behaviour*, Hodder, 2005

Fredrickson, George M., *Racism: A Short History*, Princeton University Press, 2002

French, Patrick, *Younghusband: The Last Great Imperial Adventurer*, HarperCollins, 1995

Fryer, Peter, *Staying Power: The History of Black People in Britain*, Pluto Press, 2010

Fuadmondeo, 'Top Ten Greatest Sports Countries', *The Top Tens*, 2020, https://www.thetoptens.com/sports-countries/

Furber, Holden, *Private Fortunes and Company Profits in the India Trade in the Eighteenth Century*, Variorum, 1997

Furber, Holden, 'Rival Empires of Trade in the Orient 1600–1800', *American Historical Review* 1976, 82:5, 1309–10, https://academic.oup.com/ahr/article-abstract/82/5/1309/123166?redirectedFrom=fulltext

Galbraith, John S., *Crown and Charter: The Early Years of the British South Africa Company*, University of California Press, 1992

Gallagher, John, and Robinson, Ronald, 'The Imperialism of Free Trade', *Economic History Review* 2017, 6:1, 478–98, https://onlinelibrary.wiley.com/doi/abs/10.1111/j.1468-0289.1953.tb01482.x

'Gallery 3: The British Empire: The end of the British Empire', The National Archives, https://www.nationalarchives.gov.uk/education/empire/g3/default.htm

Gandhi, Rajmohan, *A Tale of Two Revolts*, Viking, 2009

Gardner, Leigh, *Taxing Colonial Africa: The Political Economy of British Imperialism*, Oxford University Press, 2012

Gardner, Leigh, and Roy, Tirthankar, *Economic History of Colonialism*, Bristol University Press, 2020

Garland, Jon, and Rowe, Michael, *Racism and Anti-Racism in Football*, AIAA, 2001

Garvey, Marcus, 'Legendary UK Rastafarian activist, reparationist and Ethiopian scholar activist Ras Seymour McLean has joined the Ancestors', *Ligali*, 26/10/2014, http://www.ligali.org/forums/index.php?showtopic=5214

Gattey, Emma, 'A Primer for Empire: Fletcher and Kipling's School History of England', *Uncomfortable Oxford*, 26/05/2020, https://www.uncomfortableoxford.co.uk/post/a-primer-for-empire-fletcher-and-kipling-s-school-history-of-england

'General election 2019: Labour plans to teach British Empire injustice in schools', *BBC News*, 26/11/2019, https://www.bbc.co.uk/news/election-2019-50551765

Gerritsen, Anna, and Riello, Giorgio, *The Global Lives of Things: The Material Culture of Connections in the Early Modern World*, Routledge, 2015

Gerritsen, Anna, and Riello, Giorgio, *Writing Material Culture History*, Bloomsbury Academic, 2015

Gildea, Robert, *Empires of the Mind: The Colonial Past and the Politics of the Present*, Cambridge University Press, 2019

Gilmour, David, *The British in India: A Social History of the Raj*, Farrar, Straus & Giroux, 2018

Gilmour, Rachael, and Schwarz, Bill, *End of Empire and the English Novel since 1945*, Manchester University Press, 2011

Gilroy, Paul, *After Empire: Melancholia or Convivial Culture?*, Routledge, 2004

Goldberg, Maren, 'Black Hole of Calcutta', *Britannica*, 19/02/2014, https://www.britannica.com/topic/Black-Hole-of-Calcutta

Gott, Richard, *Britain's Empire: Resistance, Repression and Revolt*, Verso, 2011

Gottschalk, Peter, *Religion, Science, and Empire: Classifying Hinduism and Islam in British India*, Oxford University Press, 2013

Goulbourne, Harry, *Ethnicity and Nationalism in Post-Imperial Britain*, Cambridge University Press, 2009

Gove, Michael, 'EU referendum: Michael Gove explains why Britain should leave the EU', *Telegraph*, 20/02/2016, https://www.telegraph.co.uk/news/newstopics/eureferendum/12166345/European-referendum-Michael-Gove-explains-why-Britain-should-leave-the-EU.html

Gray, Peter, 'Famine and Land in Ireland and India, 1845–1880: James Card and the Political Economy of Hunger', *Historical Journal* 2006, 49:1, 193–215, https://www.jstor.org/stable/4091745?seq=1

Greenberg, Reesa, Ferguson, Bruce W., and Nairne, Sandy, *Thinking about Exhibitions*, Routledge, 1996

Gregory, Derek, *The Colonial Present*, Blackwell Publishing, 2004

Griffiths, Sian, 'Cambridge students topple bust of Britain's wartime ally Jan Smuts', *The Times*, 5/08/2018, https://www.thetimes.co.uk/article/cambridge-students-topple-bust-of-britains-wartime-ally-jan-smuts-d2phswhpf

Guha-Thakurta, Tapati, *Monuments, Objects, Histories: Institutions of Art in Colonial and Post-Colonial India*, Columbia University Press, 2004

'Guide to records in the V&A Archive relating to the India Museum and Indian objects', Victoria and Albert Museum, 2019, https://www.vam.ac.uk/__data/assets/pdf_file/0007/259918/Guide-to-the-India-Museum-and-Indian-Objects.pdf

Gummer, Selwyn, and Gummer, John Selwyn, *When the Coloured People Come*, TBS, 1966

Gupta, Bishnupriya, 'Falling behind and catching up: India's transition from a colonial economy', *Economic History Review* 2019, 72:3, 815–16, https://onlinelibrary.wiley.com/doi/abs/10.1111/ehr.12849

Gupta, Suman, 'On the Indian readers of Mein Kampf', *Economic and Political Weekly* 2012, 47:46, 51–8, https://www.jstor.org/stable/41720383?seq=1

Guthrie, Jonathan, 'Lex in-depth: Examining the slave trade – "Britain has a debt to repay" ', *Financial Times*, 26/06/2020, https://www.ft.com/content/945c6136-0b92-41bf-bd80-a80d944bb0b8?sharetype=blocked

Haas, Michel de, 'Measuring rural welfare in colonial Africa: did Uganda's smallholders thrive?', *Economic History Review* 2017, 70:2, 605–31, https://onlinelibrary.wiley.com/doi/abs/10.1111/ehr.12377

Hague, William, *William Pitt the Younger: A Biography*, Harper Perennial, 2005

Hall, Catherine, Draper, Nicholas, McClelland, Keith, Donington, Katie, and Lang, Rachel, *Legacies of British Slave-Ownership: Colonial Slavery and the Formation of Victorian Britain*, Cambridge University Press, 2014

Hall, Catherine, and Rose, Sonya O. (eds.), *At Home with the Empire: Metropolitan Culture and the Imperial World*, Cambridge University Press, 2009

Hall, Catherine and Rose, Sonya O., 'Introduction', in Catherine Hall and Sonya O. Rose (eds.), *At Home with the Empire: Metropolitan Culture and the Imperial World*, Cambridge University Press, 2009, pp. 1–31

Hall, Douglas, *In Miserable Slavery: Thomas Thistlewood in Jamaica, 1750–86*, Macmillan, 1989

Halperin, Sandra, and Palan, Ronen, *Legacies of Empire: Imperial Roots of the Contemporary Global Order*, Cambridge University Press, 2015

Hannan, Leonie, and Longair, Sarah, *History through Material Culture*, Manchester University Press, 2017

Hansen, Randall, *Citizenship and Immigration in Post-war Britain*, Oxford University Press, 2000

Harman, Kristyn, *Explainer: the evidence for the Tasmanian genocide*, The Conversation, 17/01/2018, https://theconversation.com/explainer-the-evidence-for-the-tasmanian-genocide-86828

Haroon Siddique, ' "Not everything was looted": British Museum to fight critics', *Guardian*, 12/10/2018 https://www.theguardian.com/culture/2018/oct/12/collected-histories-not-everything-was-looted-british-museum-defends-collections

Harris, Gareth, ' "A major step forward for Britain's colonial museums": Manchester Museum returns objects to Indigenous Australians', *Art Newspaper*, 21/11/2019, https://www.theartnewspaper.com/news/heritage-specialists-welcome-manchester-museum-s-repatriation-of-objects-to-indigenous-australians

Harrison, Rodney, *Heritage: Critical Approaches*, Routledge, 2013

Harrison, Rodney, *Understanding the Politics of Heritage*, Manchester University Press, 2010

Harrison, Simon, *Dark Trophies: Hunting and the Enemy Body in Modern War*, Berghahn, 2012

Harrison, Simon J., 'Skulls and Scientific Collecting in the Victorian Military: Keeping the Enemy Dead in British Frontier Warfare', *Comparative Studies in Society and History* 2008, 50:1, 285–303, https://www.jstor.org/stable/27563663?seq=1

Headlam, Cecil, *Ten Thousand Miles through India & Burma: An Account of the Oxford University Authentics Cricket Tour with Mr K. J. Key in the Year of the Coronation Durbar*, Dent, 1903

Heffer, Simon, *Like the Roman: The Life of Enoch Powell*, Faber & Faber, 2008

Heilpern, John, 'Town that has lost its reason', *Observer*, 14/07/1968

Hejeebu, Santhi, 'Contract Enforcement in the English East India Company', *Journal of Economic History* 2005, 65:2, 496–523, https://www.cambridge.org/core/journals/journal-of-economic-history/article/contract-enforcement-in-the-english-east-india-company/74CEE54F662764822B03CB9DB4D6A4B2

Hellen, Nicholas, 'Third of National Trust properties tainted by slave trade money', *Sunday Times*, 14/06/2020, https://www.thetimes.co.uk/article/third-of-national-trust-properties-tainted-by-slave-trade-money-p3rkbf7oh

Hemrajani, Nikhil, 'What makes Mumbai the best-paying city for expats?', *BBC Worklife*, 2/03/2018, https://www.bbc.com/worklife/article/20180302-what-makes-mumbai-the-best-paying-city-for-expats

Henare, Amiria, *Museums, Anthropology and Imperial Exchange*, Cambridge University Press, 2005

Hennessy, Alistair, 'Penrhyn Castle', *History Today* 1995, 45:1, 40–45, https://www.historytoday.com/archive/penrhyn-castle

Hensher, Philip, 'Let's be honest – we need to impose our imperial rule on Afghanistan', *Independent*, 17/10/2001

Herbertson, Andrew John, *The Oxford Survey of the British Empire, 1914*, vol. 6, Forgotten Books, 2018

Herwitz, Daniel, *Heritage, Culture, and Politics in the Postcolony*, Columbia University Press, 2012

Hevia, James, 'Loot's Fate: The Economy of Plunder and the Moral Life of Objects "From the Summer Palace of the Emperor of China"', *History and Anthropology* 1994, 6:4, 319–45

Hickel, Jason, 'The Case for Reparations', *Jason Hickel.org*, 13/10/2018, https://www.jasonhickel.org/blog/2018/10/13/the-case-for-reparations

'Highway to Hell: Europe's Worst Drivers Revealed in Tripadvisor's "Rowdy Road Runners" List', TripAdvisor, 29/06/2009, https://tripadvisor.mediaroom.com/2009-06-29-HIGHWAY-TO-HELL-EUROPE-S-WORST-DRIVERS-REVEALED-IN-TRIPADVISOR-S-ROWDY-ROAD-RUNNERS-LIST

Hirsch, Shirin, *In the Shadow of Enoch Powell: Race, Locality and Resistance*, Manchester University Press, 2018

History.com Editors, 'Charter granted to the East India Company', *History*, 21/07/2010, https://www.history.com/this-day-in-history/charter-granted-to-the-east-india-company

'History GCSE', *Education data lab*, 2020, https://results.ffteducationdatalab.org.uk/gcse/history.php?v=20190822.2

'History of the Royal Armouries in the Tower of London', Royal Armouries, 2019, https://royalarmouries.org/about-us/history-of-the-royal-armouries/history-of-the-royal-armouries-in-the-tower-of-london/

Hochschild, Adam, *Bury the Chains: The British Struggle to Abolish Slavery*, Pan Macmillan, 2005

Hoffenberg, Peter H., *An Empire on Display: English, Indian, and Australian Exhibitions from the Crystal Palace to the Great War*, University of California Press, 2001

Holmes, Rachel, *African Queen: The Real Life of the Hottentot Venus*, Random House, 2007

Hope, Christopher, 'National Trust could face inquiry into its "purpose"', *Daily Telegraph*, 23/10/2020, https://www.telegraph.co.uk/politics/2020/10/23/national-trust-could-face-inquiry-purpose/

Howe, Stephen, *Empire: A Very Short Introduction*, Oxford University Press, 2002

Hoyle, Ben, 'California first state to pass law for slavery reparations', 2/10/2020, *The Times*, https://www.thetimes.co.uk/article/california-sets-off-on-road-to-paying-reparations-for-slavery-z7hfss7z7

Hughes, Laura, 'Royal Navy "far weaker" than it was during Falklands War', *Telegraph*, 2/04/2017, https://www.telegraph.co.uk/news/2017/04/02/britains-navy-far-weaker-falklands-could-still-cripple-spain/

Hunt, Tristram, 'Maqdala 1868', V&A Blog, 4/04/2018, https://www.vam.ac.uk/blog/museum-life/maqdala-1868

Hunt, Tristram, 'Should museums return their colonial artefacts?', *Guardian*, 29/06/2019, https://www.theguardian.com/culture/2019/jun/29/should-museums-return-their-colonial-artefacts

Hutton, Brian, 'State papers 1989: Tory MP feared letting Irish politicians into Westminster', *Irish Independent*, 30/12/2019, https://www.independent.ie/irish-news/state-papers-1989-tory-mp-feared-letting-irish-politicians-into-westminster-38820995.html

Huxtable, Sally-Anne, Fowler, Corinne, Kefalas, Christo, and Slocombe, Emma, *Interim Report on the Connections between Colonialism and Properties Now in the Care of the National Trust, Including Links with Historic Slavery*, 2020, https://nt.global.ssl.fastly.net/documents/colonialism-and-historic-slavery-report.pdf

Huyssen, Andreas, *Present Pasts: Urban Palimpsests and the Politics of Memory*, Stanford University Press, 2003

Hyam, Ronald, *Britain's Imperial Century, 1815–1914: A Study of Empire and Expansion*, Palgrave Macmillan, 2003

Hyam, Ronald, 'The British Empire in the Edwardian Era', Oxford Scholarship Online, 2011, https://oxford.universitypressscholarship.com/view/10.1093/acprof:oso/9780198205647.001.0001/acprof-9780198205647-chapter-2

Hyman, Robert, *Empire and Sexuality: The British Experience*, Manchester University Press, 1990

Imtiaz, Habib, 'Indians in Shakespeare's England as "the first-fruits of India": Colonial Effacement and Postcolonial Reinscription', *Journal of Narrative Theory* 2006, 36:1, https://www.questia.com/library/journal/1P3-1163615621/indians-in-shakespeare-s-england-as-the-first-fruits

Inikori, Joseph E., 'Slavery and the Development of Industrial Capitalism in England', *Journal of Interdisciplinary History* 1987, 17:4, 771–93, https://www.jstor.org/stable/204653?seq=1

Ishiguro, Laura Mitsuyo, 'Relative Distances: Family and Empire between Britain, British Columbia and India, 1858–1901', PhD thesis, University College London, 2011

Jack, Ian, 'Four historians, two arguments, nobody dead. Does it matter? Well, yes', *Guardian*, 19/11/2011, https://www.theguardian.com/commentisfree/2011/nov/18/ian-jack-teaching-history-british-empire

Jackson, Ashley, *The British Empire: A Very Short Introduction*, Oxford University Press, 2013

Jackson, William, Review of Jeremy Paxman, *Empire: What Ruling the World Did to the British*, *Reviews in History*, No. 1216, https://reviews.history.ac.uk/review/1216

James, Lawrence, 'Nailing the lie of the evil Empire', *Sunday Times*, 18/06/2006, https://www.thetimes.co.uk/article/nailing-the-lie-of-the-evil-empire-mt56f7vkhr5

James, Lawrence, *Raj: The Making and Unmaking of British India*, Abacus, 1998

James, Lawrence, *Rise and Fall of the British Empire*, Abacus, 1995

Jasanoff, Maya, 'Collectors of Empire: Objects, Conquests and Imperial Self-Fashioning', *Past & Present* 2004, 184, 109–35, https://www.jstor.org/stable/3600699?seq=1

Jasanoff, Maya, *Edge of Empire: Conquest and Collecting in the East, 1750–1850*, Harper Perennial, 2006

Jeffreys, Henry, 'After all that arak I felt no urge to copulate in the streets', 6/02/2015, https://worldofbooze.wordpress.com/2015/02/06/after-all-that-arak-i-felt-no-urge-to-copulate-in-the-streets/

Jeffreys, Henry, *Empire of Booze*, Unbound, 2016

Jeffreys, Henry, 'How to enjoy ouzo, even when you're not on holiday', *Guardian*, 6/02/2015, https://www.theguardian.com/lifeandstyle/2015/feb/06/ouzo-arak-holiday-drinks

Jeffries, Stuart, 'The best exotic nostalgia boom: why colonial style is back', *Guardian*, 19/03/2015, https://www.theguardian.com/culture/2015/mar/19/the-best-exotic-nostalgia-boom-why-colonial-style-is-back

Jehangir, Abu Md, Anwara, and Shamuz Miah, Mohammed, 'Bangla Stories', *Bangla Stories*, 2020, https://www.banglastories.org/

Johnson, Boris, 'The rest of the world believes in Britain. It's time that we did too', *Telegraph*, 15/07/2018, https://www.telegraph.co.uk/politics/2018/07/15/rest-world-believes-britain-time-did/

Johnson, Georgie-Rose, 'Outbound Tourism Statistics', *Finder*, 14/04/2020, https://www.finder.com/uk/outbound-tourism-statistics

Johnson, Robert, *British Imperialism: Histories and Controversies*, Palgrave Macmillan, 2003

Jones, Geoffrey, 'Merchants to Multinationals: British Trading Companies in the Nineteenth and Twentieth Centuries', *Working Knowledge*, 11/03/2001, https://hbswk.hbs.edu/item/merchants-to-multinationals-british-trading-companies-in-the-nineteenth-and-twentieth-centuries

Joshi, Sonam, 'Why expats don't want to live in India', *Times of India*, 9/09/2017, https://timesofindia.indiatimes.com/india/why-expats-dont-want-to-live-in-india/articleshow/60433029.cms

Kaganof, Aryan, *Metalepsis in Black*, 2016, https://vimeo.com/193233861

Karp, Ivan, Kreamer, Christine Mullen, and Lavine, Steven D., *Museums and Communities: The Politics of Public Culture*, Smithsonian Institution Press, 1992

Karp, Ivan, and Lavine, Steven D., *Exhibiting Cultures: The Poetics and Politics of Museum Display*, Smithsonian Books, 1991

Katwala, Sunder, 'Is the British Empire to blame?', *Guardian*, 17/11/2002, https://www.theguardian.com/politics/2002/nov/17/foreignpolicy.comment

Kaufmann, Miranda, *Black Tudors: The Untold Story*, Oneworld Publications, 2017

Kaye, John William, *A History of the Sepoy War in India, 1857–58*, vol. 3, Longmans Green, 1876

Keay, John, *The Honourable Company: A History of the English East India Company*, HarperCollins, 1993

Kellaway, Lucy, 'How the office was invented', *BBC News*, 22/07/2013, https://www.bbc.co.uk/news/magazine-23372401

Kennedy, Dane, *The Imperial History Wars: Debating the British Empire*, Bloomsbury, 2018

Khan, Muhammad Mojlum, 'Great Historian of Medieval Bengal', *bmri*, http://www.bmri.org.uk/biogs/Ghulam-Husain-Salim.pdf

Khan, Stephen, 'Explainer: the evidence for the Tasmanian genocide', *The Conversation*, 17/01/2018, https://theconversation.com/explainer-the-evidence-for-the-tasmanian-genocide-86828

Khan, Yasmin, 'Refugees, Migrants, Windrush and Brexit', in Stuart Ward and Astrid Rasch (eds.), *Embers of Empire in Brexit Britain*, Bloomsbury Academic, 2019, pp. 101–10

Kidambi, Prashant, *Cricket Country: An Indian Odyssey in the Age of Empire*, Oxford University Press, 2019

King, Anthony D., *Writing the Global City: Globalisation, Postcolonialism and the Urban*, Routledge, 2016

Kingdon, Zachary, and Bersselaar, Dmitri van den, 'Collecting empire? African objects, West African trade and a Liverpool museum', in Sheryl-lynne Haggerty, Anthony Webster and J. Nicholas White (eds.), *The Empire in One City? Liverpool's Inconvenient Imperial Past*, Manchester University Press, 2008, pp. 100–122

Kinsey, Danielle C., 'Koh-i-Noor: Empire, Diamonds, and the Performance of British Material Culture', *Journal of British Studies* 2009, 48:2, 391–419, https://www.jstor.org/stable/25483040?seq=1

Klein, Christopher, 'Queen Victoria's Diamond Jubilee', *History*, 30/08/2018, https://www.history.com/news/queen-victorias-diamond-jubilee

Knell, Simon J., MacLeod, Suzanne, and Watson, Sheila (eds.), *Museum Revolutions: How Museums Change and Are Changed*, Routledge, 2007

Kobayashi, Kazuo, *Indian Cotton Textiles in West Africa: African Agency, Consumer Demand and the Making of the Global Economy*, Palgrave Macmillan, 2019

Kriegel, Lara, 'After the Exhibitionary Complex: Museum Histories and the Future of the Victorian Past', *Victorian Studies* 2006, 48:4, 681–704, https://www.jstor.org/stable/i413196

Krishna, Nakul, 'Rhodocylces', *N+1* 2016, 26, https://nplusonemag.com/issue-26/politics/rhodocycles/

Kros, Cynthia, 'Rhodes Must Fall: Archives and Counter-Archive', *Critical Arts* 2015, 29:1, 150–65, https://www.tandfonline.com/doi/abs/10.1080/02560046.2015.1102270

Kumar, Krishan, *Political Agenda of Education: A Study of Colonialist and Nationalist Ideas*, Sage Publications, 2005

Kuper, Adam, *The Invention of Primitive Society: Transformations of an Illusion*, Routledge, 1988

Kwarteng, Kwasi, *Ghosts of Empire: Britain's Legacies in the Modern World*, Bloomsbury, 2012

Landler, Mark, 'Britain Grapples with its Racist Past, from the Town Square to the Boardroom', *New York Times*, 18/07/2020, https://www.nytimes.com/2020/06/18/world/europe/uk-slavery-trade-lloyds-greene-king.html

Larson, Frances, *Severed: A History of Heads Lost and Found*, Granta, 2015

Laux, Clair, Ruggiu, François-Joseph, and Singaravélou, Pierre, *At the Top of the Empire: European Elites in the Colonies*, Presses Interuniversitaires Européennes, 2009

Leach, Anna, Voce, Antonio, and Kirk, Ashley, 'Black British history: the row over the school curriculum in England', *Guardian*, 13/07/2020, https://www.theguardian.com/education/2020/jul/13/black-british-history-school-curriculum-england

Leapman, Michael, 'How the moustache went the way of the British Empire', *Daily Telegraph*, 02/10/2007, https://www.telegraph.co.uk/news/features/3634260/How-the-moustache-went-the-way-of-the-British-Empire.html

Lee, Felicia R., 'From Noah's Curse to Slavery's Rationale', *New York Times*, 2003, 1/11/2003, https://www.nytimes.com/2003/11/01/arts/from-noah-s-curse-to-slavery-s-rationale.html

Lees, William Nassau, *Indian Musalmans*, Kessinger Legacy Reprints, 2010

Lenckos, Elisabeth, 'Daylesford', UCL Blog, 2014, https://blogs.ucl.ac.uk/eicah/daylesford-case-study/

Levine, Philippa, 'Sexuality and Empire', in Catherine Hall and Sonya O. Rose (eds.), *At Home with the Empire: Metropolitan Culture and the Imperial World*, Cambridge University Press, 2009, pp. 122–42

'List of countries that have gained independence from the United Kingdom', *World Heritage Encyclopedia*, http://self.gutenberg.org/articles/eng/List_of_countries_that_have_gained_independence_from_the_United_Kingdom

Little, Tony, 'Remember the Rights of the Savage', *Liberal History*, 20/05/2012, https://liberalhistory.org.uk/history/remember-the-rights-of-the-savage/

'Living in India', *Expat info desk*, 2020, https://www.expatinfodesk.com/expat-guide/deciding-on-the-right-country/top-expatriate-destinations/india/

'London museums urged to show more "hidden" artefacts', *BBC News*, 19/01/2011, https://www.bbc.co.uk/news/uk-england-london-12214145#:~:

text=Apercent2oBBCpercent2oFreedompercent2oofpercent2oInformation, 95percent25percent2oofpercent2oitspercent2ospecimenpercent2ocollec tions

Lonetree, Amy, *Decolonizing Museums: Representing Native America in National and Tribal Museums*, University of North Carolina Press, 2014

Longair, Sarah, and McAleer, John, *Curating Empire: Museums and the British Imperial Experience*, Manchester University Press, 2012

Longmore, Jane, ' "Cemented by the Blood of a Negro"? The Impact of the Slave Trade on Eighteenth-Century Liverpool', in David Richardson, Suzanne Schwarz and Anthony Tibbles (eds.), *Liverpool and Transatlantic Slavery*, Liverpool University Press, 2007, pp. 227–51, https://www. cambridge.org/core/books/liverpool-and-transatlantic-slavery/ cemented-by-the-blood-of-a-negro-the-impact-of-the-slave-trade-on-eighteenthcentury-liverpool/ B2CB934253DAA23B1C8BAB3233DC8BE9

Lorcin, Patricia, 'The Nostalgias for Empire', *History & Theory* 2018, 57:2, 269–85, https://onlinelibrary.wiley.com/doi/abs/10.1111/hith. 12061

Lovelace, Antonia, 'War Booty: Changing Contexts, Changing Displays: Asante "Relics" from Kumasi, Acquired by the Prince of Wales's Own Regiment of Yorkshire in 1896', *Journal of Museum Ethnography* 2000, 12, 147–60, https://www.jstor.org/stable/i40035801

Luce, Richard, 'We colonialists only wanted to serve', *The Times*, 10/07/2020, https://www.thetimes.co.uk/article/the-empire-builders-only-wanted-to-serve-pch55cqjk

Luty, Jennifer, 'Museum and gallery attendance in England 2012–2019, by age', *Statista*, 6/12/2019, https://www.statista.com/statistics/418323/museum-galery-attendance-uk-england-by-age/

McCartor, Robert Lynn, 'The John Company's College: Haileybury and the British Government's attempt to control the Indian Civil Service', PhD thesis, Texas Tech University, 1981, https://ttu-ir.tdl.org/ttu-ir/ bitstream/handle/2346/9799/31295002384690.pdf?sequence=1

Mace, Henry, 'Britain has had enough of experts, says Gove', *Financial Times*, 3/06/2016, https://www.ft.com/content/3be49734-29cb-11e6-83e4-abc22d5d108c

McGrath, Jane, 'Did the Dutch really trade Manhattan for nutmeg?', *How Stuff Works*, 2009, https://history.howstuffworks.com/history-vs-myth/nutmeg-new-netherland.htm#pt3

McKay, Alex, 'The British Invasion of Tibet, 1903–4', *Inner Asia* 2012, 14:1, 5–25, https://www.jstor.org/stable/24572145?seq=1

Mackenzie, John M., *Imperialism and Popular Culture*, Manchester University Press, 1986

Mackenzie, John M., *Propaganda and Empire: The Manipulation of British Public Opinion, 1880–1960*, Manchester University Press, 1984

Mādagāvakara, Govinda Nārāyaṇa, *Govind Narayan's Mumbai: An Urban Biography from 1863*, Anthem Press, 2008

Madley, Benjamin, *From Terror to Genocide: Britain's Tasmanian Penal Colony and Australia's History Wars, Journal of British Studies*, Vol. 47, No. 1 (Jan., 2008), pp. 77–106, Cambridge University Press

Madra, Amandeep Singh, and Singh, Parmjit, *Eyewitness at Amritsar: A Visual History of the 1919 Jallianwala Bagh Massacre*, Kashi House, 2019

Mahindru, Megha, and Khanna, Priyanka, '68 expats tell us the story of how they made India their home', *Vogue*, 4/04/2018, https://www.vogue.in/magazine-story/55-expats-tell-us-the-story-of-how-they-made-india-their-home/

Mahmud, Tayyab, 'Colonialism and Modern Constructions of Race: A Preliminary Inquiry', *University of Miami Law Review* 1999, 53:4, 1219–46, https://repository.law.miami.edu/cgi/viewcontent.cgi?article=1657&context=umlr

Mail Reporter, 'Boozy Brits abroad: Half of us drink every day on holiday, while a third admit they make a start in the departure lounge', *Daily Mail*, 26/06/2014, https://www.dailymail.co.uk/travel/article-2670592/Boozy-Brits-abroad-Half-drink-day-holiday-admit-start-drinking-DEPARTURE-LOUNGE-says-Alcohol-Concern-study.html

Maleuvre, Didier, *Museum Memories: History, Technology, Art*, Stanford University Press, 1999

Malhotra, Aanchal, *Remnants of Partition: 21 Objects from a Continent Divided*, C. Hurst, 2019

Malik, Nesrine, *We Need New Stories: Challenging the Toxic Myths behind our Age of Discontent*, Weidenfeld & Nicolson, 2019

Manning, Sanchez, 'Britain's colonial shame: Slave-owners given huge pay-outs after abolition', *Independent*, 24/02/2013, https://www.independent.co.uk/news/uk/home-news/britains-colonial-shame-slave-owners-given-huge-payouts-after-abolition-8508358.html

Mansell, Warwick, 'Michael Gove redrafts new history curriculum after outcry', *Guardian*, 21/06/2013, https://www.theguardian.com/education/2013/jun/21/michael-gove-history-curriculum

Marcus, Harold G., *A History of Ethiopia*, University of California Press, 2002

Marcus, Harold G., *The Life and Times of Menelik II: Ethiopia, 1844–1913*, The Red Sea Press, 1995

'Margaret Thatcher Speech to Conservative Rally at Cheltenham July 3, 1982', https://www.margaretthatcher.org/document/104989

Markham, Albert H., *Life of Sir Clements Markham*, Cambridge University Press, 2015

Marks, Kathy, 'Blair issues apology for Irish Potato Famine', *Independent*, 2/06/1997, https://www.independent.co.uk/news/blair-issues-apology-for-irish-potato-famine-1253790.html

Marshall, H. E., *Our Island Story*, Digireads.Com Publishing, 2013

Marshall, P. J. (ed.), *British Empire*, Cambridge University Press, 1996

Marshall, P. J., 'The British Empire at the end of the Eighteenth Century', in P. J. Marshall (ed.), *British Empire*, Cambridge University Press, 1996, pp. 16–23

Marshall, P. J., 'The Diaspora of the Africans and the Asians', in P. J. Marshall (ed.), *British Empire*, Cambridge University Press, 1996, pp. 280–95

Marshall, P. J., *East Indian Fortunes: The British in Bengal in the Eighteenth Century*, Clarendon Press, 1976

Marshall, P. J., 'Imperial Britain', in P. J. Marshall (ed.), *British Empire*, Cambridge University Press, 1996, pp. 318–37

Marshall, P. J., 'Private British Trade in the Indian Ocean before 1800', in Om Prakash (ed.), *European Commercial Expansion in Early Modern Asia*, Routledge, 2020

Marshall, P. J., and Low, Alaine, *The Oxford History of the British Empire*, vol. II: *The Eighteenth Century*, Oxford University Press, 1998, https://oxford.universitypressscholarship.com/view/10.1093/acprof:oso/9780198205630.001.0001/acprof-9780198205630

Marstine, Janet, *New Museum Theory and Practice: An Introduction*, John Wiley, 2006

Martin, James Gabriel, 'Discover the most sports mad countries in the world', *Lonely Planet*, 8/03/2019, https://www.lonelyplanet.com/articles/sportiest-countries-in-world

Mayberry, Kate, 'The innovators offering expats cheaper schools', *BBC Worklife*, 11/05/2017, https://www.bbc.com/worklife/article/20170510-the-innovators-offering-expats-more-affordable-schools

Mbembe, Achille, 'Decolonizing Knowledge and the Question of the Archive', *Africa is a Country*, 2015, https://africaisacountry.atavist.com/decolonizing-knowledge-and-the-question-of-the-archive

Mbembe, Achille, *On the Postcolony*, University of California Press, 2001

Meath, Reginald Brabazon, *Brabazon Potpourri*, Hutchinson, 1928

Meath, Reginald Brabazon, *Memories of the Nineteenth Century*, E. P. Dutton, 1923

Meath, Reginald Brabazon, *Memories of the Twentieth Century*, John Murray, 1924

Meath, Reginald Brabazon, 'What the Boy Scout Movement may do for Britain', *Windsor Magazine*, 31/12/1909

Merryman, J. H., *Imperialism, Art and Restitution*, Cambridge University Press, 2006

Meskell, Lynn, *Global Heritage*, John Wiley, 2015

Metcalf, Thomas R., 'Imperial Towns and Cities', in P. J. Marshall (ed.), *British Empire*, Cambridge University Press, 1996, pp. 224–53

Michalski, Sergiusz, *Public Monuments: Art in Political Bondage, 1870–1997*, Reaktion Books, 1998

Mignolo, Walter, *The Darker Side of Western Modernity: Global Futures, Decolonial Options*, Duke University Press, 2011

Mill, James, *The History of British India*, 3 vols. (1817–18), Cambridge University Press, 2010

Miller, David, and Reill, Peter, *Visions of Empire: Voyages, Botany and Representations of Nature*, Cambridge University Press, 1996

Miller, Phil, 'The Foreign Office is Full of Colonial Relics', *Vice*, 15/10/2018, https://www.vice.com/en_uk/article/wj9k5q/the-foreign-office-is-full-of-colonial-relics

Mills, Lennox Algernon, *Ceylon under British Rule, 1795–1932*, Psychology Press, 1964

Mishra, Pankaj, 'Guilt and Glory', *Financial Times*, 21/10/2011, https://www.ft.com/content/3b56dac0-f992-11e0-bf8f-00144feab49a

Mitchell, Peter, 'Waiting for Sargon', *Review 31*, 2020, http://review31.co.uk/essay/view/60/waiting-for-sargon

Mitchell, Timothy, 'The World as Exhibition', *Comparative Studies in Society and History* 1989, 31:2, 217–36, https://www.jstor.org/stable/178807?seq=1

Mitchell, W. J. T., and Taussig, Michael, 'Discussions in Contemporary Culture: Monuments, Monumentality, Monumentalization', Detroit Institute of Arts, 6 December 2014, https://youtu.be/caGhHQT9WYY

Moody, Oliver, 'Germany can teach us how to say sorry properly', *The Times*, 18/08/2020

Morefield, Jeanne, 'Empires without Imperialism: Anglo-American Decline and the Politics of Deflection', Oxford Scholarship Online, 2014, https://oxford.universitypressscholarship.com/view/10.1093/acprof:oso/9780199387328.001.0001/acprof-9780199387328

Morgan, Kenneth, *Slavery, Atlantic Trade and the British Economy, 1660–1800*, Cambridge University Press, 2001

Morgan, Philip D., 'The Black Experience in the British Empire, 1680–1810', in P. J. Marshall and Alaine Low (eds.), *The Oxford History of the British Empire*, vol. II: *The Eighteenth Century*, Oxford University Press, 1998, https://oxford.universitypressscholarship.com/view/10.1093/acprof:oso/9780198205630.001.0001/acprof-9780198205630-chapter-21

Morgan, Simon, 'Material Culture and the Politics of Personality in Early Victorian England', *Journal of Victorian Culture* 2012, 17:2, 127–46, https://academic.oup.com/jvc/article-abstract/17/2/127/4102463

Morris, Jan, *Farewell the Trumpets: An Imperial Retreat*, vol. III of the *Pax Britannica* trilogy, Faber & Faber, 2012

Morris, Jan, *Heaven's Command: An Imperial Progress*, vol. I of the *Pax Britannica* trilogy, Faber & Faber, 2012

Morris, Jan, *Pax Britannica: The Climax of an Empire*, vol. II of the *Pax Britannica* trilogy, Faber & Faber, 2012

Moser, Stephanie, 'The Devil is in the Detail: Museum Displays and the Creation of Knowledge', *Museum Anthropology* 2010, 33:1, https://anthrosource.onlinelibrary.wiley.com/doi/abs/10.1111/j.1548-1379.2010.01072.x

Mount, Ferdinand, 'Atrocity upon Atrocity', *Times Literary Supplement*, 23/02/2018, https://www.the-tls.co.uk/articles/atrocity-upon-atrocity-india-indian-mutiny-1857-history-british/

Mount, Ferdinand, *Tears of the Rajas: Mutiny, Money and Marriage in India, 1805–1905*, Simon & Schuster, 2015

Mrinalini, Rajagopalan, and Desai, Madhuri, *Colonial Frames, Nationalist Histories: Imperial Legacies, Architecture and Modernity*, Ashgate, 2012

Mukherjee, Aditya, 'Empire: How Colonial India Made Modern Britain', *Economic and Political Weekly* 2010, 45–50, 73–82, https://www.jstor.org/stable/25764217?seq=1

Mukherjee, Sumita, '"Narrow-majority" and "Bow-and-agree": Public Attitudes towards the Elections of the First Asian MPs in Britain, Dadabhai Naoroji and Mancherjee Merwanjee Bhownaggree, 1885–1906', *Journal of the Oxford University History Society* 2004, 1–20, https://sumita-mukherjee.files.wordpress.com/2016/01/naoroji-bhownaggree.pdf

Murphy, Tom, '"The Empire is about [to] Strike Back": Tory councillor's view after Brexit', *The Mail*, 16/02/2020, https://www.nwemail.co.uk/news/18238859.the-empire-strike-back-tory-councillors-view-brexit/

'Myall Creek massacre', National Museum of Australia, https://www.nma.gov.au/defining-moments/resources/myall-creek-massacre

Myatt, Tim, 'Looting Tibet: Conflicting Narratives and Representations of Tibetan Material Culture from the 1904 British Mission to Tibet', *Inner Asia* 2012, 4:1, 61–97, https://www.jstor.org/stable/24572147?seq=1

Nanda, B. R., 'Nehru and the British', *Modern Asian Studies* 1996, 30:2, 469–79, https://www.jstor.org/stable/313016?seq=1

Nandy, Ashis, *The Intimate Enemy: Loss and Recovery of Self under Colonialism*, Oxford India Paperbacks, 1988

Neilson, Keith, *The British Way in Warfare: Power and the International System, 1856–1956*, Routledge, 2010

Neiman, Susan, *Learning from the Germans: Confronting Race and the Memory of Evil*, Allen Lane, 2019

Nelson, Robert S., and Olin, Margaret, *Monuments and Memory, Made and Unmade*, University of Chicago Press, 2004

Netchman, Tillman W., *Nabobs: Empire and Identity in Eighteenth-Century Britain*, Cambridge University Press, 2010

Nevinson, H. W., *Ladysmith: The Diary of a Siege*, 1900, https://www.guten berg.org/files/16603/16603-h/16603-h.htm

Nubia, Onyeka, 'Who was the Ipswich Man?', *Our Migration Story*, 2020, https://www.ourmigrationstory.org.uk/oms/the-ipswich-man

Nye, John V. C., *War, Wine and Taxes: The Political Economy of Anglo-French Trade, 1689–1900*, Princeton University Press, 2007

O'Brien, Patrick K., and Prados de la Escosura, Leandro, 'Balance sheets for the acquisition, retention and loss of European empires overseas', *IFCS – Working Papers in Economic History.WH 6183* 1999, 23:3–4, https://ideas.repec.org/p/cte/whrepe/6183.html

Offer, Avner, 'The British Empire, 1870–1914: a waste of money?', *Economic History Review* 1993, 46:2, 215–38, https://www.jstor.org/stable/2598015?seq=1

Ogborn, Miles, *Global Lives: Britain and the World, 1550–1800*, Cambridge University Press, 2008

Ogborn, Miles, *Indian Ink: Script and Print in the Making of the English East India Company*, University of Chicago Press, 2008

O'Hare, Maureen, 'World's Most Powerful Passports', *CNN Travel*, 11/07/2020, https://edition.cnn.com/travel/article/henley-index-world-best-passport-2020/index.html

Okeke-Agulu, Chika, *Postcolonial Modernism: Art and Decolonization in Twentieth-Century Nigeria*, Duke University Press, 2015

Oldmixon, John, *The British Empire in America*, J. Brotherton, 1741

Olusoga, David, 'Empire 2.0 is dangerous nostalgia for something that never existed', *Guardian*, 19/03/2017, https://www.theguardian.com/commentisfree/2017/mar/19/empire-20-is-dangerous-nostalgia-for-something-that-never-existed

Olusoga, David, 'The toppling of Edward Colston's statue is not an attack on history. It is history', *Guardian*, 8/06/2020, https://www.theguardian.com/commentisfree/2020/jun/08/edward-colston-statue-history-slave-trader-bristol-protest

Onda, Will, 'Preston Empire Day, May 22nd 1909', *Colonial Film BFI*, 1909, http://www.colonialfilm.org.uk/node/461

'Opium War', National Army Museum, 2020, https://www.nam.ac.uk/explore/opium-war-1839-1842

Ormsby, Avril, 'UK law firm and bank regret slave trade links', Reuters, 1/07/2009, https://www.reuters.com/article/britain-slavery/uk-law-firm-and-bank-regret-slave-trade-links-idUSL171535320090701

Oswell, Paul, 'British tourists are "noisy, rude and badly dressed"', *Daily Mail*, 24/05/2007, https://www.dailymail.co.uk/travel/article-595852/British-tourists-noisy-rude-badly-dressed.html

O'Toole, Fintan, *Heroic Failure: Brexit and the Politics of Pain*, Apollo, 2018

O'Toole, Fintan, 'The paranoid fantasy behind Brexit', *Guardian*, 16/11/2018, https://www.theguardian.com/politics/2018/nov/16/brexit-paranoid-fantasy-fintan-otoole

Owen, Janet, 'Collecting Artefacts, Acquiring Empire: Exploring the Relationship between Enlightenment and Darwinist Collecting and Late Nineteenth-Century British Imperialism', *Journal of the History of Collections* 2006, 18:1, 9–25, https://www.researchgate.net/publication/249243526_Collecting_artefacts_acquiring_empire_Exploring_the_relationship_between_Enlightenment_and_Darwinist_collecting_and_late-nineteenth-century_British_imperialism

Oxford Union, 'Must Rhodes Fall? Full Debate', 1/01/2016, https://www.youtube.com/watch?v=y3aBDBdDIgU

Painter, Nell Irvin, *The History of White People*, Norton, 2011

Palan, Ronen, 'International Financial Centers: The British-Empire, City-States and Commercially Oriented Politics', *Theoretical Inquiries in Law* 2010, 11.1, http://www7.tau.ac.il/ojs/index.php/til/article/viewFile/736/695

Palmer, Stanley H., *Police and Protest in England and Ireland, 1780–1850*, Cambridge University Press, 1988

Panayi, Panikos, *Racial Violence in Britain in the Nineteenth and Twentieth Centuries*, Leicester University Press, 1996

Panayi, Panikos, and Virdee, Pippa, *Refugees and the End of Empire: Imperial Collapse and Forced Migration in the Twentieth Century*, Palgrave Macmillan, 2011

Pankhurst, Rita, 'The Library of Emperor Tewodros II at Maqdala', *Bulletin of the School of Oriental and African Studies* 1973, 36:1, 15–42, https://www.cambridge.org/core/journals/bulletin-of-the-school-of-oriental-and-african-studies/article/library-of-emperor-tewodros-ii-at-maqdala-magdala/719DECF41AEC2B047FB5E5925949B6DA

Parris, Matthew, 'Boris Johnson needs to take control of the cockpit', *The Times*, 8/05/2020, https://www.thetimes.co.uk/edition/comment/boris-johnson-needs-to-take-control-of-the-cockpit-25t0tw7ck

Parris, Matthew, 'Scandals in the House', *Independent*, 29/10/1995, https://www.independent.co.uk/arts-entertainment/scandals-in-the-house-1579987.html

Parry, Richard Lloyd, 'Children among dozens killed in remote Indonesian province of Papua', *The Times*, 24/09/2019, https://www.thetimes.co.uk/article/dozens-of-children-killed-in-remote-indonesian-province-of-papua-5f7jqgds9

Paxman, Jeremy, *Empire: What Ruling the World Did to the British*, Viking, 2012

Peleggi, Maurizio, 'The Social and Material Life of Colonial Hotels: Comfort Zones as Contact Zones in British Colombo and Singapore, ca. 1870–1930', *Journal of Social History* 2012, 46:1, 124–53, https://www.jstor.org/stable/41678979?seq=1

Pellew, Jill, and Goldman, Lawrence, *Dethroning Historical Reputations: Universities, Museums and the Commemoration of Benefactors*, Institute for Historical Research, 2018

Petrow, Stefan, 'Policing in a Penal Colony: Governor Arthur's Police System in Van Dieman's Land, 1826–1836', *Law and History Review* 2000, 18:2, 391–5, https://www.jstor.org/stable/744299?read-now=1&refreqid=excelsior%3A32e0fe9079f66750c6d9048f04ae01c1&seq=1

Phillips, Melanie, 'We're giving in to the race revolutionaries', *The Times*, 8/06/2020, https://www.thetimes.co.uk/article/were-giving-in-to-the-race-revolutionaries-csx59n7g8

Phillips, Richard, *Mapping Men and Empire: A Geography of Adventure*, Routledge, 1996

Phillipson, Alice, 'White Britons a minority in Leicester, Luton and Slough', *Telegraph*, 10/01/2013, https://www.telegraph.co.uk/news/uknews/immigration/9792392/White-Britons-a-minority-in-Leicester-Luton-and-Slough.htm

Phimister, I. R., 'Rhodes, Rhodesia and the Rand', *Journal of Southern African Studies* 2007, 1:1, 74–90, https://www.tandfonline.com/doi/abs/10.1080/03057077408707924

Pitzer, Andrea, 'Concentration Camps Existed Long Before Auschwitz', *Smithsonian Magazine*, 2/11/2017, https://www.smithsonianmag.com/history/concentration-camps-existed-long-before-Auschwitz-180967049/

Popović, Ana, et al., 'Late Victorian Scientific Racism and British Civilizing Mission in Pears' Soap Ads', *Pulse: The Journal of Science and Culture* 2015, 3, 99–112, https://www.ceeol.com/search/article-detail?id=674205

Popperfoto, 'British Royalty, pic: November 1921, HRH Edward, Prince of Wales pictured in Aden, as his car passes local people, with their banner "Tell Daddy we are happy under British rule"', *Getty Images*, 2020, https://www.gettyimages.co.uk/detail/news-photo/november-1921-hrh-edward-prince-of-wales-pictured-in-aden-news-photo/79621695

'Population, Houses, and Families', *Vision of Britain*, 2017, https://www.visionofbritain.org.uk/census/EW1861GEN/3

Porter, Andrew, 'Empires in the Mind', in P. J. Marshall (ed.), *British Empire*, Cambridge University Press, 1996, pp. 185–223

Porter, Andrew, *The Nineteenth Century*, Oxford University Press, 1999

Porter, Andrew, *The Oxford History of the British Empire*, vol. III: *The Nineteenth Century*, Oxford University Press, 2001

Porter, Bernard, *The Absent-Minded Imperialists: Empire, Society and Culture in Britain*, Oxford University Press, 2004

Porter, Bernard, *The Origins of the Vigilant State: The London Metropolitan Police Special Branch before the First World War*, Boydell Press, 1987

Postma, Dr J., *Tennyson*, Ardent Media, 1983

Poulter, E. K., 'Silent Witness: Tracing Narratives of Empire through Objects and Archives in the West African Collections at the Manchester Museum', *Museum History Journal* 2013, 6:1, 6–22, https://www.researchgate.net/publication/272310239_Silent_Witness_Tracing_Narratives_of_Empire_through_Objects_and_Archives_in_the_West_African_Collections_at_the_Manchester_Museum

Prakash, Gyan, and Said, Edward, *After Colonialism: Imperial Histories and Postcolonial Displacements*, Princeton University Press, 1995

Prakash, Om, 'Wildlife Destruction: A Legacy of the Colonial State in India', *Proceedings of the Indian History Congress* 2006–7, 67, 692–702, https://www.jstor.org/stable/44147988?seq=1

Prasad, Ritika, *Tracks of Change: Railways and Everyday Life in Colonial India*, Cambridge University Press, 2016

Preston Guardian, British Newspaper Archive, 29/05/1909, pp. 9, 11, 12, 15, 16

Pretorius, Fransjohan, 'Concentration camps in the South African War? Here are the real facts', *The Conversation*, 18/02/2019, https://theconversation.com/concentration-camps-in-the-south-african-war-here-are-the-real-facts-112006

Preziosi, Donald, and Farago, Claire, *Grasping the World: The Idea of the Museum*, Ashgate, 2004

'Prisons and detention camps, Kenya', House of Commons Debate, 24/02/1959, https://api.parliament.uk/historic-hansard/commons/1959/feb/24/prisons-and-detention-camps-kenya#S5CV0600P0_19590224_HOC_335

Procida, Mary A., *Married to the Empire: Gender, Politics and Imperialism in India, 1883–1947*, Manchester University Press, 2014

Procter, Alice, *The Whole Picture: The Colonial Story of the Art in our Museums and Why We Need to Talk about It*, Cassell, 2020

Proctor, Kate, ' "Tone-deaf" ministers reject BAME review of English curriculum', *Guardian*, 20/07/2020, https://www.theguardian.com/education/2020/jul/30/exclusive-tone-deaf-ministers-reject-bame-review-of-english-curriculum?CMP=twt_gu&utm_source=Twitter&utm_medium#Echobox=1596121892

Puri, Kavita, *Partition Voices*, Bloomsbury, 2019

Puri, Samir, *The Great Imperial Hangover: How Empires Have Shaped the World*, Atlantic Books, 2020

Qureshi, Sadiah, *Peoples on Parade: Exhibitions, Empire, and Anthropology in Nineteenth-Century Britain*, University of Chicago Press, 2011

Rachman, Gideon, 'Brexit reinforces Britain's imperial amnesia', *Financial Times*, 27/3/2017, https://www.ft.com/content/e3e32b38-0fc8-11e7-a88c-50ba212dce4d

Ramdin, Ron, *Reimagining Britain: 500 Years of Black and Asian History*, Pluto Press, 1999

Rao, Rahul, 'On Statues', *The Disorder of Things Part One and Two*, 2/04/2016, https://thedisorderofthings.com/2016/04/02/on-statues/

Raskin, Jonah, *The Mythology of Imperialism: A Revolutionary Critique of British Literature and Society in the Modern Age*, Monthly Review Press, 1971

Rea, Naomi, 'Jamaica Joins a Growing Number of Nations Calling on the British Museum to Repatriate its Cultural Artifacts', *ArtNetNews*, 8/08/2019, https://news.artnet.com/art-world/jamaica-repatriation-british-museum-1619821

Rees-Mogg, Jacob, 'My vision for a global-facing, outward-looking post-Brexit Britain', *Brexit Central*, 21/06/2018, https://brexitcentral.com/vision-global-facing-outward-looking-post-brexit-britain/

Reeves, Frank, *Race and Borough Politics*, Avebury, 1989

Renan, Ernest, *Qu'est-ce qu'une nation?*, Calmann Lévy, 1882, https://fr.wikisource.org/wiki/Qu%E2%80%99est-ce_qu%E2%80%99une_nation_%3F

'Responses', *Impact of Omission*, 2020, https://impactofomission.squarespace.com/survey

Rhodes, Cecil, 'Confession of Faith', *Uoregon*, 1877, https://pages.uoregon.edu/kimball/Rhodes-Confession.htm

Rhodes, Cecil, 'The Last Will and Testament of Cecil Rhodes', ed. W. T. Stead, 'Review of Reviews' Office, 1902, https://info.publicintelligence.net/RhodesLastWill.pdf

Richards, Thomas, *The Imperial Archive: Knowledge and the Fantasy of Empire*, Verso, 1993

Richardson, David, 'The British Empire and the Atlantic Slave Trade, 1660–1807', in P. J. Marshall and Alaine Low (eds.), *The Oxford History of the British Empire*, vol. II: *The Eighteenth Century*, Oxford University Press, 1998, https://oxford.universitypressscholarship.com/view/10.1093/acprof:oso/9780198205630.001.0001/acprof-9780198205630-chapter-20

Richens, Peter, 'The economic legacies of the "thin white line": indirect rule and the comparative development of Sub-Saharan Africa', *African Economic History* 2009, 37, 33–102, https://www.jstor.org/stable/41756121?seq=1

Rickett, Oscar, 'Britain Has Never Faced Up to the Shame of Empire', *Vice*, 27/05/2017, https://www.vice.com/en_uk/article/3d9jdw/britain-has-never-faced-up-to-the-shame-of-empire

Roberts, Elizabeth, 'Unsociable? British expats "fail to make local friends"', *Telegraph*, 29/10/2014, https://www.telegraph.co.uk/expat/11193034/Unsociable-British-expats-fail-to-make-local-friends.html

Robinson, Cedric J., 'Capitalism, Slavery and Bourgeois Historiography', *History Workshop Journal* 1987, 23:1, 122–40, https://academic.oup.com/hwj/article-abstract/23/1/122/614644?redirectedFrom=PDF

Roediger, David R., *How Race Survived US History*, Verso, 2010

Rotter, Andrew J., *Empires of the Senses: Bodily Encounters in Imperial India and the Philippines*, Oxford University Press, 2019

Roy, Nilanjana, 'Empire in the eyes of a cad – the lessons of Flashman', *Financial Times*, 12/07/2019, https://www.ft.com/content/e00c9d96-a184-11e9-a282-2df48f366f7d

Roy, Tirthankar, 'Economic history and modern India: redefining the link', *Journal of Economic Perspectives* 2002, 16:3, 109–30, https://www.aeaweb.org/articles?id=10.1257/089533002760278749

'Royal Pavilion', Brighton Museum, 2020, https://brightonmuseums.org.uk/royalpavilion/history/ww1-and-the-royal-pavilion/

Russell, Jenni, 'Studying History tells us who we really are', *The Times*, 7/11/2019, https://www.thetimes.co.uk/article/studying-history-tells-us-who-we-really-are-w95p6vtkt

Rutherford, Adam, *How to Argue with a Racist: History, Science, Race and Reality*, Weidenfeld & Nicolson, 2020

Sadler, Nigel, *The Legacy of Slavery in Britain*, Amberley Publishing, 2018

Said, Edward W., *Culture & Imperialism*, Vintage, 1994

Said, Edward W., *Orientalism*, Penguin, 2003

Saini, Angela, *Superior: The Return of Race Science*, Fourth Estate, 2019

Sandbrook, Dominic, 'How one corporation conquered an entire continent', review of William Dalrymple, *The Anarchy: The Relentless Rise of the East India Company*, *The Times*, 8/09/2019, https://www.thetimes.co.uk/article/the-relentless-rise-of-the-east-india-company-by-william-dalrymple-review-how-one-corporation-conquered-an-entire-continent-t3d7fx7tr

Sanderson, David, 'Beware colonial guilt, Neil MacGregor warns museums', *The Times*, 12/09/2019, https://www.thetimes.co.uk/article/beware-colonial-guilt-neil-macgregor-warns-museums-3f7mmfrp6

Sandhu, Serina, 'No Thanks, We're British: Survey Reveals UK Tourists are Offended by Thongs and Topless Sunbathing', *Independent*, 19/06/2015, https://www.independent.co.uk/travel/news-and-advice/no-thanks-were-british-survey-reveals-uk-tourists-are-offended-by-thongs-and-topless-sunbathing-10331457.html

Sanghera, Sathnam, 'Coronavirus and ethnicity: black and Asian NHS medics on the front line', *The Times*, 24/04/2020, https://www.thetimes.co.uk/article/coronavirus-and-ethnicity-black-and-asian-nhs-medics-on-the-front-line-dhznrc3kc

Sarr, Felwine, and Savoy, Bénédicte, *The Restitution of African Cultural Heritage: Toward a New Relational Ethics*, 2018, http://restitutionreport2018.com/sarr_savoy_en.pdf

Saunders, Robert, 'The myth of Brexit as imperial nostalgia', *Prospect*, 7/01/2019, https://www.prospectmagazine.co.uk/world/the-myth-of-brexit-as-imperial-nostalgia

Saunders, Robert, 'Myths from a small island: the dangers of a buccaneering view of British history', 9/10/2019, *New Statesman*, https://www.newstatesman.com/politics/uk/2019/10/myths-small-island-dangers-buccaneering-view-british-history

Saunders, Robert, *Yes to Europe!*, Cambridge University Press, 2018

Schama, Simon, 'History is better served by putting the Men in Stone in museums', *Financial Times*, 12/06/2020, https://www.ft.com/content/1117dfb6-8e51-46ec-a74b-59973a96a85a

Schildkrout, Enid, and Keim, Curtis A., *The Scramble for Art in Central Africa*, Cambridge University Press, 1998

Schofield, Camilla, *Enoch Powell and the Making of Postcolonial Britain*, Cambridge University Press, 2013

Schofield, Hugh, 'Human zoos: When real people were exhibits', *BBC News*, 2011, 27/12/2011, https://www.bbc.co.uk/news/magazine-16295827

Schorch, Philipp, and McCarthy, Conal, *Curatopia: Museums and the Future of Curatorship*, Manchester University Press, 2018

Schulz, Johannes, 'Must Rhodes Fall? The Significance of Commemoration in the Struggle for Relations of Respect', *Journal of Political Philosophy* 2018, 27:2, 1–21, https://philpapers.org/rec/SCHMRF-2

Schwarz, Bill, *The White Man's World: Memories of Empire*, Oxford University Press, 2011

Schwarz, Phillip J., ' "A Sense of their own Power": Black Virginians, 1619–1989', *Virginia Magazine of History and Biography* 1989, 97:3, 311–54, https://core.ac.uk/download/pdf/51286936.pdf

Scott, David, *Refashioning Futures: Criticism after Postcoloniality*, Princeton University Press, 1999

Seeley, J. R., *The Expansion of England*, University of Chicago Press, 1971

Segura-Garcia, Teresa, 'The illiterate boy who became a maharaja', Cambridge University, 1/07/2016, https://www.cam.ac.uk/research/features/the-illiterate-boy-who-became-a-maharaja

Seibold, Birgit Susanne, *Emily Hobhouse and the Reports on the Concentration Camps during the Boer War, 1899–1902*, Ibidem Press, 2011

Sen, Sudipta, *Empire of Free Trade: The East India Company and the Making of the Colonial Marketplace*, University of Pennsylvania Press, 1998

Sengoopta, Chandak, *Imprint of the Raj: How Fingerprinting was Born in Colonial India*, Macmillan, 2003

Sengupta, Indra, *Memory, History and Colonialism: Engaging Pierre Nora in Colonial and Postcolonial Contexts*, German Historical Institute, 2009

Shafeeq, Samuel, 'British Reaction to the Sepoy Mutiny, 1857–1858', MA thesis, University of Texas, 1970, https://digital.library.unt.edu/ark:/67531/metadc131301/m2/1/high_res_d/n_04183.pdf

Shah, Neha, 'How did British Indians become so prominent in the Conservative party?', *Guardian*, 27/02/2020, https://www.theguardian.com/commentisfree/2020/feb/27/how-did-british-indians-become-so-prominent-in-the-conservative-party

Sharma, Manimugdha S., 'Why Hitler is not a dirty word in India', *Times of India*, 29/04/2018, https://timesofindia.indiatimes.com/india/why-hitler-is-not-a-dirty-word-in-india/articleshow/63955029.cms

Sibthorpe, Jan, 'East India Company at Home, 1757–1857: Sezincote Case Study', UCL Blog, 2020, https://blogs.ucl.ac.uk/eicah/sezincote-gloucestershire/sezincote-case-study-sezincote-a-brief-description/

Siddique, Haroon, 'Home Office urged to correct false slavery information in citizenship test', *Guardian*, 22/07/2020, https://www.theguardian.com/politics/2020/jul/22/home-office-urged-to-correct-false-slavery-information-in-citizenship-test?CMP=Share_iOSApp_Other

Singh, Patwant, and Rai, Jyoti M., *Empire of the Sikhs: The Life and Times of Maharaja Ranjit Singh*, Peter Owen Publishers, 2013

Sivasubramonian, S., *National Income of India in the Twentieth Century*, Oxford University Press, 2001

'Slave trade and the British economy', *BBC Bitesize*, 2020, https://www.bbc.co.uk/bitesize/guides/zc92xnb/revision/1

'Slave trade shameful, Blair says', *BBC News*, 25/03/2007, http://news.bbc.co.uk/1/hi/uk/6493507.stm

Smith, Adam, *The Wealth of Nations: Books I–III*, Penguin Classics, 1982

Smith, Alison, Brown, David, and Jacobi, Carol (eds.), *Artist and Empire: Facing Britain's Imperial Past*, Tate Publishing, 2015

Smith, Anna Marie, *The New Right Discourse on Race and Sexuality: Britain, 1968–1990*, Cambridge University Press, 1994

Sohal, Jay Singh, 'The battle of Saragarhi: when 21 Sikh soldiers stood against 10,000 men', *History Extra*, 19/08/2019, https://www.historyextra.com/period/victorian/when-21-sikh-soldiers-stood-against-10000-men-the-battle-of-saragarhi/

Solow, Barbara L., and Engerman, Stanley L., *British Capitalism and Caribbean Slavery: The Legacy of Eric Williams*, Cambridge University Press, 2010

Spilsbury, Julian, *The Indian Mutiny*, Weidenfeld & Nicolson, 2008

Springhall, J. O., 'Lord Meath, Youth, and Empire', *Journal of Contemporary History* 1970, 5:4, 97–111, https://journals.sagepub.com/doi/abs/10.1177/002200947000500406

Stanley, Henry M., *Coomassie and Magdala: The Story of Two British Campaigns in Africa*, Naval and Military Press, 2009

Stephens, Phillip, 'British exceptionalism has reached the end of the road', *Financial Times*, 13/05/2020, https://www.ft.com/content/32b7fc68-952f-11ea-abcd-371e24b679ed

Stern, Philip J., *The Company-State: Corporate Sovereignty and the Early Modern Foundations of the British Empire in India*, Oxford University Press, 2011

Stobart, Jon, 'Culture versus Commerce: Societies and Spaces for Elites in Eighteenth-Century Liverpool', *Journal of Historical Geography* 2002, 28:4, pp. 471–85

Stocking, George W., Jr, *Objects and Others: Essays on Museums and Material Culture*, University of Wisconsin Press, 1985

Stoler, Ann Laura, *Duress: Imperial Durabilities in our Times*, Duke University Press, 2016

Stoler, Ann Laura, *Imperial Debris: On Ruins and Ruination*, Duke University Press, 2013

Storti, Craig, *The Art of Coming Home*, Nicholas Brealey Publishing, 2001

'The Story of Empire Day', ArchiveBlog, 24/05/2018, https://www.mary-evans.com/archiveBlog/?p=14632

Su, Alice, 'As trade war escalates, Chinese remember "national humiliation"', *Los Angeles Times*, 13/05/2019, https://www.latimes.com/world/la-fg-china-trade-war-tariffs-colonialism-humiliation-20190513-story.html

Subrahmanyam, Sanjay, *Merchant Networks in the Early Modern World, 1450–1800*, An Expanding World series, Ashgate, 1996

Sully, Dean, *Decolonising Conservation: Caring for Maori Meeting Houses Outside New Zealand*, Left Coast Press, 2008

Sultana, Farhana, 'The false equivalence of academic freedom and free speech: Defending academic integrity in the age of white supremacy, colonial nostalgia, and anti-intellectualism', *ACME* 2018, 17:2, https://www.acmejournal.org/index.php/acme/article/view/1715

Sunak, Rishi, and Rajeswaran, Saratha, *A Portrait of Modern Britain*, Policy Exchange, 6/05/2014, https://policyexchange.org.uk/wp-content/uploads/2016/09/a-portrait-of-modern-britain.pdf

Sutherland, Lucy, *The East India Company in Eighteenth-Century Politics*, Clarendon Press, 1952

Sweet, Matthew, 'Did Colston deserve his watery grave?', *UnHerd*, 8/06/2020, https://unherd.com/2020/06/did-colston-deserve-his-watery-grave/

Swenson, Astrid, and Mandler, Peter, *From Plunder to Preservation: Britain and the Heritage of Empire, c.1800–1940*, Oxford University Press, 2013

Tabili, Laura, 'A Homogeneous Society? Britain's Internal "Others", 1800–Present', in Catherine Hall and Sonya O. Rose (eds.), *At Home with the Empire: Metropolitan Culture and the Imperial World*, Cambridge University Press, 2009, pp. 53–76

Tandon, Prakash, *Punjabi Century, 1857–1947*, University of California Press, 1969

Terracciano, Emilia, Dohmen, Renate, Eaton, Natasha, Gray, Nicola, Allday, Louis, and Hutchens, Jessyca, ' "Artist and Empire" Part 1: Tate', *Third Text*, 12/08/2020, http://thirdtext.org/artist-empire-tate

Thackeray, David, and Toye, Richard, 'Debating Empire 2.0', in Stuart Ward and Astrid Rasch (eds.), *Embers of Empire in Brexit Britain*, Bloomsbury Academic, 2019, pp. 15–24

Tharoor, Shashi, *Inglorious Empire: What the British Did to India*, C. Hurst, 2017

'This is what we know about the government loan to pay slave owners compensation after slavery was abolished in 1833', *Full Fact*, 2/07/2020, https://fullfact.org/economy/slavery-abolition-act-loan/

Thomas, Hugh, *The Slave Trade: The History of the Atlantic Slave Trade, 1440–1870*, Phoenix, 2006

Thomas, Nicholas, *Entangled Objects: Exchange, Material Culture, and Colonialism in the Pacific*, Harvard University Press, 1991

Thomas, Nicholas, *The Return of Curiosity: What Museums are Good for in the Twenty-First Century*, Reaktion Books, 2016

Thompson, Andrew, *The Empire Strikes Back? The Impact of Imperialism on Britain from the Mid-Nineteenth Century*, Pearson Education, 2005

Thrush, Coll, *Indigenous London: Native Travelers at the Heart of Empire*, Yale University Press, 2016

'Tiger Hunting in India 1924', *National Geographic*, 2/08/2014, https://www.nationalgeographic.com/news/2014/8/140803-tiger-hunt-1924-india-maharaja-safari/

Tillotson, Michael, 'Recollections of the Indian Mutiny', *The Times*, 18/08/2007, https://www.thetimes.co.uk/article/recollections-of-the-indian-mutiny-22mbvzvdz89

Tindall, Gillian, *The House by the Thames*, Pimlico, 2007

Tolhurst, Alain, 'Coronavirus: UK's testing chief says track and trace was ditched in March due to forecast of one million cases', *Politics Home*, 22/05/2020, https://www.politicshome.com/news/article/coronavirus-uks-testing-chief-says-track-and-trace-was-abandoned-in-march-due-to-forecast-of-a-million-cases

Tombs, Robert, *The English and their History*, Penguin, 2015

Tosh, John, ' "A Fresh Access of Dignity": Masculinity and Imperial Commitment in Britain, 1815–1914', University of North London, http://www.kznhass-history.net/files/seminars/Tosh.pdf

Tosh, John, 'Home and Away: The Flight from Domesticity in Late-Nineteenth-Century England Re-visited', *Gender and History* 2015, 27:3, 561–75, https://onlinelibrary.wiley.com/doi/10.1111/1468-0424.12150

'Trans-Atlantic Slave Trade – Estimates', *Slave Voyages*, https://www.slavevoyages.org/assessment/estimates

Travis, Alan, 'Virginity tests for immigrants "reflected dark age prejudices" of 1970s Britain', *Guardian*, 8/05/2020, https://www.theguardian.com/uk/2011/may/08/virginity-tests-immigrants-prejudices-britain

Trigger, Bruce G., 'Alternative Archaeologies: Nationalist, Colonialist, Imperialist', *Man* 1984, 19:3, 355–70, https://www.jstor.org/stable/2802176?seq=1

Tunzelman, Alex von, *Indian Summer: The Secret History of the End of an Empire*, Pocket Books, 2008

Twain, Mark, *Following the Equator and Anti-Imperialist Essays*, Oxford University Press, 1996

Tythacott, Louise, 'Trophies of War: Representing "Summer Palace" Loot in Military Museums in the UK', *Museum & Society* 2015, 13:4, 469–88, https://www.researchgate.net/publication/331369050_Trophies_of_War_Representing_'Summer_Palace'_Loot_in_Military_Museums_in_the_UK

'UK economic history: slavery', *Financial Times*, 13/06/2020, https://www.ft.com/content/99e4053d-ed8c-40d0-b5c5-745a1393e596

'UK's coronavirus death toll is met with global disbelief', *The Times*, 7/05/2020, https://www.thetimes.co.uk/article/uks-coronavirus-death-toll-is-met-with-global-disbelief-t70clv9kq

Van Keuren, David K., and Brantlinger, Patrick, *Energy and Entropy: Science and Culture in Victorian Britain: Essays from Victorian Studies*, Indiana University Press, 1989

Vautier, Elaine, 'Playing the "race card": white anxieties and the expression and repression of popular racisms in the 1997 UK election', *Patterns of Prejudice* 2009, 43:2, 122–41

Visram, Rozina, *Asians in Britain: 400 Years of History*, Pluto Press, 2002

Wagner, Kim A., *Amritsar 1919: An Empire of Fear and the Making of a Massacre*, Yale University Press, 2019

Wagner, Kim A., *Rumours and Rebels: A New History of the Indian Uprising of 1857*, Peter Lang, 2017

Wagner, Kim A., *The Skull of Alum Bheg: The Life and Death of a Rebel of 1857*, C. Hurst, 2017

Waijenburg, Marlous van, 'Financing the African Colonial State: The Revenue Imperative and Forced Labor', *Journal of Economic History* 2018, 78:1, 40–80, https://www.cambridge.org/core/journals/journal-of-economic-history/article/financing-the-african-colonial-state-the-revenue-imperative-and-forced-labor/9514245BA11D58B053FBB83E4EADF565

Wallop, Harry, 'Michael Palin: British Empire was not "wicked"', *Telegraph*, 2/10/2009, https://www.telegraph.co.uk/news/uknews/6251398/Michael-Palin-British-Empire-was-not-wicked.html

Walvin, James, *The Trader, The Owner, The Slave: Parallel Lives in the Age of Slavery*, Vintage Books, 2008

Ward, Stuart, *British Culture and the End of Empire*, Manchester University Press, 2001

Ward, Stuart, 'How imperialism still stops Britain from grasping how it looks to the world', *Prospect*, 6/10/2017, https://www.prospectmagazine.co.uk/magazine/how-imperialism-still-stops-britain-from-grasping-how-it-looks-to-the-world

Ward, Stuart, and Rasch, Astrid (eds.), *Embers of Empire in Brexit Britain*, Bloomsbury Academic, 2019

Washbrook, David, 'South India 1770–1840: The Colonial Transition', *Modern Asian Studies* 2004, 38:3, 479–516, https://www.jstor.org/stable/3876680?seq=1

Watson, I. B., *Foundation for Empire: English Private Trade in India, 1659–1760*, Vikas, 1980

Webb, Denver A., 'War, Racism, and the Taking of Heads: Revisiting Military Conflict in the Cape Colony and Western Xhosaland in the Nineteenth Century', *Journal of African History* 2015, 56:1, 37–55, https://www.cambridge.org/core/journals/journal-of-african-history/article/war-racism-and-the-taking-of-heads-revisiting-military-conflict-in-the-cape-colony-and-western-xhosaland-in-the-nineteenth-century/3879DE7648B875570B39EADC9A4461EF

Webster, Anthony, and Richardson, Roger, *The Debate on the Rise of British Imperialism*, Manchester University Press, 2006

Weizmann, Fredric, 'Type and Essence: Prologue to the History of Psychology and Race', *Defining Difference: Race and Racism in the History of Psychology* 2004, 21–47, https://psycnet.apa.org/record/2003-06663-002

Weizmann, Fredric, Fancher, Raymond, and Winston, Andrew, *Defining Difference: Race and Racism in the History of Psychology*, American Psychological Association, 2004

Whitehead, Andrew, 'Entrails of Empire', *History Workshop Journal* 2013, 75, 247–51, https://www.jstor.org/stable/i40131026

Williams, Eric, *Capitalism and Slavery*, University of North Carolina Press, 1994

Williams, Eric, 'The Golden Age of the Slave System in Britain', *Journal of African American History* 1940, 25:1, 60–106, https://www.journals.uchicago.edu/doi/abs/10.2307/2714402?mobileUi=0

Williams, Luke G., *Richmond Unchained: The Biography of the World's First Black Sporting Superstar*, Amberley, 2015

Williams, Robert, A., *Loaded Like a Weapon: The Rehnquist Court, Indian Rights, and the Legal History of Racism in America*, University of Minnesota Press, 2005

Wilson, Jon, *India Conquered: Britain's Raj and the Chaos of Empire*, Simon & Schuster, 2017

Winder, Robert, *Bloody Foreigners: The Story of Immigration to Britain*, Abacus, 2013

Winks, Robin W., *Historiography*, Oxford University Press, 1999

Wintle, Claire, *Colonial Collecting and Display: Encounters with Material Culture from the Andaman and Nicobar Islands*, Berghahn Books, 2013

Woerkens, Martine van, *The Strangled Traveler: Colonial Imaginings and the Thugs of India*, University of Chicago Press, 2002

Wolfe, Patrick, *Traces of History: Elementary Structures of Race*, Verso, 2015

Wolmar, Christian, *Railways & the Raj: How the Age of Steam Transformed India*, Atlantic Books, 2018

Wood, James, 'These Etonians', *London Review of Books* 2019, 41:13, https://www.lrb.co.uk/the-paper/v41/n13/james-wood/diary

Woolcock, Nicola, 'To say grammar schools are full of rich white pupils is lazy and wrong, says Townley Grammar head teacher', *The Times*, 7/12/2019, https://www.thetimes.co.uk/article/to-say-grammar-schools-are-full-of-rich-white-pupils-is-lazy-and-wrong-says-townley-grammar-head-teacher-jr6f7djrm

'The World's Top Travelling Nations', *GetGoingInsurance*, 2020, https://getgoinginsurance.co.uk/big-travel-spenders/

Yanni, Carla, *Nature's Museums: Victorian Science and the Architecture of Display*, Athlone, 1999

Yeo, Colin, *Welcome to Britain: Fixing our Broken Immigration System*, Biteback, 2020

Yorke, Harry, 'Jeremy Corbyn promises children will be taught about evils of British Empire', *Telegraph*, 25/11/2019, https://www.telegraph.

co.uk/politics/2019/11/25/jeremy-corbyn-promises-children-will-taught-evils-british-empire/

Young, Robert J. C., *Postcolonialism: An Historical Introduction*, Wiley-Blackwell, 2001

Young, Toby, 'Britain needs Boris, the extraordinary man I've known for 35 years', *Spectator*, 11/04/2020, https://www.spectator.co.uk/article/britain-needs-boris-the-extraordinary-man-ive-known-for-35-years

Younge, Gary, 'Ambalavaner Sivanandan obituary', *Guardian*, 7/02/2018,   https://www.theguardian.com/world/2018/feb/07/ambalavaner-sivanandan

Yule, Henry, and Burnell, A. C., *Hobson-Jobson: The Definitive Glossary of British India*, Oxford University Press, 2015

Zutshi, Chitralekha, 'Designed for Eternity: Kashmiri Shawls, Empire and Cultures of Production and Consumption in Mid-Victorian Britain', *Journal of British Studies* 2009, 48:2, 420–40, https://www.cambridge.org/core/journals/journal-of-british-studies/article/designed-for-eternity-kashmiri-shawls-empire-and-cultures-of-production-and-consumption-in-midvictorian-britain/8BC637E16F9C0009A4A8097114FC630F

Notes

Acknowledgements

1 The changing composition of goods means that using 'CPI' as a measure works less well over longer periods than over shorter periods – we can't measure the price of a laptop in the eighteenth century, for example. For longer periods, a more appropriate measure is average nominal earnings. For a longer but non-technical explanation for why this method works better, see Roderick Floud, *The Economic History of the English Garden*, Allen Lane, 2019, pp. 10–13. Floud also uses this method to calculate, for instance, Capability Brown's salary in current terms.

Chapter 1: Empire Day 2.0

1 J. O. Springhall, 'Lord Meath, Youth, and Empire', *Journal of Contemporary History* 1970, 5:4, 97–111, https://journals.sagepub.com/doi/abs/10.1177/002200947000500406; Reginald Brabazon Meath, 'What the Boy Scout Movement may do for Britain', *Windsor Magazine*, 31/12/1909; Reginald Brabazon Meath, *Brabazon Potpourri*, Hutchinson, 1928; Reginald Brabazon Meath, *Memories of the Nineteenth Century*, E. P. Dutton, 1923; Reginald Brabazon Meath, *Memories of the Twentieth Century*, John Murray, 1924; Bernard Porter, *The Absent-Minded Imperialists: Empire, Society and Culture in Britain*, Oxford University Press, 2004, pp. 169–70, 182, 187–9, 202–3, 205, 208–10, 224, 232, 256, 260, 277; John Mackenzie, *Propaganda and Empire*, Manchester University Press, 1984, pp. 154, 156, 161, 163, 164, 231–3, 234.
2 Chitralekha Zutshi, 'Designed for Eternity: Kashmiri Shawls, Empire and Cultures of Production and Consumption in Mid-Victorian Britain', *Journal of British Studies* 2009, 48:2, 420–40, https://www.cambridge.org/core/journals/journal-of-british-studies/article/designed-for-

eternity-kashmiri-shawls-empire-and-cultures-of-production-and-consumption-in-midvictorian-britain/8BC637E16F9C0009A4 A8097114FC630F; Jan Morris, *Pax Britannica: The Climax of an Empire*, vol. II of the *Pax Britannica* trilogy, Faber & Faber, 2012, p. 440; the V&A Museum website http://www.vam.ac.uk/content/articles/c/consuming-south-asian-textiles/.

3 Ruaidhrí Carroll, 'Liberty London Was Built From Two Warships', *Culture Trip*, 11/9/2018, https://theculturetrip.com/europe/united-kingdom/england/london/articles/liberty-london-was-built-from-two-warships/ and https://www.libertylondon.com/uk/information/our-heritage.html

4 Lizzie Collingham, *The Hungry Empire: How Britain's Quest for Food Shaped the Modern World*, Vintage, 2018, pp. 120–21; fact-checked by Vanessa Winstone, Collections Officer at the National Brewery Centre in Burton upon Trent. She adds that sales of barrels of Bass hit their height in 1900, with 1,356,749 sold at a value of nearly £4 million.

5 Alice Procter, *The Whole Picture: The Colonial Story of the Art in our Museums and Why We Need to Talk about It*, Cassell, 2020, pp. 53–61; Phil Miller, 'The Foreign Office is Full of Colonial Relics', *Vice*, 15/10/2018, https://www.vice.com/en_uk/article/wj9k5q/the-foreign-office-is-full-of-colonial-relics.

6 Robert Gildea, *Empires of the Mind: The Colonial Past and the Politics of the Present*, Cambridge University Press, 2019, p. 37; Andrew Thompson, *The Empire Strikes Back? The Impact of Imperialism on Britain from the Mid-Nineteenth Century*, Pearson Education, 2005, p. 86.

7 Numbers from Joanna de Groot, 'Metropolitan Desires and Colonial Connections: Reflections on Consumption and Empire', in Catherine Hall and Sonya O. Rose (eds.), *At Home with the Empire: Metropolitan Culture and the Imperial World*, Cambridge University Press, 2009, p. 171.

8 Anna Davin, 'Imperialism and Motherhood', *History Workshop Journal* 1978, 5:1, 9–66, https://academic.oup.com/hwj/article-abstract/5/1/9/5e76550?redirectedFrom=PDF; Thompson, *The Empire Strikes Back?*, p. 112; Porter, *The Absent-Minded Imperialists*, p. 284; Alan Finch, 'The provision of school meals since 1906: progress or a recipe for disaster?', *History and Policy*, 14/01/2019, http://www.historyandpolicy.org/policy-papers/papers/the-provision-of-school-meals-since-1906-progress-or-a-recipe-for-disaster.

9 Gillian Tindall points out in *The House by the Thames*, Pimlico, 2007, p. 98, that British beer-drinking was also seen as key to the nation's imperial success. She quotes a writer saying in 1795 that a particular beer brewed in Southwark 'is well-known as a delicious beverage, from the frozen regions of Russia to the burning sands of Bengal and Sumatra . . . It refreshes the brave soldiers who are fighting the battles of their country in Germany, and animates with new ardour and activity the colonists of Sierra Leone and Botany Bay.'

10 Stanley H. Palmer, *Police and Protest in England and Ireland 1780–1850*, Cambridge University Press, 1988; Chandak Sengoopta, *Imprint of the Raj: How Fingerprinting was Born in Colonial India*, Macmillan, 2003; Bernard Porter, *The Origins of the Vigilant State: The London Metropolitan Police Special Branch before the First World War*, Boydell Press, 1987.

11 Mackenzie, *Propaganda and Empire*, p. 92.

12 Thompson, *The Empire Strikes Back?*, p. 192.

13 British Pathé, 'Think and Eat Imperially', 1927, https://www.youtube.com/watch?v=eg7FUp1AXqY.

Chapter 2: Imperialism and Me

1 Kim Wagner, *Amritsar 1919: An Empire of Fear and the Making of a Massacre*, Yale University Press, 2019

2 Quoted in Saul David, *Victoria's Wars: The Rise of Empire*, Penguin, 2007.

3 An elegant account of what happened can be found in Priya Atwal, *Royals and Rebels: The Rise and Fall of the Sikh Empire*, C. Hurst, 2020.

4 Robert Winder, *Bloody Foreigners: The Story of Immigration to Britain*, Abacus, 2013, p. 356.

5 Alan Travis, 'Virginity tests for immigrants "reflected dark age prejudices" of 1970s Britain', *Guardian*, 8/05/2020, https://www.theguardian.com/uk/2011/may/08/virginity-tests-immigrants-prejudices-britain.

6 Shirin Hirsch, *In the Shadow of Enoch Powell: Race, Locality and Resistance*, Manchester University Press, 2018; Frank Reeves, *Race and Borough Politics*, Avebury, 1989; David Beetham, *Transport and Turbans: A Comparative Study in Local Politics*, Oxford University Press, 1970.

7   Hirsch, *In the Shadow of Enoch Powell*; Simon Heffer, *Like the Roman: The Life of Enoch Powell*, Faber & Faber, 2008; Robert Saunders, *Yes to Europe!*, Cambridge University Press, 2018; Camilla Schofield, *Enoch Powell and the Making of Postcolonial Britain*, Cambridge University Press, 2013.

Chapter 3: *Difficult History*

1   Ronald Hyam, 'The British Empire in the Edwardian Era', in Judith M. Brown and Roger Wm. Louis, *The Oxford History of the British Empire*, vol. IV: *The Twentieth Century*, Oxford University Press, 1999, pp. 47–63, https://oxford.universitypressscholarship.com/view/10.1093/acprof: oso/9780198205647.001.0001/acprof-9780198205647-chapter-2;   Lennox Algernon Mills, *Ceylon under British Rule, 1795–1932*, Psychology Press, 1964, pp. 53, 107; 'Myall Creek massacre', NMA, https://www.nma. gov.au/defining-moments/resources/myall-creek-massacre.

2   'The British Empire at its Territorial Peak Covered Nearly the Same Area as the Moon', Brilliant Maps, 1/01/2019, https://brilliantmaps. com/british-empire-moon/, Creator: @jackmerlinbruce.

3   Leland Joseph Bellot, 'Canada versus Guadeloupe in Britain's Old Colonial Empire: A Study of George Louis Beer's Interpretation of the Peace of Paris of 1763', MA thesis, The Rice Institute, May 1960, https://scholarship.rice.edu/bitstream/handle/1911/89064/RICE0099. pdf?sequence=1, p. 19.

4   Gillian Tindall, *The House by the Thames*, Pimlico, 2007, p. 41.

5   William Dalrymple, *The Anarchy: The Relentless Rise of the East India Company*, Bloomsbury, 2019, p. 22.

6   Jane McGrath, 'Did the Dutch really trade Manhattan for nutmeg?', *How Stuff Works*, https://history.howstuffworks.com/history-vs-myth/ nutmeg-new-netherland.htm#pt3.

7   Richard Lloyd Parry, 'Children among dozens killed in remote Indonesian province of Papua', *The Times*, 24/09/2019, https://www.thetimes. co.uk/article/dozens-of-children-killed-in-remote-indonesian-province- of-papua-5f7jqgds9.

8 See Bernard Cohn, 'Representing Authority in Victorian India', in Eric Hobsbawm and Terence Ranger (eds.), *The Invention of Tradition*, Cambridge University Press, 2012, pp. 165–210.

9 In 'South India 1770–1840: The Colonial Transition', *Modern Asian Studies* 2004, 38:3, 479–516, https://www.jstor.org/stable/3876680?seq=1, David Washbrook writes: 'The binary oppositions and strict racial hierarchies, characteristic of conceptions of late nineteenth-century "colonialism" were a very long time reaching South India, if they ever did. In the meantime, local relationships were shaped by other and different influences.'

10 Tony Little, 'Remember the Rights of the Savage', *Liberal History*, 20/05/2012, https://liberalhistory.org.uk/history/remember-the-rights-of-the-savage/.

11 Harry Yorke, 'Jeremy Corbyn promises children will be taught about evils of British Empire', *Telegraph*, 25/11/2019, https://www.telegraph.co.uk/politics/2019/11/25/jeremy-corbyn-promises-children-will-taught-evils-british-empire/.

12 Andy Brown, *Political Languages of Race and the Politics of Exclusion*, Ashgate, 1999; Robert Saunders, *Yes to Europe!*, Cambridge University Press, 2018, p. 267.

13 MacKenzie proceeds, on p. 179 of *Propaganda and Empire: The Manipulation of British Public Opinion, 1880–1960*, Manchester University Press, 1984, to quote the German G. A. Rein on Seeley, published just before the First World War, saying Seeley was interested in 'uniformities', in generalization, large considerations, broad coherences, general principles, comprehensive ideas.

Chapter 4: Emotional Loot

1 Charles Allen, *Duel in the Snows: The True Story of the Younghusband Mission to Lhasa*, John Murray, 2004; Patrick French, *Younghusband: The Last Great Imperial Adventurer*, HarperCollins, 1995; Michael Carrington, 'Officers, Gentlemen and Thieves: The Looting of Monasteries during the 1903/4 Younghusband Mission to Tibet', *Modern Asian Studies* 2003, 37:1, 81-109, https://www.jstor.org/stable/3876552?seq=1.

2 Denver A. Webb, 'War, Racism, and the Taking of Heads: Revisiting Military Conflict in the Cape Colony and Western Xhosaland in the Nineteenth Century', *Journal of African History* 2015, 56:1, 37–55, https://www.cambridge.org/core/journals/journal-of-african-history/article/war-racism-and-the-taking-of-heads-revisiting-military-conflict-in-the-cape-colony-and-western-xhosaland-in-the-nineteenth-century/3879DE7648B875570B39EADC9A4461EF.

3 Sarah Cheang, 'Women, Pets and Imperialism: The British Pekinese Dog and Nostalgia for Old China', *Journal of British Studies* 2006, 45:2, 359–87, https://www.researchgate.net/publication/249106714_Women_Pets_and_Imperialism_The_British_Pekingese_Dog_and_Nostalgia_for_Old_China.

4 'History of the Royal Armouries in the Tower of London', Royal Armouries, 2019, https://royalarmouries.org/about-us/history-of-the-royal-armouries/history-of-the-royal-armouries-in-the-tower-of-london/.

5 Speech to the Asiatic Society of India in Calcutta when he first started as Viceroy, 1899, cited by Peter Gottschalk, *Religion, Science, and Empire: Classifying Hinduism and Islam in British India*, Oxford University Press, 2013, p. 278.

6 'Guide to records in the V&A Archive relating to the India Museum and Indian objects', V&A Publications, 2019, https://www.vam.ac.uk/__data/assets/pdf_file/0007/259918/Guide-to-the-India-Museum-and-Indian-Objects.pdf.

7 Janice Boddy, *Civilizing Women: British Crusades in Colonial Sudan*, Princeton University Press, 2007.

8 Albert H. Markham, *Life of Sir Clements Markham*, Cambridge University Press, 2015, pp. 207–22; Henry M. Stanley, *Coomassie and Magdala: The Story of Two British Campaigns in Africa*, Naval and Military Press, 2009, p. 470; Harold G. Marcus, *A History of Ethiopia*, University of California Press, 2002; Rita Pankhurst, 'The Library of Emperor Tewodros II at Maqdala', *Bulletin of the School of Oriental and African Studies* 1973, 36:1, 15–42, https://www.cambridge.org/core/journals/bulletin-of-the-school-of-oriental-and-african-studies/article/library-of-emperor-tewodros-ii-at-maqdala-magdala/719DECF41AEC2B047FB5E5925949B6DA.

9 A summary of this tale can be found in *The Times* of 12 January 1911.

10 Naomi Rea, 'Jamaica Joins a Growing Number of Nations Calling on the British Museum to Repatriate its Cultural Artifacts', *ArtNetNews*, 8/08/2019, https://news.artnet.com/art-world/jamaica-repatriation-british-museum-1619821.

11 Bernard Porter, *The Absent-Minded Imperialists: Empire, Society and Culture in Britain*, Oxford University Press, 2004, p. 88.

Chapter 5: *We Are Here Because You Were There*

1 They came on a diplomatic mission to solidify links with the British empire because they were in conflict with other indigenous nations. See Coll Thrush, *Indigenous London: Native Travelers at the Heart of Empire*, Yale University Press, 2016.

2 Two titles that explore this fascinating history: Ron Ramdin, *Reimagining Britain: 500 Years of Black and Asian History*, Pluto Press, 1999; Michael Fisher, *Counterflows to Colonialism: Indian Travellers and Settlers in Britain, 1600–1857*, Permanent Black, 2004.

3 Esther Addley, 'A one-way passage from India: Hackney Museum explores fate of colonial ayahs', *Guardian*, 1/03/2020, https://www.theguardian.com/culture/2020/mar/01/one-way-passage-from-india-hackney-museum-colonial-ayahs-london.

4 Robert Winder, *Bloody Foreigners: The Story of Immigration to Britain*, Abacus, 2013, p. 340.

5 Alice Phillipson, 'White Britons a minority in Leicester, Luton and Slough', *Telegraph*, 10/01/2013, https://www.telegraph.co.uk/news/uknews/immigration/9792392/White-Britons-a-minority-in-Leicester-Luton-and-Slough.html; Rishi Sunak and Saratha Rajeswaran, *A Portrait of Modern Britain*, Policy Exchange, 6/05/2014, https://policy-exchange.org.uk/wp-content/uploads/2016/09/a-portrait-of-modern-britain.pdf.

6 https://archive.bma.org.uk/news/2018/september/a-passage-from-india.

7 Habib Imtiaz, 'Indians in Shakespeare's England as "the first-fruits of India": Colonial Effacement and Postcolonial Reinscription', *Journal of Narrative Theory* 2006, 36:1, https://www.questia.com/library/journal/1P3-1163615621/indians-in-shakespeare-s-england-as-the-first-fruits.

8 Winder, *Bloody Foreigners*, pp. 131, 138, 145, 219.

9 Onyeka Nubia, 'Who was the Ipswich Man?', *Our Migration Story*, 2020, https://www.ourmigrationstory.org.uk/oms/the-ipswich-man.

10 Miranda Kaufmann, *Black Tudors: The Untold Story*, Oneworld Publications, 2017, pp. 7–8.

11 Winder, *Bloody Foreigners*, pp. 204–7.

12 John Heilpern, 'Town that has lost its reason', *Observer*, 14/07/1968.

Chapter 6: Home and Away

1 Anthony D. King, *Writing the Global City: Globalisation, Postcolonialism and the Urban*, Routledge, 2016, p. 153.

2 M. Dasgupta, *Calcutta Cookbook: A Treasury of Recipes from Pavement to Palace*, Penguin, 2000, p. 158.

3 James Evans, *Emigrants: Why the English Sailed to the New World*, Weidenfeld & Nicolson, 2017.

4 Melvin Ember, Carol R. Ember and Ian Skoggard (eds.), *Encyclopaedia of Diasporas: Immigrant and Refugee Cultures around the World*, 2 vols., Springer, 2005, vol. I: *Overviews and Topics*, p. 47.

5 Andrew Thompson, *The Empire Strikes Back? The Impact of Imperialism on Britain from the Mid-Nineteenth Century*, Pearson Education, 2005, p. 156.

6 Avner Offer, 'The British Empire, 1870–1914: a waste of money?', *Economic History Review* 1993, 46:2, p. 233, https://www.jstor.org/stable/2598015?seq=1.

7 Thompson, *The Empire Strikes Back?*, p. 61.

8 'Expatriates Worldwide', *Just Landed*, 2020, https://www.justlanded.com/english/Common/Footer/Expatriates/How-many-expats-are-there.

9 'The World's Top Travelling Nations', GetGoingInsurance, 2020, https://getgoinginsurance.co.uk/big-travel-spenders/.

10 Owen Amos, 'Is it true only 10% of Americans have passports?', *BBC News*, 9/01/2018, https://www.bbc.co.uk/news/world-us-canada-42586638.

11 Georgie-Rose Johnson, 'Outbound Tourism Statistics', *Finder*, 14/04/2020, https://www.finder.com/uk/outbound-tourism-statistics.

12 'Leisure and Tourism: Overseas travel and tourism, monthly. Table 3', ONS, 2019, https://www.ons.gov.uk/peoplepopulationandcommunity/leisureandtourism.

13 Nimah Foley and Chris Rhodes, 'Tourism: Statistics and Policy', House of Commons Library, Briefing Paper 06022, 24/09/2019, http://research-briefings.files.parliament.uk/documents/SN06022/SN06022.pdf.

14 Nikhil Hemrajani, 'What makes Mumbai the best-paying city for expats?', *BBC Worklife*, 2/03/2018, https://www.bbc.com/worklife/article/20180302-what-makes-mumbai-the-best-paying-city-for-expats.

15 Niall Ferguson, *Empire: How Britain Made the Modern World*, Penguin, 2003, pp. 72–3.

16 Maureen O'Hare, 'World's Most Powerful Passports', CNN Travel, 11/07/2020, https://edition.cnn.com/travel/article/henley-index-world-best-passport-2020/index.html.

17 Henry Jeffreys, 'After all that arak I felt no urge to copulate in the streets', 6/02/2015, https://worldofbooze.wordpress.com/2015/02/06/after-all-that-arak-i-felt-no-urge-to-copulate-in-the-streets/; Henry Jeffreys, 'How to enjoy ouzo, even when you're not on holiday', *Guardian*, 6/02/2015, https://www.theguardian.com/lifeandstyle/2015/feb/06/ouzo-arak-holiday-drinks; Henry Jeffreys, *Empire of Booze*, Unbound, 2016.

18 Almara Abgarian, 'Almost half of British people don't try the local food when on holiday', 29/05/2019, https://metro.co.uk/2019/05/29/almost-half-british-people-dont-try-local-food-holiday-9723200f/.

19 David Gilmour, *The British in India: A Social History of the Raj*, Farrar, Straus & Giroux, 2018, p. 350.

20 Ibid.

21 David Gilmour, *The British in India: A Social History of the Raj*, Farrar, Straus & Giroux, 2018, p. 368.

22 Jon Wilson, *India Conquered: Britain's Raj and the Chaos of Empire*, Simon & Schuster, 2017, p. 493.

23 Clair Laux, François-Joseph Ruggiu and Pierre Singaravélou, *At the Top of the Empire: European Elites in the Colonies*, Presses Interuniversitaires Européennes, 2009; Gilmour, *The British in India*.

24 Richard Phillips, *Mapping Men and Empire: A Geography of Adventure*, Routledge, 1996, p. 34.

25 John Tosh, 'Home and Away: The Flight from Domesticity in Late-Nineteenth-Century England Revisited', *Gender and History* 2015, 27:3, 561–75, https://onlinelibrary.wiley.com/doi/10.1111/1468-0424.12150.

26 Phillips, *Mapping Men and Empire*, p. 3.

27 John Darwin, *Unfinished Empire: The Global Expansion of Britain*, Penguin, 2011, p. 99.

28 Jeremy Clarkson, 'Stand still, wimp – only failures run off to be expats', *Sunday Times*, 29/3/2009.

29 John M. MacKenzie, *Propaganda and Empire: The Manipulation of British Public Opinion, 1880–1960*, Manchester University Press, 1984, p. 160.

30 Ibid.

31 For more on this, see Robert Aldrich, *Cultural Encounters and Homoeroticism in Sri Lanka: Sex and Serendipity*, Routledge, 2014.

32 Tillman W. Netchman, *Nabobs: Empire and Identity in Eighteenth-Century Britain*, Cambridge University Press, 2010, p. 175.

Chapter 7: World-Beating Politics

1 Cited by Robert Gildea, *Empires of the Mind: The Colonial Past and the Politics of the Present*, Cambridge University Press, 2019, p. 123.

2 John Mackenzie, *Propaganda and Empire: The Manipulation of British Public Opinion, 1880–1960*, Manchester University Press, 1984, p. 11.

3 Margaret Thatcher speech, 3/07/1982, https://www.margaretthatcher.org/document/104989.

4 For a photograph of the scene, see https://www.gettyimages.co.uk/detail/news-photo/november-1921-hrh-edward-prince-of-wales-pictured-in-aden-news-photo/79621695.

5 John A. Davis, *Naples and Napoleon: Southern Italy and the European Revolutions, 1780–1860*, Oxford University Press, 2006, p. 326.

6 George Curzon, *The Place of India in the Empire: Being an Address Delivered before the Philosophical Institute of Edinburgh*, John Murray, 1909.

7 Boris Johnson speech, Conservative Party Conference, 2/10/2016, https://www.spectator.co.uk/article/full-text-boris-johnson-s-conference-speech.

8 Robert Tombs, *The English and their History*, Penguin, 2015, p. 535.

9 A comment placed on the *FT* website, under the article 'Johnson under fire as coronavirus enters dangerous phase', 12/03/2020, https://www.ft.com/content/c43b9c3e-6470-11ea-a6cd-df28cc3c6a68.

10 International opinion was neatly summarized in one article: 'UK's coronavirus death toll is met with global disbelief', *The Times*, 7/05/2020, https://www.thetimes.co.uk/article/uks-coronavirus-death-toll-is-met-with-global-disbelief-t70clv9kq.

Chapter 8: Dirty Money

1 Elisabeth Lenckos, 'Daylesford', UCL Blogs, 20/08/2014, https://blogs.ucl.ac.uk/eicah/daylesford-case-study/; Jan Sibthorpe, 'East India Company at Home, 1757–1857: Sezincote Case Study', UCL Blog, 2020, https://blogs.ucl.ac.uk/eicah/sezincote-gloucestershire/sezincote-case-study-sezincote-a-brief-description/.

2 Lenckos, 'Daylesford'.

3 Sanchez Manning, 'Britain's colonial shame: Slave-owners given huge payouts after abolition', *Independent*, 24/02/2013, https://www.independent.co.uk/news/uk/home-news/britains-colonial-shame-slave-owners-given-huge-payouts-after-abolition-8508358.html.

4 'UK economic history: slavery', *Financial Times*, 13/06/2020, https://www.ft.com/content/99e4053d-ed8c-40d0-b5c5-745a1393e596; Jonathan Guthrie, 'Lex in-depth: Examining the slave trade – "Britain has a debt to repay"', *Financial Times*, 26/06/2020, https://www.ft.com/content/945c6136-0b92-41bf-bd80-a80d944bb0b8?sharetype=blocked.

5 Adam Hochschild, *Bury the Chains: The British Struggle to Abolish Slavery*, Pan Macmillan, 2005.

6 Dave Donaldson, 'Railroads of the raj: estimating the impact of transportation infrastructure', *American Economic Review* 2018, 108:4–5, 899–934, https://www.aeaweb.org/articles?id=10.1257/aer.20101199; Dan Bogart and Latika Chaudhary, 'Extractive institutions? Investor returns to Indian railway companies in the age of high imperialism', *Journal of Institutional Economics* 2019, 15:5, 751–75, https://econpapers.repec.org/article/cupjinsec/v_3a15_3ay_3a2019_3ai_3a05_3ap_3a751-774_5f00.htm.

7 Peter Richens, 'The economic legacies of the "thin white line": indirect rule and the comparative development of Sub-Saharan Africa', *African Economic History* 2009, 37, 33–102 at p. 52, https://www.jstor.org/stable/41756121?seq=1.

8 Avner Offer, 'The British Empire, 1870–1914: a waste of money?', *Economic History Review* 1993, 46:2, p. 222, https://www.jstor.org/stable/2598015?seq=1.

9 Sally-Anne Huxtable, Corinne Fowler, Christo Kefalas and Emma Slocombe, *Interim Report on the Connections between Colonialism and Properties Now in the Care of the National Trust, Including Links with Historic Slavery*, 2020, https://nt.global.ssl.fastly.net/documents/colionialism-and-historic-slavery-report.pdf, p. 20.

10 Jane Longmore, ' "Cemented by the Blood of a Negro"? The Impact of the Slave Trade on Eighteenth-Century Liverpool', in David Richardson, Suzanne Schwarz and Anthony Tibbles (eds.), *Liverpool and Transatlantic Slavery*, Liverpool University Press, 2007, pp. 227–51, https://www.cambridge.org/core/books/liverpool-and-transatlantic-slavery/cemented-by-the-blood-of-a-negro-the-impact-of-the-slave-trade-on-eighteenthcentury-liverpool/B2CB934253DAA23B1C8BAB3233DC8BE9.

11 Huxtable et al., *Interim Report*, p. 20.

12 H. V. Bowen, *The Business of Empire: The East India Company and Imperial Britain, 1756–1833*, Cambridge University Press, 2006; Lucy Kellaway, 'How the office was invented', *BBC News*, 22/07/2013, https://www.bbc.co.uk/news/magazine-23372401.

13 Geoffrey Jones, 'Merchants to Multinationals: British Trading Companies in the Nineteenth and Twentieth Centuries', *Working Knowledge*, 11/03/2001, https://hbswk.hbs.edu/item/merchants-to-multinationals-british-trading-companies-in-the-nineteenth-and-twentieth-centuries.

14 Mark Landler, 'Britain Grapples with its Racist Past, from the Town Square to the Boardroom', *New York Times*, 18/06/2020, https://www.nytimes.com/2020/06/18/world/europe/uk-slavery-trade-lloyds-greene-king.html.

15 See Nick Draper's initial research in *The Price of Emancipation*, Cambridge University Press, 2010; Catherine Hall, Nicholas Draper, Keith

McClelland, Katie Donington and Rachel Land, *Legacies of British Slave-ownership: Colonial Slavery and the Formation of Victorian Britain*, Cambridge University Press, 2014; and all the articles posted at https://www.ucl.ac.uk/lbs/.

16 Avril Ormsby, 'UK law firm and bank regret slave trade links', Reuters, 1/07/2009, https://www.reuters.com/article/britain-slavery/uk-law-firm-and-bank-regret-slave-trade-links-idUSL171535320090701.

17 Robert Winder, *Bloody Foreigners: The Story of Immigration to Britain*, Abacus, 2013, p. 129.

18 https://ehs.org.uk/multimedia/tawney-lecture-2017-falling-behind-and-catching-up-indias-transition-from-a-colonial-economy/.

19 Patrick K. O'Brien and Leandro Prados de la Escosura, 'Balance sheets for the acquisition, retention and loss of European empires overseas', *IFCS – Working Papers in Economic History.WH 6183* 1999, 23:3–4, p. 32, https://ideas.repec.org/p/cte/whrepe/6183.html.

20 Joshua Barrie, 'How taxpayers were still paying for British slave trade nearly 200 years later', *Mirror*, 13/02/2018, https://www.mirror.co.uk/news/uk-news/taxpayers-still-paying-british-slave-12019829.

Chapter 9: *The Origins of Our Racism*

1 A. D. Cameron, 'The Vellore Mutiny', PhD thesis, University of Edinburgh, 1984, https://era.ed.ac.uk/handle/1842/6856.

2 Andrew J. Rotter, *Empires of the Senses: Bodily Encounters in Imperial India and the Philippines*, Oxford University Press, 2019, p. 64.

3 Jan Morris, *Heaven's Command: An Imperial Progress*, vol. I of the *Pax Britannica* trilogy, Faber & Faber, 2012, pp. 447–67; Jeremy Paxman, *Empire: What Ruling the World Did to the British*, Viking, 2012, pp. 164–6; Piers Brendon, *The Decline and Fall of the British Empire, 1781–1997*, Vintage, 2008, pp. 68–9; Kristyn Harman, *Explainer: the evidence for the Tasmanian genocide*, The Conversation, 17/01/2018, https://theconversation.com/explainer-the-evidence-for-the-tasmanian-genocide-86828; Benjamin Madley, *From Terror to Genocide: Britain's Tasmanian Penal Colony and Australia's History Wars, Journal of British Studies*, Vol. 47, No. 1 (Jan., 2008), pp. 77–106, Cambridge University Press.

4 Even though indigenous communities were thought of as unchanged 'cavemen' by Europeans in the past, we now know that their cultures were actually always changing and complex. In *The Invention of Primitive Society: Transformations of an Illusion*, Routledge, 1988, Adam Kuper has done important work on how the notion of the 'primitive' was constructed.

5 Stephen Khan, 'Explainer: the evidence for the Tasmanian genocide', *The Conversation*, 17/01/2018, https://theconversation.com/explainer-the-evidence-for-the-tasmanian-genocide-86828.

6 Marcus Collins, 'Pride and Prejudice: West Indian Men in Mid-Twentieth-Century Britain', *Journal of British Studies* 2001, 40:3, 391–418, https://www.jstor.org/stable/3070729?seq=1.

7 Richard Cavendish, 'The Black Hole of Calcutta', *History Today* 2006, 56:6, https://www.historytoday.com/archive/black-hole-calcutta.

8 Sahil Ahujja, 'St. James' Church and Fakhr-ul-Masjid, Delhi', *Pixelated Memories*, 12/01/2016, http://pixels-memories.blogspot.com/2016/01/st-james-church-and-fakhr-ul-masjid.html; William Dalrymple, *The Last Mughal: The Fall of a Dynasty, Delhi, 1857*, Bloomsbury, 2009, p. 160; Rajmohan Gandhi, *A Tale of Two Revolts*, Viking, 2009.

9 Lawrence James, *Raj: The Making of British India*, Abacus, 1998, p. 256.

10 More on this in Tayyab Mahmud, 'Colonialism and Modern Constructions of Race: A Preliminary Inquiry', https://repository.law.miami.edu/cgi/viewcontent.cgi?article=1657&context=umlr; and Tony Ballantyne, *Orientalism and Race: Aryanism in the British Empire*, Palgrave Macmillan, 2002, p. 4.

11 Two articles on the theme: Zubair Ahmed, 'Hitler memorabilia "attracts young Indians"', *BBC News*, 15/06/2010, http://news.bbc.co.uk/1/hi/world/south_asia/8660064.stm; Manimugdha S. Sharma, 'Why Hitler is not a dirty word in India', *Times of India*, 29/04/2018, https://timesofindia.indiatimes.com/india/why-hitler-is-not-a-dirty-word-in-india/articleshow/63955029.cms.

12 Maren Goldberg, 'Black Hole of Calcutta', *Britannica*, 19/02/2014, https://www.britannica.com/topic/Black-Hole-of-Calcutta.

13 Miles Ogborn, *Indian Ink: Script and Print in the Making of the English East India Company*, University of Chicago Press, 2008, p. 250.

14 George M. Fredrickson, *Racism: A Short History*, Princeton University Press, 2002, p. 56.

15 Statistics from David Richardson, 'The British Empire and the Atlantic Slave Trade, 1660–1807', and Philip D. Morgan, 'The Black Experience in the British Empire, 1680–1810', in P. J. Marshall and Alaine Low (eds.), *The Oxford History of the British Empire*, vol. II: *The Eighteenth Century*, Oxford University Press, 1998, pp. 440 and 465.

16 Angela Saini, *Superior: The Return of Race Science*, Fourth Estate, 2019, pp. 47–50; Hugh Schofield, 'Human zoos: When real people were exhibits', *BBC News*, 27/12/2011, https://www.bbc.co.uk/news/magazine-16295827.

17 Ana Popović et al., 'Late Victorian Scientific Racism and British Civilizing Mission in Pears' Soap Ads', *Pulse: The Journal of Science and Culture* 2015, 3, 99–112, https://www.ceeol.com/search/article-detail?id=674205.

18 Judith M. Brown, *Nehru*, Routledge, 2014, p. 13; Mary A. Procida, *Married to the Empire: Gender, Politics and Imperialism in India, 1883–1947*, Manchester University Press, 2014; David Gilmour, *The British in India: A Social History of the Raj*, Farrar, Straus & Giroux, 2018.

19 Mahmud, 'Colonialism and Modern Constructions of Race'; Pradeep Barua, 'Inventing Race: The British and India's Martial Races', *Historian* 1995, 58:1, 107–16, https://www.jstor.org/stable/24449614.

20 Sanjoy Chakravorty, *The Truth about Us: The Politics of Information from Manu to Modi*, Hachette India, 2019. In a piece for the BBC (Sanjoy Chakravorty, 'Viewpoint: How the British reshaped India's caste system', *BBC News*, 18/06/2019, https://www.bbc.co.uk/news/world-asia-india-48619734) he argued that caste-based reservations in independent India were created by Brits who took 'a very large, complex and regionally diverse system of faiths and social identities' and simplified them 'to a degree that probably has no parallel in world history', creating entirely new categories and hierarchies, stuffing incompatible or mismatched parts together, creating new boundaries and hardening flexible boundaries.

21 Randall Hansen, *Citizenship and Immigration in Post-war Britain*, Oxford University Press, 2000.

22 'Prisons and detention camps, Kenya', House of Commons Debate, 24/02/1959, https://api.parliament.uk/historic-hansard/commons/

1959/feb/24/prisons-and-detention-camps-kenya#S5CV0600P0_19590
224_HOC_335.

23 Emma Gattey, 'A Primer for Empire: Fletcher and Kipling's School History of England', Uncomfortable Oxford, 26/05/2020, https://www.uncomfortableoxford.co.uk/post/a-primer-for-empire-fletcher-and-kipling-s-school-history-of-england.

24 Cecil Headlam, *Ten Thousand Miles through India & Burma: An Account of the Oxford University Authentics Cricket Tour with Mr K. J. Key in the Year of the Coronation Durbar*, Dent, 1903, p. 47.

25 Morris, *Heaven's Command*, pp. 460, 465–6.

Chapter 10: Empire State of Mind

1 John Tosh, ' "A Fresh Access of Dignity": Masculinity and Imperial Commitment in Britain, 1815–1914', University of North London, p. 4, http://www.kznhass-history.net/files/seminars/Tosh.pdf; James Epstein, 'Taking Class Notes on Empire', in Catherine Hall and Sonya O. Rose (eds.), *At Home with the Empire: Metropolitan Culture and the Imperial World*, Cambridge University Press, 2009, p. 256; Jeremy Paxman, *Empire: What Ruling the World Did to the British*, Viking, 2012, pp. 10–11, 195–8.

2 Quoted by Shirin Hirsch, *In the Shadow of Enoch Powell: Race, Locality and Resistance*, Manchester University Press, 2018.

3 Lawrence James, *Raj: The Making of British India*, Abacus, 1998, pp. 333–5; Teresa Segura-Garcia, 'The illiterate boy who became a maharaja', Cambridge University, 1/07/2016, https://www.cam.ac.uk/research/features/the-illiterate-boy-who-became-a-maharaja.

4 Michael Alexander and Sushila Anand, *Queen Victoria's Maharaj: Duleep Singh, 1838–93*, Weidenfeld & Nicolson, 2001; Arthur Christopher Benson and Viscount Esher, *The Letters of Queen Victoria: A Selection from Her Majesty's Correspondence between the Years 1837 and 1861*, vol. III: *1854–1861*, John Murray, 1908, https://www.gutenberg.org/files/28649/28649-h/28649-h.htm.

5 B. R. Nanda, 'Nehru and the British', *Modern Asian Studies* 1996, 30:2, 470, https://www.jstor.org/stable/313016?seq=1.

6 Surendranath Banerjea, *A Nation in Making: Being the Reminiscences of Fifty Years of Public Life*, Oxford University Press, 1925, p. 21.

7 Paxman, *Empire*, pp. 200–205.

8 Bernard Porter, *The Absent-Minded Imperialists: Empire, Society and Culture in Britain*, Oxford University Press, 2004, p. 63, in turn quoting from Peter Fleming, *Invasion 1940*, Common Reader, 2000, p. 192.

9 Paxman, *Empire*, pp. 178–9.

10 Andrew Thompson, *The Empire Strikes Back? The Impact of Imperialism on Britain from the Mid-Nineteenth Century*, Pearson Education, 2005, p. 41.

11 Jan Morris, *Pax Britannica: The Climax of an Empire*, vol. II of the *Pax Britannica* trilogy, Faber & Faber, 2012, p. 32.

12 Thompson, *The Empire Strikes Back?*, p. 19.

Chapter 11: Selective Amnesia

1 Stuart Jeffries, 'The best exotic nostalgia boom: why colonial style is back', *Guardian*, 19/03/2015, https://www.theguardian.com/culture/2015/mar/19/the-best-exotic-nostalgia-boom-why-colonial-style-is-back.

2 Shirin Hirsch, *In the Shadow of Enoch Powell: Race, Locality and Resistance*, Manchester University Press, 2018: 'Wolverhampton grew rapidly during the Industrial Revolution as a large town famous for its work making locks and iron goods of all kinds. Most violently, the early history of industrialisation in Wolverhampton was integrated into the international slave trade in ways still uncomfortable to acknowledge within its public heritage. The foundries and workshops of Wolverhampton produced chains, fetters, collars, padlocks and manacles, all of which would be taken to the ports of Liverpool and Bristol and used on the slave ships from Africa and in the British plantations during slavery in the Caribbean and North America. Such was the extent of this trade that Henry Waldram, a Wolverhampton ironmaker, advertised his specialism in the directory of 1770 as "Negro Collar and Handcuff Maker".'

3 Andrew Thompson, *The Empire Strikes Back? The Impact of Imperialism on Britain from the Mid-Nineteenth Century*, Pearson Education, 2005, p. 177.

4 'What role did the British Empire play in the war?', *BBC Bitesize*, 2020, https://www.bbc.co.uk/bitesize/topics/zqhyb9q/articles/z749xyc.

5 Robert Winder, *Bloody Foreigners: The Story of Immigration to Britain*, Abacus, 2013, pp. 278–9.

6 Niall Ferguson, *Empire: How Britain Made the Modern World*, Penguin, 2003, p. 165.

7 Andrew Pitzer, 'Concentration Camps Existed Long before Auschwitz', *Smithsonian Magazine*, 2/11/2017, https://www.smithsonianmag.com/history/concentration-camps-existed-long-before-Auschwitz-180967049/; Fransjohan Pretorius, 'Concentration camps in the South African War? Here are the real facts', *The Conversation*, 18/02/2019, https://theconversation.com/concentration-camps-in-the-south-african-war-here-are-the-real-facts-112006.

8 Cobain, Ian, Bowcott, Owen, and Norton-Taylor, Richard, 'Britain destroyed records of colonial crimes', *Guardian*, 18/04/2012, https://www.theguardian.com/uk/2012/apr/18/britain-destroyed-records-colonial-crime.

9 Neal Ascherson, 'Scotland, Brexit and the Persistence of Empire', in Stuart Ward and Astrid Rasch (eds.), *Embers of Empire in Brexit Britain*, Bloomsbury Academic, 2019, pp. 71–8.

10 Bernard Porter, *The Absent-Minded Imperialists: Empire, Society and Culture in Britain*, Oxford University Press, 2004, p. 267.

11 George E. Brooks, *Eurafricans in Western Africa: Commerce, Social Status, Gender, and Religious Observance from the Sixteenth to Eighteenth Century*, James Currey, 2003.

Chapter 12: Working Off the Past

1 Matthew Sweet, 'Did Colston deserve his watery grave?', *UnHerd*, 8/06/2020, https://unherd.com/2020/06/did-colston-deserve-his-watery-grave/.

2 William Dalrymple, 'Robert Clive was a vicious asset-stripper. His statue has no place on Whitehall', *Guardian*, 11/07/2020, https://www.theguardian.com/commentisfree/2020/jun/11/robert-clive-statue-whitehall-british-imperial.

3 Lucy Campbell, 'V&A in talks over returning looted Ethiopian treasures in "decolonisation" purge', *Guardian*, 7/10/2020, https://www.theguardian.com/artanddesign/2020/oct/07/va-in-talks-over-returning-looted-ethiopian-treasures-in-decolonisation-purge.

4 Nicola Bartlett, 'Boris Johnson defends appointing aide who attacked "grievance culture" to race review role', Mirror, 17/06/2020, https://www.mirror.co.uk/news/politics/boris-johnson-defends-appointing-aide-22206451.

5 Ben Hoyle, 'California first state to pass law for slavery reparations', 2/10/2020, *The Times*, https://www.thetimes.co.uk/article/california-sets-off-on-road-to-paying-reparations-for-slavery-z7hfss7z7.

6 Abu Md Jehangir, Anwara and Mohammed Shamuz Miah, 'Bangla Stories', *Bangla Stories*, 2020, https://www.banglastories.org/.

7 Nicola Woolcock, 'To say grammar schools are full of rich white pupils is lazy and wrong, says Townley Grammar head teacher', *The Times*, 7/12/2019, https://www.thetimes.co.uk/article/to-say-grammar-schools-are-full-of-rich-white-pupils-is-lazy-and-wrong-says-townley-grammar-head-teacher-jr6f7djrm.

8 Alison Flood, 'UK needs a museum of colonialism, says historian William Dalrymple', *Guardian*, 16/09/2020, https://www.theguardian.com/books/2020/sep/16/uk-needs-a-museum-of-colonialism-says-historian-william-dalrymple.

9 Martin Booth, 'Anti-Slavery Day Marked by New Artwork in Front of Edward Colston Statue', *B24/7*, 18/10/2018, https://www.bristol247.com/news-and-features/news/anti-slavery-day-marked-by-new-artwork-in-front-of-edward-colston-statue/.

10 Alice Procter, *The Whole Picture: The Colonial Story of the Art in our Museums and Why We Need to Talk about It*, Cassell, 2020, pp. 144–5.

11 Peter Mitchell, 'Waiting for Sargon', *Review 31*, 2020, http://review31.co.uk/essay/view/60/waiting-for-sargon.

Index